COLLINS BRITISH COMMON WILD FLOWER GUIDE

DAVID STREETER

ILLUSTRATED BY
CHRISTINA HART-DAVIES,
AUDREY HARDCASTLE,
FELICITY COLE & LIZZIE HARPER

WILLIAM
COLLINS

Author's Acknowledgements

It would not have been possible to write a guide of this kind without the generous help and encouragement of a large number of people, who in countless ways have helped to make the book better than it would otherwise have been. Whether it be for answering queries, offering suggestions, providing specimens, introducing me to plants in the field or trying out the keys, I would like to thank especially Frances Abrahams, Ros Bennett, Rachel Hamilton, David Harper, Jo Parmenter, David Pearman, John Poland, Ann Sankey, Jackie Thompson, Robin Walls and Kevin Warwick. Also I owe a debt of gratitude to all those literature sources from which I have derived inspiration and ideas, whether they be descriptions, keys or illustrations, all of which are gratefully acknowledged in the Bibliography. Errors are inevitable and are entirely mine and suggestions for improvement will be welcomed.

Finally a particular thank you to Myles Archibald and Helen Brocklehurst of HarperCollins for suggesting that I write the text in the first place and for all the time and commitment that they have devoted to it, and especially to Jilly MacLeod and Julia Koppitz for the conscientious way in which they fostered the book through the editorial stages with unfailing patience and good humour.

Artists' Acknowledgements

The artists wish to thank all the many individuals and organisations who provided support, information or specimens, especially Robin Walls, Bob Gibbons, David Mardon, Richard Marriott, Bryan Edwards of DERC, staff at the Sir Harold Hillier Gardens and Andy Dix for his unstinting support.

William Collins
An imprint of HarperCollins*Publishers*
1 London Bridge Street
London SE1 9GF

WilliamCollinsBooks.com

First published in 2009 as *Collins Flower Guide*
This amended edition published in 2015

Text © David Streeter
Illustrations © HarperCollins*Publishers*

21 20 19 18 17 16 15
10 9 8 7 6 5 4 3 2 1

ISBN 978-0-00-745125-8

A catalogue record for this book is available from the British Library.

Designed by D & N Publishing
Printed and bound in Hong Kong by Printing Express

CONTENTS

HOW TO USE THIS BOOK

The *Collins British Common Wild Flower Guide* is based on the comprehensive *Collins Wild Flower Guide* and is designed as an accessible field guide to the identification of those plants commonly found growing wild in the British Isles. It covers flowering plants, but excludes trees, most shrubs, grasses and sedges as well as the ferns and their allies.

About 3,500 species of flowering plants are regularly found growing wild in the British Isles, of which about 960 are apomictic micro-species of brambles, hawkweeds and dandelions (*see* 'Choice of Species' below). Of the remaining 2,500, about 1,500 are native and 1,000 are introductions. The number of species endemic to the British Isles – that is, those confined to the region and found nowhere else – is relatively small. Rich (1999) lists 470 such species, but most of these are apomicts, leaving only about 10 non-critical species. However, all these figures are only approximate as views on the status of species are constantly changing, as are views on the number of introductions that have become established.

There are two parts to the guide, the species accounts and the illustrations. These are intended to be used together to enable the user to name with confidence those plants most likely to be met with in the field. Wherever possible, characters are used that are visible to the naked eye or can be seen with a ×10 lens.

CHOICE OF SPECIES

In addition to native plants, the flora of the British Isles includes many hundreds of species growing wild that originate in other parts of the world that have a temperate climate similar to ours. The choice of which of these increasing numbers of introductions to include in a guide is necessarily somewhat arbitrary. As a rule of thumb, only those that have become

well-established and are able to reproduce and maintain themselves in the wild and have become relatively common or widespread have been considered for inclusion.

The distinction between what is a 'native' species as opposed to an 'introduction' is sometimes almost impossible to determine. For instance, many introductions arrived as weeds of agriculture in antiquity and to all intents and purposes have become established members of the native flora, so for these the distinction is merely academic. On the other hand, a large and increasing number of species are known to be more recent arrivals. These two groups are now usually distinguished by the terms *archaeophyte* and *neophyte*, which are separated by the wholly arbitrary date of about 1500. In the *Common British Wild Flower Guide*, the status of British plants is designated as either *native*, *archaeophyte* or *introduced*, the last being equivalent to those otherwise referred to as neophytes. Introduced plants that don't persist for more than a year or two are termed *casuals*. The status accorded to the individual species follows that in *New Atlas of the British and Irish Flora* by Preston, Pearman and Dines (2002).

Some groups of plants regularly produce seeds without fertilisation, these germinating into seedlings that are identical to the parent – in effect, cloning by seed. This can produce large numbers of so-called 'micro-species'. For instance, at the last count there were 412 species of hawkweeds, *Hieracium*; 232 species of dandelions, *Taraxacum*; and 320 species of brambles, *Rubus*. Such plants are termed *apomicts* and no attempt has been made here to distinguish between the micro-species.

GEOGRAPHICAL COVERAGE

The *British Wild Flower Guide* covers the British Isles (the United Kingdom, the Isle of Man, the Channel Isles and Republic of Ireland). Altitudinal ranges are taken from Pearman and Corner (2003).

PLANT NAMES

Many familiar wild flowers are known by different **English names** in different parts of the country. Some, such as Lords-and-ladies, have accumulated almost a hundred local and vernacular names. The English names in this book follow a recommended list, *English Names of Wild Flowers* (1974) by Dony, Perring and Rob, produced by the Botanical Society of the British Isles. However, in some cases, where an alternative name is equally familiar or in widespread use, this has been added. English names of non-British species, where they don't already exist, are translations of the vernacular.

Latin names have a depressing habit of changing with irritating frequency. The reasons for these changes, although often obscure, are usually perfectly good and governed by international rules that, theoretically at least, should ensure that the frequency of such changes decreases with time. Latin names in the *British Wild Flower Guide* follow those of the standard British flora, the 3rd edition of *New Flora of the British Isles* (2010) by C.A. Stace. There are two exceptions to this. First, recent research using new techniques in molecular genetics has resulted in several changes to orchid names that have been adopted, together with their more familiar synonyms. Latin names of non-British species follow those in the five-volume *Flora Europaea* (Tutin *et al.*, 1964–80).

TECHNICAL TERMS

A real attempt has been made to keep unnecessary technical terms to a minimum. However, the use of a basic botanical vocabulary is unavoidable in the description of a plant. All terms are described in the Glossary (p.259) and some are illustrated. Those relating to specific groups, such as the grasses, are also illustrated

and explained in the text in the introduction to the family. Readers will find that they will soon become familiar with the more common terms.

SPECIES ACCOUNTS

The species accounts all follow a standard pattern and appear in the text opposite the relevant plate:
- English name(s) and Latin name (*see* above).
- Conservation status and legal protection (*see* 'Symbols and Abbreviations' below).
- Species description.
- Habitat.
- British distribution and status, e.g. native, archaeophyte, introduced, casual (*see* above), endemic.
- Summary of European distribution.
- Flowering time.

USING A LENS

A lens is an indispensable piece of equipment for any naturalist, and the botanist is no exception. A magnification of ×10 is ideal for most purposes, and there are a number of lenses on the market offered by dealers in natural history equipment.

When using a lens for the first time, I suggest that you hold it between thumb and forefinger and bring it up to your eye such that you just touch the tip of your nose with your forefinger. You can then bring the specimen up to the lens until it comes into focus.

CONSERVATION

Northwest Europe is one of the most densely populated parts of the world and as a result the pressures on the countryside are enormous. Urban development, agricultural intensification, pollution and the spread of invasive introductions have had an inevitable effect on the abundance of a large number of species, about 20 of which have actually become extinct in the last 100 years. In addition, climate change is affecting both the abundance and distribution of many species, threatening some while favouring the spread of others.

When visiting the countryside and studying plants, great care should always be taken not to trample and compact the soil around species. In addition, botanists should avoid drawing attention to uncommon species. It is important that the local Wildlife Trust or BSBI County Recorder is told of the discovery of any rare or interesting species so that appropriate steps can be taken for its protection and the record properly noted.

The most recent edition of the British Red Data List for plants, *The Vascular Plant Red Data List for Great Britain* (Cheffings & Farrell, 2005), lists all British species along with the threat level of the most endangered, using the standard IUCN (International Union for Conservation of Nature) categories: EX, extinct (in British Isles); EW, extinct in the wild; CR, critically endangered; EN, endangered; VU, vulnerable; and NT, near threatened. These categories, except NT, are identified in the individual species accounts in the *British Wild Flower Guide* (*see* 'Symbols and Abbreviations' below).

The legislation relating to the protection of wild plants is complex and the following notes are not a definitive statement of the law but intended only as guidance. Under the Wildlife and Countryside Act 1981 (WCA), which covers Great Britain, it is illegal to uproot any wild plant without the permission of the landowner or occupier. It should be remembered that all wild plants belong to someone, and that under the Theft Act 1968 it is an offence to uproot plants for commercial purposes without authorisation.

Schedule 8 of the Wildlife and Countryside Act 1981 gives special protection to a list of 112 particularly rare and endangered plants that it is illegal to pick, uproot, destroy or offer for sale. The equivalent legislation in Northern Ireland, the Wildlife (Northern Ireland) Order 1985, lists 56 such species. In the Republic of Ireland, the Flora Protection Order 1987 lists 68 specially protected species. These species are all identified in the relevant species accounts in this guide (*see* 'Symbols and Abbreviations' below). Two species, the Bluebell in Britain and the Primrose in Northern Ireland, are protected against being offered for sale only. By-laws prohibiting the uprooting or picking of plants are also in operation on most statutory national and local nature reserves and National Trust properties.

In addition to the above, nine internationally rare British species are listed under the 1992 EEC Habitats Directive as being legally protected throughout the European Community: Creeping Marshwort *Apium repens*, Early Gentian *Gentianella anglica*, Fen Orchid *Liparis loeselii*, Floating Water-plantain *Luronium natans*, Killarney Fern *Trichomanes speciosum*, Lady's-slipper *Cypripedium calceolus*, Marsh Saxifrage *Saxifraga hirculus*, Shore Dock *Rumex rupestris* and Slender Naiad *Najas flexilis*.

One of the biggest threats to our native flora comes from the spread of invasive introductions, especially aquatic species. Recent examples are New Zealand Pigmyweed *Crassula helmsii*, Parrot's-feather *Myriophyllum aquaticum* and Floating Pennywort *Hydrocotyle ranunculoides*. Water Primrose *Ludwigia grandiflora* is spreading rapidly northwards through western Europe and has already been recorded in a few localities in England. Great care should be taken to avoid releasing such plants into the countryside as throw-outs, and if any are found in the wild they should be reported to the local Wildlife Trust.

RECORDING

It is important that the local Wildlife Trust, Biological Record Centre or BSBI County Recorder is told of the discovery of rare or interesting species so that appropriate steps can be taken for its protection and the find properly recorded.

Making records, whether they be of individual species or lists from specific sites, contributes significantly to our knowledge of our wild plants as well as aids their conservation. They can be sent to one of the organisations listed above together with all the relevant information, which should include your name, the date and details of the locality. The locality should include the Ordnance Survey grid reference. Since the C19th, biological recording has also been based on a system of vice-counties, the continued use of which enables us to track changes in distribution over the last 150 years.

COLLECTING

If possible, it is generally better to try to identify an unfamiliar plant by taking the book to the plant rather than to pick the plant and take it to the book. However, there are occasions when certain identification will require a more detailed examination, and in these cases only as much of the plant as is needed should be removed. That said, an appreciation of wild plants can be fostered by the moderate collection of common species for detailed examination and appreciation, and little harm is done providing that common sense is exercised. The encouragement of a responsible familiarity with, and an interest in, the detailed structure of plants can only benefit conservation.

The Botanical Society of the British Isles (BSBI) has published a *Code of Conduct for the Conservation and Enjoyment of Wild Plants* that can also be accessed on its website (www.bsbi. org.uk).

PHOTOGRAPHY

Nature photography is increasingly becoming an important and popular aspect of all areas of natural history, partly fuelled by the availability

of ever more sophisticated digital technology. When photographing a particular species, the area around it should not be 'gardened' as this may unnaturally expose it or remove the support of neighbouring plants. Care should also be taken not to damage surrounding vegetation or draw attention to rare species. The well-being of the subject should always take precedence over the quality of the photograph. If the photograph is intended to aid identification, it should be remembered that several shots might be needed to illustrate all the important diagnostic characters.

HOW TO GET INVOLVED AND FIND OUT MORE

Joining a botanical society or conservation organisation

Botanical Society of Britain and Ireland (BSBI)

The BSBI is the leading scientific society in Britain and Ireland for the study of plant distribution and taxonomy. It publishes handbooks on identification, runs national surveys, publishes the journal *Watsonia* and newsletter *BSBI News*, and holds field meetings and conferences. www.bsbi.org.uk

Plantlife

Plantlife is the conservation charity working to protect Britain's wild flowers, plants and fungi. It publishes the magazine *Plantlife*, owns and manages nature reserves, runs the 'Back from the Brink' conservation programme and involves its members in its practical conservation work. www.plantlife.org.uk

The Wildlife Trusts

The UK's 47 Wildlife Trusts together form the largest voluntary organisation concerned with all aspects of wildlife and the countryside. The trusts are mostly county-based, with separate bodies in Scotland, the Isle of Man and Alderney. The trusts are all members of the Royal Society of Wildlife Trusts (RSWT) and between them manage 2200 nature reserves, run courses and involve members in practical conservation work. The junior branch, Wildlife Watch, has 108,000 members. www.wildlifetrusts.org

Attending courses

Field Studies Council (FSC)

The FSC runs a comprehensive series of courses on plant identification and habitats at their 14 residential centres throughout the UK. These include such subjects as grasses, composites, orchids, water plants, alpines, coastal plants and how to use a key, as well as courses on painting and photography and a whole range of other natural history subjects. www.field-studies-council.org

Further reading

The *Collins British Common Wild Flower Guide* is based on the *Collins Wild Flower Guide* which is a comprehensive guide to the whole British flora including trees and shrubs, and the grasses and sedges, together with the ferns and their allies. In addition to the species descriptions and colour illustrations, it incorporates detailed identification keys to all the main groups.

The standard work on the British flora is the 3rd edition of *New Flora of the British Isles* by Clive Stace (2010), which is the most up-to-date and comprehensive account of all British species.

The BSBI publishes a series of illustrated handbooks on particular groups of plants. To date these include grasses, roses, pondweeds, umbellifers, crucifers, willows and poplars, docks and knotweeds, sedges, dandelions, starworts, fumitories and alien grasses. *Plant Crib 1998* by Tim Rich and Clive Jermy, published by the BSBI, is an indispensable aid to the identification of the more difficult plant groups.

The *New Atlas of the British and Irish Flora* by C.D. Preston, D.A. Pearman and T.D. Dines (2002) is a monumental work containing not only distribution maps of all British plants but also habitat and historical notes. Fortunately, it comes with an interactive CD that can be uploaded onto your computer.

The Vegetative Key to the British Flora (2009) by John Poland and Eric Clement provides a set of keys that enables the identification of plants using vegetative characters only.

A number of good general books on British plant life are available, but one of the best is still *Wild Flowers* by John Gilmour and Max Walters, one of the early classic volumes in the Collins New Naturalist series (No. 4), now republished as a facsimile.

Symbols and Abbreviations

Red Data Book categories:
EX = extinct (in British Isles)
EW = extinct in the wild
CR = critically endangered
EN = endangered
VU = vulnerable

* = specially protected by law:
   *B = in Britain
   *NI = in Northern Ireland
   *R = in the Republic of Ireland
Dist. = distribution
Fls = flowering time
BI = British Isles
sp. (plural spp.) = species
ssp. (plural sspp.) = subspecies
agg. = aggregate
× (as in 2×) = times (twice)
× (as in *Mentha* × *piperita*) indicates that the plant is a hybrid
N, E, S, W = points of the compass
c. (*circa*) = about
± = more or less
> = more than
< = less than
≥ = equal to or more than
≤ = equal to or less than

BIBLIOGRAPHY

Cheffings, C.M. & Farrell, L. (eds) (2005). *The Vascular Plant Red Data List for Great Britain*. Joint Nature Conservation Committee, Peterborough.

Clapham, A.R., Tutin, T.G. & Warburg, E.F. (1962). *Flora of the British Isles*. CUP, Cambridge.

Cope, T. & Gray, A. (2009) *Grasses of the British Isles*. BSBI, London.

Dony, J.G., Perring, F.H. & Rob, C.M. (1974). *English Names of Wild Flowers*. BSBI, London.

Foley, M. & Clarke, S. (2005). *Orchids of the British Isles*. Griffin Press, Maidenhead.

Fournier, P. (1977). *Les Quatre Flores de la France*. Éditions Lechevalier, Paris.

Garrard, I. & Streeter, D. (1998). *The Wild Flowers of the British Isles*. Midsummer Books, London.

Gilmour, J. & Walters, M. (2008). *Wild Flowers*. New Naturalist No. 5, facsimile edition. HarperCollins, London.

Graham, G.G. & Primavesi, A.L. (1993). *Roses of Great Britain and Ireland*. BSBI, London.

Haslam, S., Sinker, C. & Wolseley, P. (1975). British water plants. *Field Studies* 4, 243.

Hickey, M. & King, C. (1997). *Common Families of Flowering Plants*. CUP, Cambridge.

Hubbard, C.E. (1984). *Grasses*. Penguin, Harmondsworth.

Jalas, J. & Suominen, J. (eds) (1972–2007). *Atlas Florae Europaeae*. Finnish Museum of Natural History, Helsinki.

Jermy, A.C. & Camus, J. (1991). *The Illustrated Field Guide to Ferns and Allied Plants of the British Isles*. Natural History Museum, London.

Jermy, A.C., Simpson, D.A., Foley, M.J.Y. & Porter, M.S. (2007). *Sedges of the British Isles*. BSBI, London.

Kent, D.H. (1992). *List of Vascular Plants of the British Isles*. BSBI, London.

Lambinon, J., Delvosalle, L. & Duvigneaud, J. (2004). *Nouvelle Flore de la Belgique, du Grand-Duché de Luxembourg, du Nord de la France et des Régions voisines*. Jardin botanique national de Belgique, Brussels.

Lansdown, R.V. (2008). *Water-starworts Callitriche of Europe*. BSBI, London.

Lousley, J.E. & Kent, D.H. (1981). *Docks and Knotweeds of the British Isles*. BSBI, London.

Meikle, R.D. (1984). *Willows and Poplars of Great Britain and Ireland*. BSBI, London.

Murphy, R.J. (2009). *Fumitories of Britain and Ireland*. BSBI, London.

Pearman, D.A. & Corner, R.W.M. (2003). *Altitudinal Limits of British and Irish Vascular Plants*. BSBI, London.

Poland, J. & Clement, E. (2009). *The Vegetative Key to the British Flora*. BSBI, London.

Preston, C.D. (1995). *Pondweeds of Great Britain and Ireland*. BSBI, London.

Preston, C.D. & Croft, J.M. (1997). *Aquatic Plants in Britain and Ireland*. Harley Books, Colchester.

Preston, C.D., Pearman, D.A. & Dines, T.D. (eds) (2002). *New Atlas of the British and Irish Flora*. OUP, Oxford.

Rich, T.C.G. (1999). List of plants endemic to the British Isles. *BSBI News* 80, 23.

Rich, T.C.G. (2001). 'Flowering Plants' in Hawksworth, D.L. (ed.). *The Changing Wildlife of Great Britain and Ireland*. Taylor & Francis, London.

Rich, T.C.G. & Jermy, A.C. (1998). *Plant Crib 1998*. BSBI, London.

Rose, F. (1989). *Colour Identification Guide to the Grasses, Sedges, Rushes and Ferns of the British Isles and north-western Europe*. Viking, London.

Rose, F. & O'Reilly, C. (2006). *The Wild Flower Key*. Warne, London.

Sell, P. & Murrell, G. (1996–2006). *Flora of Great Britain and Ireland*. CUP, Cambridge.

Stace, C. (2010). *New Flora of the British Isles*. CUP, Cambridge.

Tutin, T.G., Heywood, V.H., Burges, N.A., Valentine, D.H., Walters, S.M. & Webb, D.A. (eds) (1964–80). *Flora Europaea. Vols 1–5*. CUP, Cambridge.

Wigginton, M.J. (ed.) (1999). *British Red Data Books. 1. Vascular Plants*. 3rd ed. Joint Nature Conservation Committee, Peterborough.

FLOWERING PLANTS

Flowering plants have dominated life on Earth for the last 100 million years and more than 250,000 have so far been described in about 500 families. They differ from the conifers in the unique structure of their flowers, and in particular in that the *seed*, the fertilised *ovule*, is wholly enclosed within the *ovary* (*see* 'The Fruit' below). With the exception of the grasses, sedges and most temperate trees, the majority of flowering plants are pollinated by animals (in Britain predominantly by insects), while conifers are all wind pollinated. The *fruit* of flowering plants consists of the mature ovary together with its enclosed seeds.

Flowering plants are traditionally divided into two main groups: the dicotyledons and the monocotyledons. The names refer to the number of seed leaves, *cotyledons*, that appear when the plant first germinates: the dicotyledons have two, while the monocotyledons have just one. Modern classifications based on molecular data now recognise about six separate groups of flowering plants, but more than 90 per cent of species still fall within the two traditional groups. These can usually be separated as follows:

- **Dicotyledons** Leaves usually 'net-veined', with a single midrib and numerous branching lateral veins; basic number of flower parts usually four or five.
- **Monocotyledons** Leaves usually narrow and strap-like, with a single midrib with parallel lateral veins arising at the base of the leaf blade and converging towards the tip; basic number of flower parts usually three or six.

The Flower

The most obvious feature that distinguishes flowering plants is the flower. A typical flower consists of two sets of sterile organs and two sets of fertile organs arranged sequentially in a series of whorls. They are attached to the *receptacle*, the swollen tip of the flower stalk, or *pedicel*.

The outer whorl of *sepals*, comprising the *calyx*, are typically green, but may be coloured, and protect the flower while it is in bud. The inner whorl of *petals*, comprising the *corolla*, are usually brightly coloured and help attract pollinators. The calyx and corolla together comprise the *perianth*. In some flowers the sepals and petals are similar and indistinguishable, or there may be only a single whorl; in these cases the individual parts are usually termed *tepals*.

The sepals and petals may be separate and free from each other right to their point of attachment, or the lower part may be joined to form a tube, the *calyx tube* or *corolla tube*.

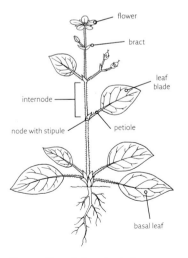

Figure labels: flower, bract, leaf blade, internode, node with stipule, petiole, basal leaf

Figure 1. Parts of a flowering plant

The fertile parts of the flower consist of the male *stamens* and the female *carpels*. The stamens consist of the *anthers*, which contain the pollen, and which are attached to the tips of slender stalks, the *filaments*.

The female organs, the *carpels*, consist of three parts. At the base is the *ovary*, which encloses the *ovules* that after fertilisation develop into the *seeds*. Surmounting the ovary is usually a stalk, the *style*, the tip of which is a swollen or branched *stigma* that forms the receptive surface for the pollen.

Most plants have several carpels (*see*

Figure 2). If the individual carpels are separate, as in a buttercup, the flower is *apocarpous*. If the carpels are fused together into a single structure the flower is *syncarpous* and the whole structure is the ovary.

The receptacle to which the parts of the flower are attached may be swollen and convex, or concave and saucer- or cup-shaped (*see* Figure 3). In the first case the sepals and petals are inserted around the base of the ovary, while in the latter they will be attached to the rim of the receptacle. In both cases the ovary is termed *superior*. In some flowers the receptacle completely encloses the ovary and is fused to it; in this case the insertion of the sepals and petals will be at the top of the ovary and the ovary is *inferior* (think of an apple).

Some flowers are unisexual, possessing only stamens or carpels. In these cases the male and female flowers may be on the same plant, as in an oak tree, in which case the plant is termed *monoecious*, or on separate male and female plants, as in a holly bush, in which case the plant is *dioecious*.

Flowers vary greatly in shape and size. If the petals and sepals are all of the same shape and size and the flowers are radially symmetrical, the flowers are described as *regular*, e.g. a Primrose. If the petals and sepals are not all of the same shape and size and it is possible to divide the flower only in one plane to produce two identical halves, then the flowers are *irregular*, e.g. a sweet pea.

In classifying plants into their separate families the important characters include:

- The numbers of sepals, petals, stamens and carpels.
- Whether flowers are apocarpous or syncarpous.
- Whether the ovary is superior or inferior.
- Whether the flowers are regular or irregular.
- Whether the sepals and petals are free or whether the lower parts are joined to form a tube.

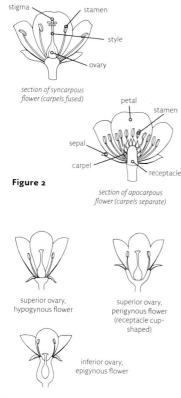

stigma
stamen
style
ovary

section of syncarpous flower (carpels fused)

Figure 2

petal
stamen
sepal
carpel
receptacle

section of apocarpous flower (carpels separate)

superior ovary, hypogynous flower

superior ovary, perigynous flower (receptacle cup-shaped)

inferior ovary, epigynous flower

Figure 3. Position of the ovary and shape of the flower receptacle

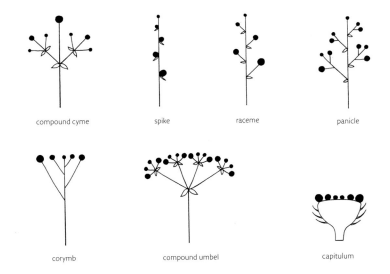

compound cyme

spike

raceme

panicle

corymb

compound umbel

capitulum

Figure 4. Inflorescence types

The Inflorescence

The flowers are either *solitary*, borne singly on the plant, as in a Primrose or dandelion, or grouped together in an *inflorescence*. The stem of a solitary flower is termed the *scape*.

Inflorescences take many forms; the more common types are illustrated above in Figure. 4.

The Fruit

The fruit in flowering plants consists of the mature ovary together with the enclosed seeds. Fruits are either dry, like a nut, or fleshy, like a berry. Dry fruits are either *dehiscent* like a pod, splitting open to release the seeds, or are *indehiscent* like a nut. Fleshy fruits are either fleshy throughout with many seeds as in a tomato – known as a *berry* – or the innermost layer of the fruit is woody and contains a single seed like a plum, known as a *drupe*.

NYMPHAEACEAE
Water-lilies
••

White Water-lily
Nymphaea alba

Perennial aquatic. **Leaves** Large, 5–30 cm diam., ± circular, floating, with *veins radiating from petiole insertion*. **Flowers** *Large, 10–20 cm diam.*, floating; 4 green sepals; *petals numerous, outermost ones longer than sepals*. **Habitat** Lowland ponds, lakes, drainage dykes, canals. **Dist.** Native throughout BI. (Europe.) **Fls** Jul–Aug.

Comments Two subspecies are recognised in Britain: ssp. *occidentalis* and ssp. *alba.* Ssp. *occidentalis* has smaller leaves (9–13 cm diam.) and flowers (5–12 cm diam.), and is restricted to W Ireland and N and W Scotland.

Yellow Water-lily
Nuphar lutea

Perennial aquatic. **Leaves** *Large*, up to 30 cm long, ovate-oblong, floating and submerged, *with up to 28 veins in herringbone arrangement.* **Flowers** 4–6 cm diam., *long-stalked above the water*; sepals yellow inside, longer than petals. *Top of ovary not lobed.*

Habitat Rivers, canals, lakes, ponds. **Dist.** Native throughout most of BI except N Scotland. (Europe.) **Fls** Jun–Aug.

Least Water-lily
Nuphar pumila

Differs from *N. lutea* in being smaller in all parts. **Leaves** *Up to 13 cm, with up to 18 lateral veins.* **Flowers** *1.5–3.5 cm diam. Top of ovary deeply lobed.* **Habitat** Lochs and lochans in Highlands, meres in Shropshire. **Dist.** Scottish Highlands and Shropshire. Rare. (Central and N Europe.) **Fls** Jul–Aug. **Comments** In some localities, hybrid between *N. lutea* and *N. pumila* occurs in absence of *N. pumila.*

CERATOPHYLLACEAE
Hornworts
••••••••••••••••••••••••••••••••••••••

Submerged aquatic herbs. Leaves whorled, divided into fine segments. Flowers minute, unisexual, in axils of leaves. Not to be confused with milfoils (*Myriophyllum*), which have pinnate leaves (p.120).

Rigid Hornwort
Ceratophyllum demersum

Dark green, rather stiff aquatic perennial. **Stems** Up to 1 m long. **Leaves** *Once or twice forked*, segments finely toothed, 1–2 cm.

Habitat Eutrophic lowland lakes, ponds, ditches, canals. Tolerant of mildly brackish conditions. **Dist.** Widespread and often abundant in England; scarce in rest of BI. (Most of Europe.) **Fls** Jul–Sep.

RANUNCULACEAE
Hellebores, anemones, buttercups and crowfoots
••••••••••••••••••••••••••••••••••••••

Annual or perennial herbs or woody climbers. Leaves are usually spirally arranged and lack stipules (except for the water-crowfoots and Thalictrum). Flowers have distinct sepals and petals, or perianth is undifferentiated; numerous stamens; one to numerous carpels, usually free; one to numerous ovules. Fruit is a cluster of achenes or of one to several follicles. Most members of the family are very poisonous.

Hellebores ▶ *Helleborus*
Perennial herbs. Leaves palmate with toothed margins. Flowers with 5 greenish sepals; petals reduced to nectaries.

Stinking Hellebore
Helleborus foetidus

Perennial with strong, unpleasant smell. **Stems** *Leafy, evergreen*, to 80 cm. **Leaves** Basal leaves absent. **Flowers** Numerous, *drooping, bowl-shaped*, 1–3 cm across, greenish edged with purple. *Bracts ovate, entire.* **Habitat** Woodlands and scrub on shallow calcareous soils. **Dist.** Native as far N as Wales; often occurring as garden escape. Rare. (SW and W Europe.) **Fls** Jan–Apr.

Green Hellebore
Helleborus viridis

Stems To 40 cm. **Leaves** *2, both basal, not evergreen.* **Flowers** *2–4, flat*, 3–5 cm diam. *Bracts divided.* **Habitat** Woodlands and scrub on damp calcareous soils. **Dist.** Native as far N as N England; often occurring as garden escape. Scarce. (W and central Europe.) **Fls** Mar–Apr.

GREEN HELLEBORE

Marsh-marigold
Caltha palustris

Perennial glabrous herb with creeping rhizomes. **Flowers** *15–50 mm diam.; 5–8 petal-like sepals.* **Habitat** Marshes, fens, wet meadows, ditches, wet woodlands, river and lake margins, mountain flushes. **Dist.** Native throughout BI; to 1100 m. **Fls** Mar–Jul.

Globeflower
Trollius europaeus *(NI, R)

Tall, glabrous perennial to 60 cm. **Leaves** *Palmate.* **Flowers** 2.5–3.0 cm, *usually single, cup-shaped; usually 10 sepals, petal-like.* **Habitat** Hay meadows, alpine pastures, fens, damp woodland, banks of streams and rivers. **Dist.** Native. N Britain, Wales; to 1005 m. Declining. (Europe.) **Fls** Jun–Aug.

Winter Aconite
Eranthis hyemalis

Erect, glabrous perennial herb to 15 cm. **Leaves** Basal leaves palmately lobed, deeply divided. **Flowers** Single, 2–3 cm diam.; 6 petal-like sepals; *3 deeply divided leaf-like bracts form whorl beneath each flower.* **Habitat** Parks and woodland. **Dist.** Introduced as garden plant in sixteenth century; now naturalised, especially in E England. (S Europe and Turkey.) **Fls** Jan–Mar.

Larkspur
Consolida ajacis

Pubescent annual herb to 60 cm.
Leaves Palmate, divided into linear
segments. **Flowers** *4–16* form an
inflorescence; *zygomorphic*;
5 petal-like sepals with
a single 15 mm
spur. **Habitat**
Waste ground
or on well-
drained soils.
Dist. Introduced.
Cultivated since
sixteenth century;
occasional garden
escape or arable
weed, especially
in E England.
(S Europe.)
Fls Jun–Jul.

Monk's-hood
Aconitum napellus

Tall perennial herb to 1.5 m.
Leaves *Deeply palmately
lobed.* **Flowers** Form a
raceme; *zygomorphic; 5
petal-like sepals, rear
sepal forming large
helmet-shaped hood.*
Habitat Damp
open woodlands,
shady stream
banks, damp
meadows; also
waste ground,
roadsides. **Dist.** Native
in SW England
and S Wales as
ssp. *napellus*, but
commonly cultivated forms that
occur widely as garden escapes are
not native plants (W and central Europe).
Fls (Ssp. *napellus*) May–Jun.

Wood Anemone
Anemone nemorosa

Glabrous to sparsely hairy perennial, to
30 cm. **Leaves** 1–2 basal leaves; 3 stem
leaves, stalked, borne about ⅔ up stem,
divided into 3 lobes. **Flowers** Comprise
6–7 white sepals, sometimes tinged pink.
Habitat Abundant in woodlands, especially
coppice, and on acid or waterlogged
soils; also hedge banks, grassy heathland,
limestone pavement. **Dist.** Native.
Throughout BI; to 1190 m. (Most of
Europe, rare in S.) **Fls** Mar–May.

Baneberry
Actaea spicata

Perennial with an unpleasant smell. **Stem** To
60 cm, glabrous. **Leaves** Basal leaves large,
leaflets coarsely toothed, hairy beneath.
Flowers *Small, in dense inflorescence;
4 sepals; 0–6 petals.* **Fruits** *Berry*, green
turning shiny black. **Habitat** Open or light
woodland. **Dist.** Native. Rare and local,
confined to limestone of N England; to
450 m. (Throughout Europe, N to Norway,
E to China.) **Fls** May–Jun.

BANEBERRY

Traveller's-joy/Old Man's Beard
Clematis vitalba

Perennial woody climber, to 30 m. **Flowers** Fragrant, 2 cm diam.; sepals greenish white, hairy beneath. **Fruits** Achenes with long silky plumes (hence alternative common name). **Habitat** Scrub, hedgerows, wood margins, railway embankments, on calcareous soils. **Dist.** Native. Widespread in lowland England and Wales, introduced further N. (Europe S to N Africa, E to Caucasus.) **Fls** Jul–Aug.

Buttercups and spearworts ▶
Ranunculus

Meadow Buttercup
Ranunculus acris

Hairy perennial to 100 cm. **Stem** Not stoloniferous. **Leaves** *Terminal lobe of leaf sessile.* **Flowers** 18–25 mm diam., stalks not furrowed, *sepals erect.* **Fruits** Glabrous

achenes. **Dist.** Native. Common throughout BI; to 1220 m. (Europe.) **Habitat** Damp pastures and meadows, road verges, upland rock ledges. **Fls** May–Aug.

Creeping Buttercup
Ranunculus repens

Hairy perennial to 60 cm. **Stem** Long leafy stolons, rooting at nodes. **Leaves** *Leaf lobes stalked.* **Flowers** 20–30 mm diam., stalks furrowed, *sepals erect.* **Fruits** Glabrous achenes. **Habitat** Damp grassland, marshes, fens, woodland clearings and rides, pond and lake

CREEPING BUTTERCUP

margins, and as arable weed. **Dist.** Native.
Common throughout BI; to 1035 m.
(Europe.) **Fls** May–Aug.

Bulbous Buttercup
Ranunculus bulbosus

Hairy perennial to 40 cm.
Stem Base swollen to
form rounded corm-
like tuber. **Leaves**
Lobes stalked. **Flowers**
15–30 mm diam.,
stalks furrowed, *sepals
strongly reflexed.* **Habitat**
Grasslands on dry, well-
drained soils. **Dist.** Native.
Common throughout most
of BI; lowland to 580 m.
(Most of Europe.) **Fls** Apr to
Jun (earlier than *R. acris* and
R. repens).

Hairy Buttercup
Ranunculus sardous

Hairy annual to 45 cm. Similar to
R. bulbosus, but without swollen stem base
and *with whole plant covered by spreading
hairs;* basal leaves rather glossy, leaflets
stalked; and flowers 12–25 mm, *sepals*

reflexed. **Habitat** Damp
grazed pastures,
pond margins. **Dist.**
Common near coast
in E and S England;
rare inland. Rare in
Scotland. Absent
from Ireland.
(Central and S
Europe.) **Fls**
Jun–Oct.

Small-flowered Buttercup
Ranunculus parviflorus

Small, prostrate, hairy
annual herb. **Leaves** Distinct
yellowish green. **Flowers**
Small, 3–6 mm di-am.,
often buried among leaves;

**HAIRY
BUTTERCUP**

stalks short, furrowed, opposite leaves;
sepals reflexed. **Habitat** Broken ground,
cliff edges, grassy banks, usually near coast.
Dist. Native. England, Wales. Scarce and
decreasing. (S and SW Europe.) **Fls** Apr–
Jun.

Corn Buttercup
Ranunculus arvensis CR.

Erect annual to 60 cm. **Leaves** *Lower
leaves shallowly lobed, upper deeply divided.*
Flowers 4–12 mm diam., sepals not
reflexed. **Fruits** *Achenes with prominent
spines, >1 mm.* **Habitat** Arable weed of wide
range of soils. **Dist.** Long-established alien.

England. Scarce and in rapid decline. (All Europe.) **Fls** Jun–Jul.

Goldilocks Buttercup
Ranunculus auricomus

Erect, sparsely hairy perennial to 40 cm. **Leaves** *Very variable: lowest leaves long-stalked, rounded, hardly lobed; upper leaves deeply divided.* **Flowers** 15–25 mm diam.; sepals erect; *0–5 petals, variable in number on same plant.* **Habitat** Deciduous woodland, especially on heavy basic soils. **Dist.** Native. Throughout BI; lowland to 1090 m. (All Europe.) **Fls** Apr–May.

Celery-leaved Buttercup
Ranunculus sceleratus

Erect annual to 60 cm. **Leaves** Lower *leaves deeply 3-lobed, glabrous, shiny.* **Flowers** 5–10 mm diam., sepals reflexed. **Fruits** Achenes, *receptacle elongating when ripe.* **Habitat** Marshes, muddy margins of ponds, ditches and dykes; especially coastal and tolerant of brackish conditions. **Dist.** Native. Throughout BI; lowland. (N and central Europe.) **Fls** May–Sep.

Greater Spearwort
Ranunculus lingua

Tall stoloniferous perennial to 120 cm. **Leaves** *Stem leaves to 25 cm, entire* or obscurely toothed. **Flowers** *2–5 cm diam.* **Habitat** Marshes, fens, ditch and pond margins. Frequently planted and establishing in wild. **Dist.** Native. Local throughout BI except N Scotland; lowland. (All Europe.) **Fls** Jun–Sep.

Lesser Spearwort
Ranunculus flammula

Prostrate or erect perennial to 50 cm, often rooting at lower nodes. Very variable. **Leaves** *Typically lanceolate to linear, tapering to base.* **Flowers** *8–20 mm diam.* **Habitat** Marshes, fens, woodland flushes, stream sides, pond margins, lake shores. **Dist.** Native. Common throughout BI. (Most of Europe.) **Fls** May–Sep.

Lesser Celandine
Ficaria verna

Glabrous perennial to 25 cm. Roots with numerous spindle-shaped tubers. **Leaves** *Basal leaves 1–4 cm,* stem leaves smaller. **Flowers** 2–4 cm diam., *3 sepals, 7–12 petals.* **Habitat** Woods, hedgerows, damp pastures, road verges, river and stream sides. **Dist.** Native. Throughout BI; to 750 m. (All Europe.) **Comments** Ssp. *verna* has bulbils developing in leaf axils

after flowering and is more characteristic of disturbed ground and gardens; ssp. *fertilis* has no bulbils. **Fls** Mar–May.

Water-crowfoots ▶ *Ranunculus*
Water-crowfoots are not always easy to identify and can only be named with certainty when in flower. They show great morphological variation and frequently hybridise. Two kinds of leaves can be produced: finely divided submerged leaves; and rounded, lobed floating or terrestrial leaves. The shape of the nectaries at the base of the petals is important (remove the petals and examine with a lens). Characters of the receptacle are also important.

Ivy-leaved Crowfoot
Ranunculus hederaceus

Prostrate annual or perennial, growing on mud or floating in shallow water. **Leaves** *1–3 cm wide,* shallowly lobed, *lobes broadest at base.* No finely divided leaves. **Flowers** *3–6 mm diam., petals hardly longer than sepals.* **Habitat** Mud and shallow water of pond edges, ditches, streams, wet paths, cattle tracks. **Dist.** Native. Throughout BI; to 770 m. (W Europe.) **Fls** Jun–Sep.

Round-leaved Crowfoot
Ranunculus omiophyllus

Prostrate annual or perennial, growing on mud or in shallow water. **Leaves** *8–30 mm wide,* shallowly lobed, *lobes narrowest at*

base. No finely divided leaves. **Flowers**
8–12 mm diam., petals c.*2× as long as*
sepals. **Habitat** Small, slow-moving streams,
ditches, pools, damp depressions in pastures
and heathland, on acid, nutrient-poor
soils. **Dist.** Native. Wales, W England,
SW Scotland, S Ireland; to 1005 m. (W
Europe.) **Fls** Jun–Aug.

Common Water-crowfoot
Ranunculus aquatilis

Annual or perennial aquatic with *both*
floating and finely divided submerged leaves.
Leaves Submerged leaves shorter than
internodes, segments spreading; floating
leaves deeply lobed. **Flowers** *12–18 mm*
diam., petals <10 mm, nectaries circular.
Habitat Shallow ponds, drainage dykes,
small streams. **Dist.** Native.
Throughout most of BI, but
scarce in Scotland; lowland
to 445 m. (All Europe.)
Fls May–Sep.

Pond Water-crowfoot
Ranunculus peltatus

Annual or perennial aquatic with both
floating and finely divided leaves. **Leaves**
Like *R. aquatilis* but floating leaves less
deeply lobed. **Flowers** *15–22 mm diam.,*
petals >10 mm, nectaries pear-shaped.
Habitat Wide range of shallow waters, from
small pools and drainage dykes to small
lakes and streams. **Dist.** Native. Throughout
BI, but scarce in Scotland; lowland to
500 m. (Most of Europe.) **Fls** May–Aug.

Stream Water-crowfoot
Ranunculus penicillatus

Very variable aquatic perennial.
Leaves Ssp. *penicillatus* has floating
leaves similar to those of *R. aquatilis* and
R. peltatus. Ssp. *pseudofluitans* similar

to *R. fluitans*, with submerged leaves only. **Habitat** Ssp. *penicillatus* forms dense stands in fast-flowing rivers; ssp. *pseudofluitans* found in rivers and streams. **Dist.** Native. Ssp. *penicillatus* scarce in SW England, Wales, Ireland. Ssp. *pseudofluitans* frequent in England and Wales; rare in Scotland and Ireland. (Most of Europe.) **Fls** May–Aug.

Mousetail
Myosurus minimus VU.

Small, inconspicuous annual to 10 cm. **Leaves** *Linear, in basal rosette*. **Flowers** Solitary, 5 sepals, 5 petals. **Fruits** *With elongated receptacle (the 'mousetail').* **Habitat** Bare patches on damp arable soils, such as pathsides and cattle troughs. **Dist.** Native. Scattered throughout lowland England; local and declining. (Central and S Europe.) **Fls** Midsummer.

Columbine
Aquilegia vulgaris

Glabrous or finely hairy perennial to 100 cm. **Leaves** Basal leaves long-stalked. **Flowers** 3–5 cm diam., *sepals petal-like, petals each with curved spur with swollen tip*. **Habitat** Damp woodland glades,

marshes, fens, especially on calcareous soils. Often occurs as garden escape. (S and central Europe.) **Dist.** Native. Local throughout BI; to 470 m. **Fls** May–Jun.

Meadow-rue ▶ *Thalictrum*

Common Meadow-rue
Thalictrum flavum

Erect rhizomatous *perennial to 120 cm.* **Leaves** Ultimate *leaflets distinctly longer than broad*. **Flowers** In dense clusters, *stamens erect*. **Habitat** Marshes, fens, wet meadows, stream sides, on base-rich soils. **Dist.** Native. Locally abundant in lowland England. (All Europe.) **Fls** Jul–Aug.

Lesser Meadow-rue
Thalictrum minus

Erect perennial to 120 cm. **Leaves** *Ultimate leaflets about as long as broad*. **Flowers** In loose clusters, *stamens drooping*. **Habitat** Very variable: calcareous grassland, limestone pavement, sand-dunes, lake and stream margins. **Dist.** Native throughout BI

except for much of S, where it is naturalised; to 855 m. (All Europe.) **Fls** Jun–Aug.

Alpine Meadow-rue
Thalictrum alpinum

Small, erect, stoloniferous *perennial to 15 cm.* **Leaves** *Stem leaves absent.* **Flowers** Form *unbranched inflorescence*, purplish, stamens drooping. **Habitat** Mountain grassland, rock ledges, stream sides, on base-rich soils. (Arctic and alpine Europe.) **Dist.** Native. Widespread in Scottish Highlands, also mts of

N Wales and N England; to 1190 m. **Fls** Midsummer.

PAPAVERACEAE
Poppies
....

A distinctive family of herbaceous annuals and perennials, with 2 sepals (which fall early) and 4 showy petals (in the garden plume poppies *Macleaya*, the petals are absent), and a milky or yellow latex. Leaves are spirally arranged, often deeply lobed and lack stipules. Flowers are regular; 2 sepals; 2+2 petals (or absent); numerous stamens; ovary superior. Fruit is usually a capsule.

Common Poppy
Papaver rhoeas

Annual branched herb to 20 cm. **Leaves** Hairy, deeply lobed, lowest stalked, upper sessile. **Flowers** 7–10 cm diam., petals often with black blotch at base. **Fruits** *Globose capsule, slightly longer than wide, glabrous.* **Habitat** Arable fields, disturbed ground, roadside verges, especially on calcareous soils.

Dist. Introduced in antiquity. Common on lowland throughout BI, but rare in Scotland and N Ireland. (Europe N to S Sweden.) **Fls** Jun–Sep.

Long-headed Poppy
Papaver dubium

Annual herb. Similar to *P. rhoeas*, but leaves glaucous; flowers smaller, 3–7 cm diam., paler; and *capsule ≥2× as long as wide, glabrous*. **Habitat** Similar to *P. rhoeas* (p.25) and sometimes mixed with it, but

less frequent. **Dist.** Introduced in antiquity. Throughout BI but scarcer in N; lowland to 450 m. (Europe N to S Sweden.) **Fls** Jun–Jul.

Prickly Poppy
Papaver argemone VU.

Annual herb to 45 cm. Similar to *P. rhoeas*, but *flowers* smaller, *2–6 cm diam.*, petals not overlapping and with black spot at base; *capsule elongated, ribbed and bristly*. **Habitat**

Arable fields on light sandy or chalky soils. **Dist.** Introduced with agriculture. Widespread but scattered in lowland England; rare elsewhere. (Europe N to S Sweden.) **Fls** Jun–Jul.

Welsh Poppy
Meconopsis cambrica

Branched, glabrous perennial to 60 cm. **Flowers** *5–7.5 cm diam., solitary in leaf axils.* **Fruits** Ribbed capsule, 2.5–3 cm. **Habitat** Damp rocky woodlands in native range; also hedge banks, walls, waste ground. **Dist.** Native in Wales, SW England, Ireland; to 640 m. Naturalised throughout rest of BI, especially in N. (W Europe: N Spain, Pyrenees, S France.) **Fls** Jun–Sep.

Greater Celandine
Chelidonium majus

Erect perennial to 90 cm. **Stem** Sparsely hairy, *producing bright orange latex when cut.* **Flowers** *In umbels; 2–2.5 cm diam.*, 2 sepals (soon falling), 4 petals. **Fruits** Capsule, 3–5 cm. **Habitat** Hedge banks, hedgerows, walls, especially near buildings. **Dist.** Introduced and originally cultivated for medicinal purposes, but whole plant is very poisonous. Naturalised throughout BI but rare in Scotland and W Ireland. (All Europe except far N.) **Fls** May–Aug.

Yellow Horned-poppy
Glaucium flavum

Extremely glaucous, branched, short-lived perennial to 90 cm. **Stem** Glabrous. **Leaves** Much lobed and divided, roughly hairy. **Flowers** *6–9 cm diam.* **Fruits** *Distinctive long, curved, rough pod, 15–30 cm.* **Habitat** Characteristic plant of shingle beaches; also less commonly on cliffs, sand-dunes, waste ground close to sea. **Dist.** Native. All round coast of Britain as far N as Solway; also S Ireland. (Coasts of S and W Europe.) **Fls** Jun–Sep.

FUMARIACEAE
Fumitories
••

Annuals or perennials, often climbing or scrambling, with much-divided leaves. Inflorescence usually a raceme, flowers zygomorphic, 2 sepals, 4 petals with 1 or 2 spurs, 2 stamens. The fumitories are not easy to identify. Details of the flowers and fruits are important, including colour and petal shape; sepals and fruits are illustrated within each species description. Flowers are measured from the tip of the spur to the tip of the longest petal. Petal colour excludes the dark tips. Some species are highly variable, with several subspecies and varieties.

COMMON RAMPING-FUMITORY

Common Fumitory
Fumaria officinalis

Commonest small-flowered *Fumaria*. Variable species with several named varieties. **Leaves** *Lobes flat, narrow*. **Flowers** ≥6 mm, lower petal paddle-shaped; inflorescence longer than peduncle; *bracts shorter than flower stalks*. **Fruits** Rough, tip truncate or slightly notched. **Habitat** Arable fields, gardens on light sandy or calcareous soils. **Dist.** Archaeophyte. Throughout BI; to 305 m. (All Europe.) **Fls** May–Oct.

Common Ramping-fumitory
Fumaria muralis

Commonest large-flowered *Fumaria*. Very variable species whose commonest form is ssp. *boraei*. **Leaves** Lobes flat, wedge-shaped. **Flowers** 9–12 mm, *lower petal not paddle-shaped and with erect margins*. **Fruits** *Smooth*, bracts >½ as long as pedicels. **Habitat** Arable fields, waste ground, hedge banks, walls. **Dist.** Native. Throughout BI. (W Europe.) **Fls** May–Oct.

White Ramping-fumitory
Fumaria capreolata

Leaves Lobes flat, oblong or wedge-shaped. **Flowers** *10–12 mm, cream, upper petal strongly laterally compressed, wings not concealing keel*; inflorescence shorter than

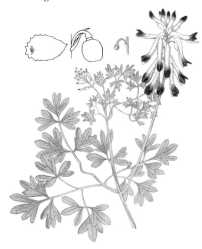

peduncle. **Fruits** Pedicels strongly recurved;
bracts narrow, equalling or shorter than
pedicels. **Habitat** Hedge banks, scrub, cliffs.
Dist. Native, scattered throughout BI. (S
and W Europe.) **Fls** May–Sep.

Climbing Corydalis
Ceratocapnos claviculata

Much-branched scrambling annual to 80 cm.
Leaves *Pinnate, ending in a branched
tendril.* **Flowers** *Cream*, 5–6 mm; *c.*6
forming inflorescence arising opposite
leaves. **Habitat** Acid woodlands, shaded
rocky hillsides; also heathy ground, peat.
Dist. Native. Throughout BI, but rare in
Ireland; lowland to 430 m. (W Europe.)
Fls Jun–Sep.

Yellow Corydalis
Pseudofumaria lutea

Much-branched erect perennial to 30 cm.
Leaves *Pinnate, ending in a leaflet.*
Flowers *Yellow,* 12–18 mm; 5–10 forming
inflorescence arising opposite leaves.
Habitat Found especially on old mortared
walls. **Dist.** Introduced; commonly
cultivated since sixteenth century. Widely
naturalised throughout BI, but rare in

Scotland and Ireland. (Native of Italian
Alps.) **Fls** May–Aug.

CANNABACEAE
Hops and hemp
······················

Hop
Humulus lupulus

Perennial, dioecious *evergreen climber.*
Leaves *Opposite, 3–5-lobed, toothed.*
Flowers Male inflorescence branched,
flowers small, 5 stamens; *female inflorescence*

a stalked cone-like spike with broad, overlapping, membranous bracts, persisting in fruit. **Habitat** Hedgerows, fen carr, woodland edges, on moist soils; often occurring as relic of cultivation. **Dist.** Native to England, Wales; introduced to Scotland, Ireland. Cultivated since sixteenth century. (All Europe except extreme N.) **Fls** Jul–Aug.

URTICACEAE
Nettles

Common Nettle
Urtica dioica

Erect, dioecious perennial to 150 cm. **Stems** With stinging hairs. **Leaves** *Cordate*, with stinging hairs, *lower leaves longer than petioles.* **Flowers** Small, perianth with 4 segments; in elongated spike-like inflorescence. **Habitat** Woodlands, fens, ditches, riverbanks, stream sides, areas associated with habitation on fertile or enriched soils; to 850 m. **Dist.** Native. Common throughout BI. (All Europe.) **Fls** Jun–Aug. **Note** Plants growing in wet fen woodland at Wicken Fen, Cambridgeshire, without stinging hairs and with narrower, more elongated leaves, densely hairy on the underside, have been named as *Urtica galeopsifolia*, but they need further study.

Small Nettle
Urtica urens

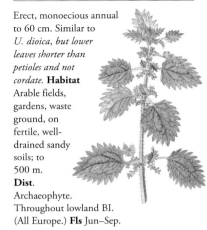

Erect, monoecious annual to 60 cm. Similar to *U. dioica, but lower leaves shorter than petioles and not cordate.* **Habitat** Arable fields, gardens, waste ground, on fertile, well-drained sandy soils; to 500 m. **Dist.** Archaeophyte. Throughout lowland BI. (All Europe.) **Fls** Jun–Sep.

Pellitory-of-the-wall
Parietaria judaica

Much-branched, softly hairy perennial to *c.*50 cm. **Leaves** *Alternate.* **Flowers** Unisexual, perianth with 4 segments. **Habitat** Crevices in old mortared walls, cliffs, steep-sided hedge banks, on dry, well-drained soils. **Dist.** Native. Throughout England, Wales; rare in Scotland, N Ireland. (W, central and S Europe.) **Fls** Jun–Oct.

Mind-your-own-business
Soleirolia soleirolii

Small, creeping, mat-forming evergreen perennial. **Stems** Slender, rooting at nodes. **Leaves** *2–6 mm, alternate*. **Flowers** Unisexual, perianth 4-lobed. **Habitat** Damp walls, banks, pathsides, gardens. (Endemic to islands of W Mediterranean.) **Dist**. Introduced; cultivated since 1905. Throughout BI, spreading from SW, but rare in Scotland and most of Ireland. **Fls** Jun–Oct.

MYRICACEAE
Bog-myrtle family

Bog-myrtle
Myrica gale

Suckering deciduous shrub to 2 m. Usually dioecious, occasionally monoecious or

hermaphrodite. **Leaves** *Grey-green*, glabrous above, downy beneath, *toothed towards apex, strongly aromatic* when crushed. **Flowers** *In catkins, perianth absent*. **Habitat** Abundant in wetter parts of acid bogs and fens, especially where there is moving ground water; lowland to 520 m. **Dist**. Native. Widespread in N and W BI, and on heaths in S. (NW Europe.) **Fls** Apr–May.

AIZOACEAE
Hottentot-fig family

Hottentot-fig
Carpobrotus edulis

Succulent, mat-forming perennial. **Leaves** 7–10 cm, triangular in section. **Flowers** *Yellow or purple*. **Habitat** Sea cliffs, rocks, walls, sand-dunes. **Dist**. Introduced in 1690 (native of S Africa). Abundant in coastal SW England, where it is a serious threat to native vegetation. (S and SW Europe.) **Fls** May–Jul.

AMARANTHACEAE
Goosefoots and oraches

A family of annual or perennial, often succulent herbs or shrubs with small, inconspicuous flowers. Leaves are alternate, simple, without stipules, and often 'mealy' with a whitish bloom. Flowers are greenish, regular, hermaphrodite or unisexual; 3–5 tepals in 1 whorl; as many or fewer stamens as tepals; ovary superior or half-inferior, 2–3 stigmas. Fruit is an achene.

Goosefoots ▶ *Chenopodium*

The goosefoots are a difficult group, and certain identification is often possible only by examining the sculpturing on the seed coat.

Good-King-Henry
Chenopodium bonus-henricus

Erect perennial to 50 cm **Leaves** To 10 cm, *dull green, broadly spear-shaped, margins wavy, untoothed.* **Flowers** Stigmas long, exserted. **Habitat** Enriched soil around farmyards, hedge banks, near old buildings. **Dist.** Archaeophyte. Widely distributed as relic of cultivation; rare in Scotland, Ireland. (All Europe except N and SW.) **Fls** May–Jul.

Red Goosefoot
Chenopodium rubrum

Prostrate to erect, *glabrous, often reddish annual*, to 70 cm. Vegetative plants superficially similar to *Atriplex prostrata* (p.34), and prostrate coastal forms very similar to *C. chenopodioides*. **Leaves** *Glossy, triangular, coarsely and irregularly toothed.* **Habitat** Farmyards, manure heaps, exposed mud of lake and pond margins, brackish marshes, dune slacks. **Dist.** Native. Throughout BI; lowland, coastal in N and W. (W, central and E Europe.) **Fls** Jun–Sep.

**FIG-LEAVED
GOOSEFOOT**

Fat-hen
Chenopodium album

Erect, usually mealy annual. **Stem** Often
red-tinged. **Branches** Usually short,

Many-seeded Goosefoot/
All-seed
Chenopodium polyspermum

Erect, glabrous annual to 1 m. **Leaves**
*Unlobed, almost untoothed, often with
purplish tinge.* **Habitat** Weed of arable crops,
gardens, waste ground. **Dist**. Archaeophyte.
Common but local in England and Wales;
rare in Scotland and Ireland. (All Europe
except N and SW.) **Fls** Jul–Aug.

Fig-leaved Goosefoot
Chenopodium ficifolium

Erect, slightly mealy annual to 90 cm.
Leaves To 8 cm, *3-lobed; middle lobe long, ±
parallel-sided; lateral lobes short,* usually with
1 tooth on lower margin. **Habitat** Arable
weed of rich fertile soils, manure heaps,
farmyards. **Dist**. Archaeophyte. Frequent in
lowland central and S England, S Wales. (W,
central and E Europe.) **Fls** Jul–Sep.

stiffly erect. **Leaves** *Toothed, variable in shape*. **Similar spp**. Several other closely related species occur less commonly in similar habitats, but can only be reliably distinguished from *C. album* by details of seed coat. **Habitat** Abundant weed of arable crops, waste ground, gardens, manure heaps, roadsides; lowland to 435 m. **Dist**. Native. Common throughout BI. (All Europe.) **Fls** Jul–Oct.

Oraches ▶ *Atriplex*

The oraches are superficially very similar to the goosefoots and they often grow together on disturbed and enriched ground. They differ in having unisexual flowers and fruits that are enclosed between a pair of enlarged bracteoles (note that these only develop as the seeds ripen and are scarcely evident during flowering).

Spear-leaved Orache
Atriplex prostrata

Erect or decumbent, glabrous to slightly mealy annual, to 100 cm. **Leaves** *Broadly triangular, upper leaves narrower*. **Flowers**

bracteole

Bracteoles sessile, 2–6 mm, joined only in basal ¼. **Habitat** Brackish marshes, dykes, shingle (where it needs to be distinguished carefully from *A. glabriuscula*); weed of disturbed soils, gardens, arable land and roadsides inland. Lowland to 415 m. **Dist**. Native. Throughout BI, but mainly coastal in N and W. (All Europe.) **Fls** Jul–Sep.

Grass-leaved Orache
Atriplex littoralis

bracteole

Much-branched, ± mealy annual to 100 cm. **Leaves** *Narrow, remotely toothed or entire*. **Fruits** Fruiting bracteoles triangular, rough. **Habitat** Upper part of salt marshes, drift lines, brackish grassland, sea walls, waste ground close to sea; sometimes forms dense stands. Spreading inland along salted road verges. **Dist**. Native. All round coasts of BI, except NW Scotland, W Ireland. (Coasts of Europe, except SE Mediterranean.) **Fls** Jul–Aug.

Common Orache
Atriplex patula

Prostrate to erect annual, to 100 cm. Similar to *A. prostrata*, *but leaves narrowly*

rhomboidal and tapering into petiole; and fruiting bracteoles triangular, fused to c. ½ their length. **Habitat** Annual weed of arable land, gardens, open ground near sea; lowland to 435 m. **Dist.** Native. Common throughout most BI, but rare in N Scotland. (All Europe.) **Fls** Jul–Sep.

Frosted Orache
Atriplex laciniata

Mealy white or silvery, prostrate annual to 30 cm. **Stems** Yellow or reddish. **Leaves** Small, 1.5–2 cm. **Fruits** *Fruiting bracteoles broader than long, warty on back and hardened at base.* **Habitat** Drift line on fine shingle and sandy shores, foot of sand-dunes, often with *Salsola kali.* **Dist.** Native. All round coasts of BI. (Coasts of W Europe, SW Spain.) **Fls** Aug–Sep.

Sea Beet
Beta vulgaris ssp. *maritima*

Much-branched, straggling perennial, usually with red pigmentation in stems and leaves.

Leaves To 10 cm, usually thick, glossy. **Flowers** *In large, branched inflorescence.* **Fruits** *Bracteoles absent; perianth and receptacle swelling.* **Habitat** Drift line on salt marshes, sand and shingle beaches, sea walls, cliffs and waste ground near sea, especially where nutrient-enriched. **Dist.** Native. All round coasts of BI, but rare in Scotland. (Coasts of Europe, N to Denmark.) **Fls** Jul–Sep. **Similar spp**. Beetroot, Sugar Beet and Mangel-wurzel, cultivated annuals with swollen roots, are forms of *B. vulgaris* ssp. *vulgaris* and sometimes occur as casuals.

Glassworts ▶ *Salicornia*

Glassworts are distinctive-looking succulent plants, with no apparent leaves and with the stems appearing jointed. In fact, the succulent sheath is composed of opposite pairs of fused leaves that surround the stem. The small flowers, which are embedded in the succulent tissue, develop in groups of three (except for *Salicornia pusilla*, where the flowers are solitary). All are plants of salt marshes and intertidal mud flats, and are physiologically adapted to growing in saline conditions (halophytes).

Glassworts are extremely variable and very difficult to identify as the distinction between species is not clear. Four taxa are reasonably distinctive. *Salicornia* species are annual. Of these, *S. pusilla* is distinguished by its solitary flowers while the rest can be divided into two aggregate species, *S. europaea* and *S. procumbens*. The last two have been further subdivided into a variable number of ill-defined species. Identification should only be attempted on groups of well-developed plants in late summer when the plants are in flower or fruiting and they develop their characteristic late-season coloration. Many populations will be found that cannot be named with confidence as they do not fit any of the descriptions precisely.

Salicornia europaea agg.

Purple Glasswort
Salicornia ramosissima

Very variable erect or prostrate annual; commonest member of genus. **Stems** Branching very variable. *Dark glossy green, becoming dark glossy purplish red, especially in prostrate forms.* Fertile segments conspicuously swollen, giving 'beaded' or 'waisted' appearance. Pale margin of segment tip conspicuous, >0.1 mm broad, internal angle of apex >90°. **Flowers** Central flower much larger than laterals. **Habitat** Upper and middle levels of marshes, creek sides, muddy shingle. **Dist.** Native. British coasts except NW Scotland. **Fls** Aug–Sep.

Salicornia procumbens agg.

Yellow Glasswort
Salicornia fragilis

Erect annual to 40 cm. **Stems** Usually with primary branches only. Green, becoming yellowish green to yellow. Fertile segments cylindrical, *terminal spikes with 8–16 fertile segments.* **Flowers** Central flower hardly larger than laterals. **Habitat** *Often forming dense stands* on bare mud on lower parts of salt marshes. **Dist.** Native. British coasts N to S Scotland; absent from SW. **Fls** Aug–Sep.

Annual Sea-blite
Suaeda maritima

Erect to prostrate annual, to *c.*30 cm. Very variable, with several named forms. **Stems** Glaucous, becoming purplish. **Leaves** Colour as stems, glabrous, 3–25 × 1–2 mm, ± *half-round in section, tip acute.* **Flowers** In groups of 1–3; 2 stigmas. **Habitat** Middle and lower levels of salt marshes, creeks, muddy shingle, dune slacks, often with *Salicornia.* **Dist.** Native. All round British coasts. (Coasts of Europe except extreme N.) **Fls** Jul–Aug.

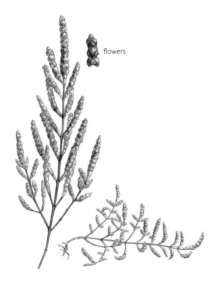

flowers

flower

**ANNUAL
SEA-BLITE**

Prickly Saltwort
Salsola kali VU.

Prostrate prickly, usually rough annual to 60 cm. **Stems** Much branched, with reddish stripes. **Leaves** Succulent, 1–4 cm, ± *half-round in section, with spiny tip.* **Flowers** Solitary, tepals spine-tipped. **Fruits** Tepals winged. **Habitat** Drift line of sandy shores, foot of sand-dunes, often with *Atriplex laciniata* and *Cakile maritima*. **Dist**. Native. All round British coasts, except extreme N. (Coasts of Europe N to latitude of N Scotland.) **Fls** Jul–Sep.

flower

PORTULACACEAE
Purslanes
••

Similar to Caryophyllaceae, *but calyx has only 2 sepals.* Annual or perennial glabrous herbs. Flowers hermaphrodite, actinomorphic, with 2 sepals, 2–6 petals (sometimes absent), 3–20 stamens, ovary superior.

Blinks
Montia fontana

Annual to perennial; erect, prostrate or floating. **Stems** Branched, 1–20 cm. **Leaves** Opposite, 2–20 × 1.5–6 mm. **Flowers** *Tiny, inconspicuous, 2–3 mm diam.; 5 white petals; 3–5 stamens.* **Habitat** Springs, flushes, stream sides, wet rocks, marshes, damp meadows, trackways, on acid soils; to 945 m. **Dist**. Native. Widespread throughout BI. (All Europe, but rare in S.) **Fls** May–Oct. **Note** Usually divided into 4 subspecies, separable only by sculpturing of seed coat. Non-flowering plants can look similar to starworts or water-purslanes.

flowers

Pink Purslane
Claytonia sibirica

Erect, glabrous annual to perennial, to 40 cm. **Leaves** Basal leaves long-stalked; *2 stem leaves, opposite, sessile but not fused across stem.* **Flowers** 15–20 mm diam.; 5 petals pink, deeply notched; 5 stamens.

Habitat Damp
woodland, shaded
stream banks on
sandy soils. **Dist**.
Introduced in
1768 (native
of Siberia and W
North America).
Well
established
throughout
BI; rare in
Ireland. (NW
Europe.) **Fls** Apr–Jul.

**PINK
PURSLANE**

CARYOPHYLLACEAE
Chickweeds, pinks and campions
••••••••••••••••••••••••••••••••••••••

A large but distinctive family of annuals and
perennials, including the pinks, campions,
chickweeds and stitchworts. Leaves
are usually in opposite and alternating
pairs, narrow, simple and entire, and
mostly without stipules. Inflorescence is
usually a characteristic dichasial cyme
(see Introduction). Flowers are normally
hermaphrodite (occasionally dioecious),
regular; 4–5 sepals, free or joined below;
4–5 petals (rarely absent), often notched or
bifid; 8 or 10 stamens; ovary superior; 2–5
styles. Fruit is a capsule or, rarely, a berry or
1-seeded nutlet (achene).

Thyme-leaved Sandwort
Arenaria serpyllifolia

Slender, erect to ascending annual or biennial
herb, to 25 cm. **Leaves** Hairy, to 6 mm.
Flowers *5–8 mm diam., sepals 3–4 mm,
petals shorter than sepals, 10 stamens, 3 styles,
capsule flask-shaped.* **Habitat** Common
on bare ground in rough grassland, grassy

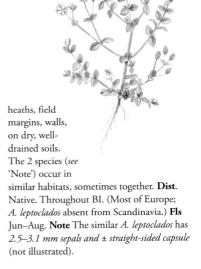

heaths, field
margins, walls,
on dry, well-
drained soils.
The 2 species (*see*
'Note') occur in
similar habitats, sometimes together. **Dist**.
Native. Throughout BI. (Most of Europe;
A. leptoclados absent from Scandinavia.) **Fls**
Jun–Aug. **Note** The similar *A. leptoclados* has
2.5–3.1 mm sepals and ± straight-sided capsule
(not illustrated).

Three-nerved Sandwort
Moehringia trinervia

Slender, branched,
prostrate to ascending
pubescent annual.
Leaves 6–25 mm,
*conspicuously
3-veined below.*
Flowers *c*.6 mm
diam., petals
shorter than
sepals, 10
stamens, 3
styles. **Habitat**
Deciduous
woodland, on
fertile, well-drained
soils; lowland to
425 m.

Dist. Native. Throughout BI except extreme N. (Most of Europe.) **Fls** May–Jun.

Sea Sandwort
Honckenya peploides

Succulent maritime, dioecious *perennial*.

Flowering and non-flowering shoots arising from long, creeping stolons. **Leaves** *Glabrous, fleshy*, 6–18 mm. **Flowers** 6–10 mm diam., *petals greenish*, 10 stamens. **Fruits** Globular, 8 mm diam., longer than sepals. **Habitat** Sand and sand-shingle shores. **Dist**. Native. Common all round British coasts. (W and NW Europe.) **Fls** May–Aug.

Spring Sandwort
Minuartia verna

Cushion-forming perennial with flowering and non-flowering shoots, to 15 cm. **Leaves** 3-veined, 6–15 mm. **Flowers** Stalks glandular-hairy, sepals 3-veined, petals longer than sepals, 3 styles. **Habitat** Open rocky habitats, scree, spoil heaps of old lead mines; to 875 m. **Dist**. Native. Local. Carboniferous limestone in N England, scattered elsewhere. (Montane Europe, except Scandinavia.) **Fls** May–Sep.

Cyphel
Minuartia sedoides VU.

Yellow-green mossy cushion-forming alpine perennial with densely leafy flowering and non-flowering shoots. **Leaves** Crowded, channelled above, 5–15 mm. **Flowers** *Greenish*, 4–5 mm diam., sepals 3-veined, *petals absent*. **Habitat** Bare open mountain ledges, flushed grassland on base-rich soils; to 1190 m. **Dist**. Native. Scottish Highlands, Inner Hebrides. (Alpine Europe.) **Fls** Jun–Aug.

Stitchworts and chickweeds ►
Stellaria and *Myosoton* | mouse-ears
► *Cerastium*

Common Chickweed
Stellaria media

Very variable prostrate to erect, much-branched annual, to 40 cm. **Stem** With single line of hairs down length. **Leaves** Lower leaves long-stalked, 3–20 mm. **Flowers** *Sepals 4.5–5 mm*; petals deeply bifid,

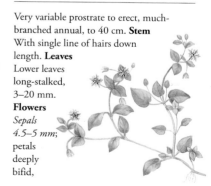

≤sepals, sometimes absent; *3–8 stamens; red-violet anthers*. **Habitat** Persistent weed of arable crops, gardens, roadsides, waste ground, on fertile soils; also coastal seabird and seal colonies, shore drift lines. **Dist**. Native. Abundant throughout BI. (All Europe.) **Fls** Year-round.

Lesser Chickweed
Stellaria pallida

Much-branched, prostrate annual to 40 cm. Similar to *S. media*, but more slender; leaves all short-stalked, <7 mm; *sepals 2–3.5 mm*, petals minute or absent, *1–2 stamens, and grey-violet anthers*. **Habitat** Coastal sand-dunes, waste ground, arable land, heath grassland, woodland rides, on light, sandy soils. **Dist**. Native. Local throughout BI, rare in NW Scotland, Ireland. (Europe, except Scandinavia.) **Fls** May–Aug.

Greater Chickweed
Stellaria neglecta

Prostrate to erect annual or perennial, to 90 cm. Similar to *S. media*, but larger in all parts, flowers c.*10 mm diam., sepals 5–6.5 mm, petals ≥sepals, and 10 stamens*. **Habitat** Wet woodlands, shady stream sides;

lowland to 440 m. **Dist**. Native. Local in England, Wales; rare in Scotland; absent from Ireland. (W, central and S Europe.) **Fls** Apr–Jul.

GREATER CHICKWEED

Greater Stitchwort
Stellaria holostea

Ascending to erect perennial, to 60 cm. **Stems** *4-angled, rough*, glabrous below, hairy above. **Leaves** 4–8 cm. **Flowers** *20–30 mm diam., petals much longer than sepals*, 10 stamens. **Habitat** Hedgerows, open woodland, roadsides, on well-drained soils. **Dist**. Native. Common throughout BI. (All Europe, except Scandinavia and extreme SW.) **Fls** Apr–Jun.

Lesser Stitchwort
Stellaria graminea

Prostrate to erect perennial, to 75 cm. **Stems** 4-angled, smooth, glabrous. **Leaves** 1.5–4 cm, linear-lanceolate, sessile; *bracts pale, without central green stripe, margins hairy.* **Flowers** 5–12 mm diam.; sepals 3-veined; *petals as long as or longer than sepals, split to >halfway;* 10 stamens. **Habitat** Rough grassland, permanent pasture, woodland rides, roadsides, on well-drained acid soils; to 740 m. **Dist**. Common throughout BI. (All Europe except Mediterranean.) **Fls** May–Aug.

Bog Stitchwort
Stellaria alsine

Prostrate to erect perennial, to 30 cm. **Stems** 4-angled, smooth, glabrous. **Leaves** 5–10 mm, sessile, narrowly ovate; *bracts*

pale with central green stripe. **Flowers** 6 mm across; sepals 3-veined; *petals shorter than sepals, split almost to base;* 10 stamens. **Habitat** Wet woodland, stream sides, marshes, spring lines, on acid soils; to 1005 m. **Dist**. Widely distributed throughout BI. (Central and W Europe.) **Fls** May–Jun.

Field Mouse-ear
Cerastium arvense

Pubescent, glandular perennial with prostrate and erect non-flowering and flowering shoots to 30 cm. **Leaves** 5–20 mm, *lower leaves with axillary bunches of small leaves.* **Flowers** 12–20 mm diam., petals about 2× as long as sepals, 10 stamens, 5 styles. **Habitat** Well-drained permanent grassland, hedge banks, road verges, sand-dunes, on calcareous to slightly acid sandy soils; lowland to 300 m. **Dist**. Native. Local throughout BI but rare in W. (Most of Europe; introduced in Scandinavia.) **Fls** Apr–Aug.

Common Mouse-ear
Cerastium fontanum

Pubescent, mat-forming perennial *with prostrate non-flowering shoots* and erect flowering shoots to *c.*40 cm. **Leaves** Dark green, covered with white hairs. **Flowers** *Petals as long as or slightly longer than sepals*, deeply split; 10 stamens; *5 styles.*

Habitat Meadows, pastures, montane grassland, cultivated soils, road verges, sand-dunes, shingle; to 1220 m. **Dist**. Native. Common throughout BI. (All Europe.) **Fls** Apr–Sep. **Note** Very variable species with a number of named subspecies; the common British plant is ssp. *vulgare*.

Sticky Mouse-ear
Cerastium glomeratum

Erect, pubescent, glandular annual. **Leaves** *Yellow-green, broader than* C. fontanum. **Flowers** Clustered into compact heads, flower stalks very short; *sepals glandular with long white hairs extending beyond tips*; petals about equalling sepals, split to *c*.¾ of their length; 10 stamens; 5 styles. **Habitat** Arable weed, improved grassland, walls, roadsides, sand-dunes; lowland to 610 m. **Dist**. Native. Common throughout BI. (Most of Europe except extreme N.) **Fls** Apr–Sep.

Sea Mouse-ear
Cerastium diffusum

Slender, prostrate to erect, branched, glandular annual, to 30 cm. **Leaves** *Bracts and bracteoles wholly green without pale*

margins. **Flowers** 3–6 mm diam.; *usually 4 sepals and petals*, sepals glandular-hairy but hairs not projecting beyond tips, petals shorter than sepals; *4 stamens; 4 styles*. **Habitat** Sand-dunes, open grassland, sandy and gravelly habitats, close to sea; lowland and coastal. **Dist**. Native. Throughout BI. (W Europe.) **Fls** May–Jul.

Water Chickweed
Myosoton aquaticum

Prostrate to erect, somewhat trailing or scrambling perennial, to 100 cm. Stems Glabrous below, hairy and glandular above. Leaves 2–5 cm; base cordate, often with wavy margin. Flowers 12–15 cm diam.; stalks glandular; petals longer than sepals, split almost to base. Habitat Marshes, wet meadows, riverbanks, sides of ponds, streams and ditches.

Dist. Native. Lowland England, W Wales. (W, central and E Europe.) Fls Jul–Aug.

Pearlworts ▶ *Sagina*

Knotted Pearlwort
Sagina nodosa

Tufted, procumbent to erect, glabrous or glandular-hairy perennial, to 15 cm, with basal leaf rosettes. **Leaves** Linear; *upper leaves with bunches of short leaves in their axils,* giving characteristic 'knotted' appearance. **Flowers** 0.5–1.0 cm diam.; *5 petals, 2× as long as sepals*; sepals glandular; 10 stamens; 5 styles. **Habitat** Short, wet, broken turf on calcareous or peaty soils, mires, dune slacks; lowland to 850 m. **Dist**. Native. Throughout BI, but rare and declining in S. (All Europe except S.) **Fls** Jul–Sep.

Flowers Stalks glabrous; 4–5 sepals, blunt-tipped, hooded, spreading in fruit; *petals minute or absent*. **Habitat** Paths, banks, wall tops, grass verges, waste ground; to 1150 m. **Dist**. Native. Abundant throughout BI. (All Europe.) **Fls** May–Sep.

Annual Pearlwort
Sagina apetala, S. filicaulis

Erect, branching annual to 15 cm, with 2 closely related species. **Stems** Main stem flowering. **Leaves** *Tapering to a fine point.* **Flowers** 4 sepals, petals minute or absent; in *S. filicaulis* sepals spread in fruit and all 4 are blunt; in *S. apetala* sepals are erect in fruit, the outer acute and the inner blunt. **Habitat** Walls, paths, bare ground, on dry sandy or gravelly soils. **Dist**. Native. Both species occur throughout BI. (All Europe except Scandinavia.) **Fls** May–Aug.

Procumbent Pearlwort
Sagina procumbens

Tufted, mat-forming perennial with a tight rosette of leaves and long, prostrate side-shoots that root at nodes.

PROCUMBENT PEARLWORT

glabrous. **Habitat** Open, disturbed ground of grassy heaths, arable land, on dry sandy soils; lowland to 365 m. **Dist**. Native. Scattered and local throughout BI; rare in N and Ireland. (All Europe except extreme N.) **Fls** Jun–Aug.

Spurreys ▶ *Spergula* and *Spergularia*

Sea Pearlwort
Sagina maritima

Erect, branching annual to 15 cm. Similar *S. apetala*, but *leaves are blunt with a short point (<0.1 mm), not tapering to a fine point.* **Habitat** Bare patches in dune slacks, cliff tops, fine shingle, roadsides. **Dist**. Native. All round British coasts. (All European coasts.) **Fls** May–Sep.

Knawels ▶ *Scleranthus*
Much-branched annuals or perennials, with opposite pairs of linear leaves that meet across the stem. Flowers inconspicuous, greenish white, in dense inflorescences; 5 sepals, petals absent.

Annual Knawel
Scleranthus annuus

Erect, branched annual to 20 cm. **Leaves** 5–15 mm. **Flowers** *c.*4 mm diam., *calyx*

Corn Spurrey
Spergula arvensis VU.

Very variable weak-stemmed, rather scrambling, glandular annual to 40 cm.
Leaves Linear, channelled beneath, 1–3 cm; stipules deciduous.
Flowers 4–7 mm diam., petals slightly longer than sepals, 10 stamens, *5 stigmas.* **Habitat** Arable weed of light, sandy, acid soils; lowland to 450 m. **Dist**. Archaeophyte. Common throughout BI. (All Europe.) **Fls** Jun–Sep.

Rock Sea-spurrey
Spergularia rupicola

Densely glandular, hairy perennial to 15 cm. **Stems** Not ridged, often purplish. **Leaves**

Fleshy, slightly flattened, 5–15 mm; stipules silvery. **Flowers** 8–10 mm diam.; petals as long as or slightly longer than sepals, deep pink. **Habitat** Short turf and broken ground on cliffs, scree, rocks, walls and bird colonies close to sea. **Dist**. Native. Local. S and W coasts of BI as far N as N Uist. (W coast of Europe.) **Fls** Jun–Sep.

Greater Sea-spurrey
Spergularia media

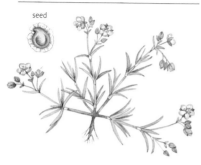

Prostrate to ascending, glabrous perennial, to 30 cm. **Leaves** Linear, fleshy, 1–2.5 cm; stipules triangular, pale but not silvery. **Flowers** 7.5–12 mm diam.; *petals slightly longer than sepals, pale pink*. **Fruits** *Seeds pale yellowish brown, winged, with broad pale border*. **Habitat** Salt and brackish marshes on sandy and muddy shores; also occasionally on salt-treated roadsides. **Dist**. Native. Common all round coasts of BI. (All round coasts of Europe; inland in E.) **Fls** Jun–Sep.

Lesser Sea-spurrey
Spergularia marina

Prostrate, glabrous or slightly glandular-hairy annual to 20 cm. **Leaves** Yellowish green. **Flowers** Similar to *S. media*, but smaller, 6–8 mm diam., *petals shorter than sepals, deep pink*. **Fruits** *Seeds mostly without a border*. **Habitat** Drier parts of salt and brackish marshes on sandy and muddy

shores, often with *S. media*; also saline lagoons inland, and spreading along salt-treated road verges. **Dist**. Native. All round coasts of BI. (All coasts of Europe; also saline soils inland.) **Fls** Jun–Aug.

Sand Spurrey
Spergularia rubra

Prostrate, glandular-hairy annual or biennial to 25 cm. **Leaves** Not fleshy, tapering to a fine point, 4–25 mm; *stipules conspicuous, silvery*, narrow, torn at tip. **Flowers** *3–5 mm diam., stalk longer than sepals; petals deep pink*, pale at base, shorter than sepals. **Habitat** Open ground on heathland, cliff tops, dunes, tracks, quarries, waste ground, on dry, acid, sandy soils; lowland to 560 m. **Dist**. Native. Throughout BI, but rare in Ireland. (All Europe except extreme N.) **Fls** May–Sep.

Corncockle
Agrostemma githago

Erect, pubescent annual to 100 cm. **Flowers** Large, conspicuous, 3–5 cm diam.; *calyx*

CORNCOCKLE

tube 10-ribbed, with long, narrow, spreading teeth, 3–5 cm, longer than petals. **Dist**. Archaeophyte, introduced with agriculture in Iron Age. Originally most of BI but now extinct as an arable weed. Frequently introduced in wildflower mixes. (Native in most of Europe except extreme N.) **Fls** Jun–Aug.

Campions and catchflies ►
Silene

Ragged-robin
Silene flos-cuculi

Erect, glabrous or sparsely hairy perennial to *c*.70 cm. **Flowers** 3–4 cm diam.; calyx tube reddish, strongly 10-veined; *petals deeply divided into 4 narrow lobes*; 10 stamens; 5 styles. **Habitat** Marshes, fens, wet meadows, woodlands, avoiding acid soils; to 750 m. **Dist**. Native. Common throughout BI. (All Europe, except extreme S.) **Fls** May–Jun.

Bladder Campion
Silene vulgaris

Erect, usually glabrous but sometimes pubescent, rather glaucous perennial to 90 cm. **Flowers** Male, female or hermaphrodite, drooping, *c*.18 mm diam.; calyx strongly inflated, narrowed at apex, pale or pinkish, net-veined with 20 main veins; petals deeply notched. **Fruits** *Teeth of capsule erect.* **Habitat** Permanent grassland, arable fields, hedge banks, roadsides, disturbed ground on dry calcareous soils; to 350 m. **Dist**. Native. All BI except for Northern Isles. (All Europe.) **Fls** Jun–Aug.

Sea Campion
Silene uniflora

Prostrate maritime perennial *with cushion of non-flowering shoots*, to 25 cm. **Leaves** Similar to *S. vulgaris*. **Flowers** Similar to *S. vulgaris*, but larger, 20–25 mm diam.; *calyx not narrowed at apex and calyx teeth recurved*. **Habitat** Sea cliffs, bird colonies, rocky ground, shingle beaches; also grows as an alpine plant of cliff ledges and lake margins to 970 m in Scotland. **Dist**. Native. Common all round coasts of BI. (Coasts of W Europe.) **Fls** Jun–Aug.

Moss Campion
Silene acaulis *(NI)

Densely tufted, cushion-forming alpine perennial to 10 cm.

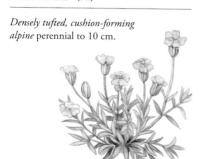

Leaves In tight rosettes, linear, fringed with stiff hairs. **Flowers** 9–12 mm diam., solitary; calyx glabrous, faintly 10-veined, reddish. **Habitat** Rock ledges, scree, crevices, mountain-top detritus, on basic soils; to 1305 m. **Dist**. Native. Widespread in Scottish Highlands; scattered in N Wales, Lake District. (Arctic and alpine Europe.) **Fls** Jul–Aug.

White Campion
Silene latifolia

Erect, hairy, slightly glandular, dioecious perennial to 100 cm. **Flowers** 25–30 mm diam., unisexual; calyx tube hairy, glandular, 10- or 20-veined, 18–25 mm long; *5 styles*. **Fruits** Capsule teeth ± erect. **Habitat** Cultivated ground, waste places, roadsides, on dry, especially calcareous soils; lowland to 425 m. **Dist**. Archaeophyte. Throughout BI. (All Europe except extreme N.) **Fls** May–Sep.

Soapwort
Saponaria officinalis

Erect, stoloniferous, *glabrous perennial to 90 cm*. **Flowers** *2.5 cm diam.*; sepals joined at base; calyx tube glabrous, 18–20 mm, reddish; 2 styles. **Fruits** Capsule with 4 unequal teeth. **Habitat** Hedge banks, roadsides, damp, shady habitats, usually near habitation. **Dist**. Archaeophyte. Naturalised throughout BI except extreme NW. (Native throughout Europe except Scandinavia.) **Fls** Jul–Sep.

Red Campion
Silene dioica

Erect, hairy, dioecious biennial or perennial to 90 cm, with numerous prostrate non-flowering shoots. **Flowers** 18–25 mm diam., unisexual; calyx tube hairy, glandular, 10- or 20-veined, 10–15 mm long; *5 styles*. **Fruits** Capsule teeth recurved. **Habitat** Deciduous woodland, hedgerows, hedge banks, on fertile, base-rich soils; also cliffs (including bird cliffs), scree. To 1065 m. **Dist**. Native. Common throughout BI. (Most of Europe except extreme SW.) **Fls** May–Jun. **Note** Hybrids between *S. dioica* and *S. latifolia*, *S.* × *hampeana*, with pink flowers and intermediate characters, are common where the parents grow together.

RED CAMPION

POLYGONACEAE
Knotweeds, sorrels and docks
• •

A family of herbs, shrubs and climbers, usually with rather small, inconspicuous flowers. Leaves are alternate, simple and usually entire, with characteristic sheathing stipules that surround the stem above the petiole. Flowers are regular, and hermaphrodite or unisexual; 3–6 greenish, brownish, white or pink tepals in 2 whorls; 6–9 stamens; ovary superior, 2–3 stigmas. Fruit is an achene.

Common Bistort
Persicaria bistorta

Erect, almost glabrous, *unbranched perennial to 50 cm*. **Leaves** *Petiole of basal leaves winged*, stem leaves sessile. **Flowers** In a dense terminal spike; tepals 4–5 mm, pink.

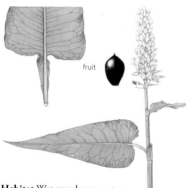

fruit

Habitat Wet meadows, pastures, damp roadsides, alder carr; to 430 m. Often occurs as garden escape. **Dist**. Native. Throughout BI, but rare in Ireland. (Most of Europe except Scandinavia and Mediterranean.) **Fls** Jun–Aug.

Amphibious Bistort
Persicaria amphibia *(R)

Creeping, rhizomatous perennial. Occurs in both terrestrial and aquatic forms. **Stems** Erect in terrestrial plant, rooting at nodes. **Leaves** *Rounded or cordate at base*; ± sessile and pubescent in terrestrial plant; floating and glabrous with long petiole in aquatic. **Flowers** In dense inflorescence; tepals 3.5 mm, pink; *stamens protruding*; 2 styles. **Habitat** Terrestrial form on margins of dykes,

lakes and ponds and as arable weed; aquatic form in ponds, lakes, canals, dykes, streams; to 570 m. **Dist**. Native. Throughout BI. (All Europe.) **Fls** Jul–Sep.

fruit

Redshank
Persicaria maculosa

Prostrate to erect, ± glabrous annual, to 75 cm. **Leaves** 3–11 cm, *often with large black blotch*. **Flowers** *In dense inflorescence;*

fruit

peduncle and flowers without glands, glabrous; tepals bright pink, sometimes whitish. **Habitat** Weed of cultivated land, gardens, waste ground, roadsides; also banks of ponds, rivers, streams. Lowland to 450 m. **Dist**. Native. Common throughout BI. (All Europe except extreme N.) **Fls** Jun–Oct.

Pale Persicaria
Persicaria lapathifolia

Prostrate to erect, often pubescent annual, to 60 cm. **Leaves** 5–15 cm, often with large black blotch. **Flowers** In dense inflorescence; *peduncle and flowers with numerous yellow glands*; tepals dull pink to white or greenish (but note that colour of flower is not a reliable difference from *P. maculosa*). **Habitat** Similar to *P. maculosa*, with which it sometimes grows; lowland to 450 m. **Dist**. Native. Throughout BI, but scarce in extreme N. (All Europe.) **Fls** Jun–Aug.

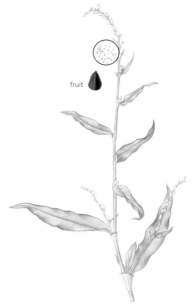

fruit

fruit

Water-pepper
Persicaria hydropiper

Erect, glabrous annual, with stems rooting at nodes. **Leaves** Mid-stem stipule teeth *c*.0.3 mm; *with burning, acrid taste* (hence 'pepper'). **Flowers** *Glandular*, ≥4 mm, pale pink to greenish white, *in long, slender, interrupted, nodding inflorescence*. **Fruits** Dull nuts. **Habitat** Margins of ponds, lakes, rivers, streams and dykes, woodland rides where water stands in winter. **Dist**. Native. Common throughout BI, but rare in extreme N. (All Europe except extreme N.) **Fls** Jul–Sep.

Alpine Bistort
Persicaria vivipara *(R)

Slender, erect, unbranched, glabrous perennial to 30 cm. **Leaves** *Basal leaves stalked, unwinged; upper leaves sessile.*

BUCKWHEAT

Flowers In slender *inflorescence spike, flowers in upper part only, lower part consisting of purple bulbils*; tepals 3–4 mm, pink-white. **Habitat** Mountain grassland and pastures, scree, wet rocks; uplands to 1210 m. **Dist**. Native. N England, Scotland. (N and alpine Europe.) **Fls** Jun–Aug.

Buckwheat
Fagopyrum esculentum

Erect, thinly pubescent, little-branched annual to 60 cm. **Leaves** *Triangular, cordate.* **Flowers** *Inflorescence of compact clusters at ends of long peduncles*; 5 tepals, 3–4 mm, white to pale pink. **Fruits** Tepals neither keeled nor winged. **Habitat** Casual of waste ground, rubbish tips, field borders; also a relic of cultivation. **Dist**. Introduced (native of SW China). (W, central and E Europe.) **Fls** Jul–Aug.

Knotgrasses ▶ *Polygonum*

Equal-leaved Knotgrass
Polygonum arenastrum

Much-branched, prostrate, mat-forming annual to 30 cm. **Leaves** *All ± same size, crowded and overlapping.* **Flowers** *Tepals greenish white to pinkish, c.1.5 mm, fused for ⅓–½ of their length.* **Fruits**

fruit

Nut, about as long as perianth. **Habitat** Compacted sandy, gravelly soils of tracks, footpaths, gateways, waste ground. **Dist**. Archaeophyte. Common throughout BI. (All Europe except extreme N.) **Fls** Jul–Nov.

Knotgrass
Polygonum aviculare

Much-branched, prostrate to erect annual, to 200 cm. **Leaves** *Of markedly different sizes*, those on main stem much larger, >5 mm wide, than those on branches and flowering stems; petioles enclosed within stipules. **Flowers** *Tepals c.2 mm, fused for up to ¼ of their length*, overlapping almost to tip. **Fruits** Nut, 2.5–3.5 mm. **Habitat** Waste and disturbed ground, roadsides, seashores; also garden and arable weed. To 550 m. **Dist**. Native. Common throughout BI (except Shetland). (All Europe.) **Fls** Jul–Nov.

fruit and flowers

NORTHERN KNOTGRASS

flower

fruit

Mountain Sorrel
Oxyria digyna

Tufted, glabrous, dioecious perennial to 30 cm. **Leaves** *Basal, kidney-shaped, acid to the taste*, becoming reddish in late summer. **Flowers** In branched inflorescence. **Fruits** Broadly winged nut, 3–4 mm. **Habitat** Wet rock ledges, damp rocks by streams, river

fruit

Northern Knotgrass
Polygonum boreale

Prostrate to erect, scrambling annual, to 100 cm. Similar to *P. aviculare*, *but petioles longer than stipules and nut larger, 3.5–4.5 mm*. **Habitat** Similar to *P. aviculare*. **Dist**. Native. N Scotland, Outer Hebrides, Orkney, Shetland (where it replaces *P. aviculare*). (N Scandinavia, Iceland, Faeroes.) **Fls** Jun–Oct.

shingle; to 1190 m. **Dist**. Native. Locally common in mts of N Wales, Lake District, Scotland, Ireland. (Arctic and alpine Europe.) **Fls** Jul–Aug.

Knotweeds ▶ *Fallopia*

Japanese Knotweed
Fallopia japonica

Tall, erect, clump- or thicket-forming perennial to 200 cm. **Stems** Annual, glaucous to reddish. **Leaves** *Truncate at base*, 6–12 cm, *glabrous*. **Flowers** Inflorescence branches slender, shorter than leaves. **Habitat** Roadsides, railways, riverbanks, waste ground. **Dist**. Introduced as a garden plant from Japan in 1825. Established and persistent throughout BI. Highly invasive. (Established in W, central and E Europe.) **Fls** Aug–Oct.

fruit

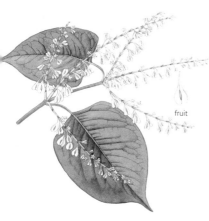

fruit

Giant Knotweed
Fallopia sachalinensis

Similar to *F. japonica*, but taller, to 400 cm; **Leaves** *larger, 15–40 cm, cordate at base, undersides sparsely pubescent.* **Habitat** Forms extensive thickets on roadsides, waste ground, riverbanks, and lake and loch shores. **Dist**. Introduced as a garden plant in 1869 from Sakhalin I. Established throughout BI, but less common than *F. japonica*. (Established in W and central Europe.) **Fls** Aug–Sep.

Black-bindweed
Fallopia convolvulus

Scrambling or climbing, slightly mealy annual to 120 cm. **Fruits** *Dull* black nut, 4–5 mm; *fruiting pedicels 1–3 mm, jointed above middle; outer tepals narrowly winged in fruit.* **Habitat** Weed of arable land, gardens, rubbish tips, waste ground, roadsides; to 450 m. **Dist**. Archaeophyte. Common throughout BI. (All Europe.) **Fls** Jul–Oct.

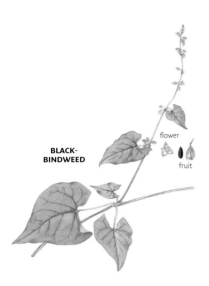

BLACK-BINDWEED

flower

fruit

Sorrels and docks ▶ *Rumex*

Sheep's Sorrel
Rumex acetosella

Slender, erect, glabrous, dioecious perennial to 30 cm. **Leaves** To 4 cm, with *narrow, spreading basal lobes*; upper leaves distinctly stalked. **Flowers** Outer tepals remain appressed to inner. **Fruits** Glossy nut, 1.3–1.5 mm. **Habitat** Acid grassland, heaths, commons, on well-drained sandy soils; to 1050 m. **Dist**. Native. Common throughout BI. (All Europe.) **Fls** May–Sep.

fruit

Common Sorrel
Rumex acetosa

Erect, glabrous, tufted, dioecious perennial to 50(–100) cm. **Leaves** *4–7 cm; basal lobes pointing downwards or slightly convergent*; upper leaves sessile, clasping stem. **Flowers** Outer tepals reflexed after flowering. **Fruits** Glossy nut, 2–2.5 mm. **Habitat** Grassland, woodland rides, roadside verges, riverbanks, coastal shingle, mountain ledges; to 1215 m. **Dist**. Native. Common throughout BI. (All Europe.) **Fls** May–Jun.

Northern Dock
Rumex longifolius

Robust perennial to 120 cm. Similar to *R. aquaticus*, but *basal leaves to 60 cm, broadly lanceolate, margins undulate; fruiting tepals kidney-shaped, about as long as wide, without teeth or tubercles*. **Habitat** Wet meadows, banks of rivers, streams and lakes, farmland; to 520 m. **Dist**. Native. Widespread in N England, Scotland. (NW Europe, Pyrenees.) **Fls** Jun–Aug.

fruit

Water Dock
Rumex hydrolapathum

fruit

Tall, robust, erect, much-branched, tufted perennial to 200 cm. **Leaves** *Basal leaves to 110 cm.* **Flowers** In dense inflorescence. **Fruits** *Fruiting tepals ± triangular, without teeth, each with elongated tubercle.* **Habitat** Margins of lakes, ponds, rivers, ditches, dykes and canal, fens, marshes; lowland. **Dist**. Native. Widespread in England, rare in rest of BI. (W, central and E Europe.) **Fls** Jul–Sep.

Curled Dock
Rumex crispus

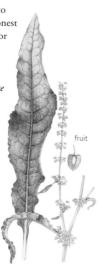
fruit

Tall, erect perennial to 100 cm. The commonest British dock, with 2 or 3 subspecies. **Leaves** *Basal leaves narrow, almost parallel-sided, edges strongly undulate or crisped*, to 35 cm. **Flowers** In open inflorescence in ssp. *crispus*; in dense inflorescence in ssp. *littoreus.* **Fruits** *Fruiting tepals triangular, without teeth*, variously 1–3 tubercles, unequal or subequal in size. In ssp. *crispus*, tubercles on fruiting tepals unequal or

only 1, nuts ≤2.5 mm; in ssp. *littoreus*, usually 3 tubercles, ± equal, nuts ≥2.5 mm. **Habitat** Cultivated soils, waste places, roadsides, hedge banks, water margins; ssp. *littoreus* found on coastal shingle, sand-dunes. To 845 m. **Dist**. Native. Throughout BI. (All Europe except extreme N.) **Fls** Jun–Oct.

Clustered Dock
Rumex conglomeratus

Erect, branched perennial to 60 cm. **Leaves** To 30 cm, petiole often as long as leaf blade. **Flowers** In whorls, forming much-branched, *leafy inflorescence*, branches making wide angle of ≥30° with main stem. **Fruits** *Fruiting tepals narrow, without teeth, each with oblong tubercle* (perianth with 3 tubercles). **Habitat** Banks of ponds, ditches, streams and rivers, marshes, wet places where water stands in winter. **Dist**. Native. Common throughout BI except N Scotland. (Most of Europe except Scandinavia.) **Fls** Jul–Oct.

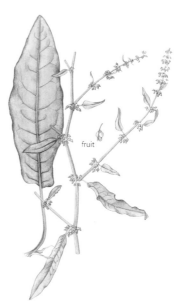
fruit

Wood Dock
Rumex sanguineus

Erect, sparsely branched perennial to 60 cm. Similar to *R. conglomeratus*, but *inflorescence* branches less wide-spreading (angle ≤30° to main stem), *not leafy to top*; fruiting tepals narrow, without teeth, *perianth with 1 tubercle*, rounded. **Habitat** Woodland rides, clearings, roadside verges, hedgerows, waste ground; lowland to 350 m. **Dist**. Native. Common throughout BI except extreme N Scotland. (Most of Europe except Spain and Scandinavia.) **Fls** Jun–Jul.

fruit

Fiddle Dock
Rumex pulcher

Much-branched, spreading biennial or perennial to 40 cm. **Stems** *Branches tangled, making wide angle with stem.* **Leaves** To 10 cm, *distinctly constricted above base.* **Flowers** In whorls; inflorescence a tangle of wide-spreading branches. **Fruits** *Fruiting tepals toothed, each with rough tubercle (perianth with 3 tubercles).* **Habitat** Well-drained, short coastal grassland, village greens, churchyards, roadsides. **Dist**. Native. S and SE England. (S and SW Europe.) **Fls** Jun–Jul.

Broad-leaved Dock
Rumex obtusifolius

Tall, robust perennial to 100 cm. **Leaves** *Basal leaves to 100 cm, broad, strongly cordate at base, glabrous above, hairy below.* **Flowers** In open inflorescence, leafy below. **Fruits** *Fruiting tepals triangular, with prominent teeth, 1 with a tubercle (perianth with 1 tubercle).* **Habitat** Waste places, hedge banks, pastures, roadsides, water margins, disturbed ground. **Dist**. Native. Abundant throughout BI. (Most Europe except N Scandinavia.) **Fls** Jun–Oct.

fruit

PLUMBAGINACEAE
Sea-lavenders and thrifts

Characteristic and unmistakable plants of coastal habitats, with purple or pink flowers. Leaves are all basal. Flowers are regular; 5 petals and sepals, fused below; 5 stamens; ovary superior.

Sea-lavenders ▶ *Limonium*
The small flowers of the sea-lavenders are arranged in 1–5-flowered spikelets, each of which has 3 scale-like bracts; the spikelets are further grouped together into spikes at the end of the branches of the inflorescence.

Common Sea-lavender
Limonium vulgare

Erect perennial to 40 cm. **Leaves** Pinnately veined, tip with short recurved spine.

Flowers In dense, rather flat-topped inflorescence, *branching from above middle of stem*; outer bract of flower clusters ≤3 mm, rounded on back; *anthers yellow*. **Habitat** Intermediate zone of inter-tidal salt marsh. **Dist**. Native. Abundant on coasts of BI except extreme SW Wales, Scotland, Ireland. (W and S Europe.) **Fls** Jun–Oct.

Lax-flowered Sea-lavender
Limonium humile

Erect perennial to 40 cm. Similar to *L. vulgare* (with which it frequently hybridises, giving rise to intermediate individuals), but inflorescence more open, *branching from below middle of stem*; outer bract of flower clusters ≥3 mm, usually keeled; *anthers reddish. In cases of doubt, certain identification is possible only by microscopic examination of the pollen.*

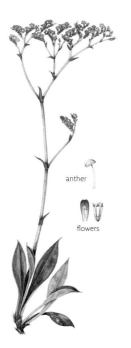

anther

flowers

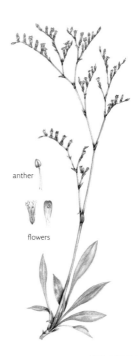

anther

flowers

Habitat Intermediate zone of inter-tidal salt marsh. **Dist**. Native. Coasts of BI as for *L. vulgare*, but also including SW Wales, Ireland. (W Europe.) **Fls** Jun–Oct.

Rock Sea-lavender
Limonium binervosum agg. *(NI)

Erect evergreen perennial to 30 cm. **Leaves** *Narrowly obovate, with 1–3 veins*. **Flowers** In variable inflorescence. **Habitat** Dry maritime cliffs, rocks, consolidated shingle. **Dist**. Native. Local on coasts of BI except NE England, Scotland. (Coasts of SW Europe.) **Fls** Jul–Sep. **Note** Extremely variable species; *L. binervosum* has been separated into more than 20 closely related and very variable species and subspecies that are very difficult to distinguish. Most are restricted to single localities or small areas of coast.

flowers

Thrift
Armeria maritima

Dense mat- or cushion-forming perennial with 2 subspecies: ssp. *maritima* and ssp. *elongata*. **Stems** Flowering stems erect, unbranched, to 30 cm. Stems hairy in ssp. *maritima*, glabrous in ssp. *elongata*. **Leaves** Linear, narrow, <2 mm wide, with 1 vein. **Flowers** In heads, 15–25 mm across; in ssp. *maritima*, sheath surrounding bracts ≤15 mm, outer bracts shorter than inner; in ssp. *elongata*, sheath surrounding bracts 12–25 mm, outer bracts as long as inner. **Habitat** Ssp. *maritima* in middle zone of salt marshes, maritime rocks, cliffs; alpine habitats inland on mountain rocks, cliffs, moss heaths; metal-rich waste, salted road verges; to 1270 m. Ssp. *elongata* on sandy soil. **Dist**. Native. Ssp. *maritima* common on all coasts of BI and inland; ssp. *elongata* CR. in only 2 localities in Lincolnshire. (W Europe.) **Fls** Apr–Oct.

HYPERICACEAE
St John's-worts
•••

An easily recognised family of annuals or perennials or small shrubs with opposite leaves without stipules and yellow flowers. Leaves sessile, often with translucent or colourless glands; flowers regular; sepals and petals 5, often glandular; stamens numerous and grouped in bundles; ovary superior; fruit a capsule or berry-like.

Tutsan
Hypericum androsaemum

Erect, branched, half-evergreen, shrubby, mildly aromatic perennial to 100 cm. **Stems** With 2 raised lines. **Leaves** Glabrous, to 10 cm. **Flowers** *c.2 cm across*, in few-flowered inflorescence; sepals unequal; *stamens as long as petals*; styles shorter than

stamens. **Fruits** Red, turning black. **Habitat** Damp deciduous woodland, hedge banks, grikes in limestone pavement. **Dist**. Native. Widely distributed throughout W and S BI; frequently naturalised outside native range. (W and S Europe.) **Fls** Jun–Aug.

Perforate St John's-wort
Hypericum perforatum

Erect, glabrous, rhizomatous perennial to 90 cm. **Stems** *With 2 raised lines.* **Leaves**

To 2 cm, with abundant small yellowish translucent glandular dots (visible when held up to light). **Flowers** *c.*2 cm across; *sepals glandular, shorter than petals*. **Habitat** Rough grassland, meadows, road verges, hedge banks, open woodland. **Dist**. Native. Common throughout BI except extreme N Scotland. (All Europe except extreme N.) **Fls** Jun–Sep.

Imperforate St John's-wort
Hypericum maculatum

Erect, glabrous, rhizomatous perennial to 60 cm. **Stems** *With 4 raised lines.* **Leaves** Narrowed to base, not clasping stem. **Flowers** Bright yellow, *c.*2 cm across, *petals ≥2× as long as sepals*, sepals and petals with black glands. **Habitat** Damp wood margins, rough grassland, hedge banks, roadsides; lowland to 320 m. **Dist**. Native. (Central and N Europe.) **Fls** Jun–Aug. **Comments** Ssp. *maculatum* sparsely branched, branches making angle of 30° with stem; leaves without transparent glands; sepals 2–3 mm wide, tip entire. Rare, in scattered localities in Scotland only Ssp. *obtusiusculum* more branched, branches making angle of *c.*50° with main stem; leaves usually with transparent glands; sepals 1.2–2 mm wide, tip toothed. Local throughout most of BI.

Square-stalked St John's-wort
Hypericum tetrapterum

Erect stoloniferous glabrous perennial to 70 cm. **Stems** *Square in section, angles winged.* **Leaves** To 2 cm, half-clasping stem, with small translucent glands. **Flowers** *Pale yellow, c.1 cm across; sepals c.⅔ length of petals.* **Habitat** Damp grassland, woodland clearings, road verges, pond and stream margins; lowland to 380 m. **Dist**. Native. Frequent throughout BI except extreme N Scotland. (All Europe.) **Fls** Jun–Sep.

Trailing St John's-wort
Hypericum humifusum

Slender, prostrate, glabrous perennial to 20 cm. **Stems** With 2 raised lines. **Leaves** Elliptic, to 1 cm, with translucent glands.

Flowers *c.*1 cm across; *petals ≤2× as long as sepals;* sepals unequal, glandular. **Habitat** Open patches in woodland paths and clearings, heaths, moors, on acid soils; lowland to 530 m. **Dist**. Native. Most of BI. (W and central Europe.) **Fls** Jun–Sep.

Slender St John's-wort
Hypericum pulchrum

Erect, glabrous perennial to 60 cm. **Stems** *Without raised lines.* **Leaves** To 1 cm, with transparent glands, *broadly cordate, their bases clasping and meeting across stem.* **Flowers** 1.5 cm across, petals red-tinged, sepals fringed with stalked black glands. **Habitat** Grassy heaths, commons, woodland clearings, rides, on well-drained acid soils; to 820 m. **Dist**. Native. Throughout BI. (W and central Europe.) **Fls** Jun–Aug.

Hairy St John's-wort
Hypericum hirsutum *(R)

Erect, pubescent, little-branched perennial to 100 cm. **Stems** *Without raised lines*. **Flowers** *c*.1.5 cm across, in many-flowered inflorescence; petals pale yellow; sepals ½ length of petals, fringed with stalked black glands. **Habitat** Rough grassland, scrub, open woodland, chiefly on calcareous soils. **Dist**. Native. Most of BI, but rare or absent in N Scotland and W. (N and central Europe.) **Fls** Jul–Aug.

Marsh St John's-wort
Hypericum elodes

Prostrate to erect, *stoloniferous, densely hairy perennial*, to 30 cm. **Stems** *Without raised lines*, rooting at nodes. **Leaves** *Rounded, ± clasping*. **Flowers** *c*.1.5 cm across, in few-flowered inflorescence; *sepals with stalked red glandular teeth*. **Habitat** Margins of acid pools, streams, flushes on heaths, bogs. **Dist**. Native. Local and declining. W BI, S England; scattered elsewhere. (W Europe.) **Fls** Jun–Sep.

MALVACEAE
Mallows
••

Herbs or shrubs, usually with showy pink or purplish flowers. Leaves are alternate, often palmately lobed. Flowers are in racemes or solitary in axils of leaves, regular and with an epicalyx of 3 to several sepal-like segments below calyx (looks like an outer ring of sepals); 5 sepals; 5 petals, free; numerous stamens, the filaments joined below into a tube that divides above into branches; ovary superior. Fruit is a capsule or consists of a group of nutlets.

Musk Mallow
Malva moschata

Erect, branched, sparsely hairy perennial to 80 cm. **Leaves** Basal leaves kidney-shaped, 3-lobed; *stem leaves deeply divided, with narrow linear lobes*. **Flowers** 3–6 cm across; epicalyx ½ as long as calyx; petals 3× as long as sepals. **Habitat** Roadsides, hedge banks, pastures, field borders, on well-drained soils; lowland to 305 m. **Dist**. Native in England, Wales; introduced in Scotland, Ireland. (Most of Europe.) **Fls** Jul–Aug.

Common Mallow
Malva sylvestris

Prostrate to erect, sparsely
hairy perennial, to
100 cm. **Leaves**
Basal leaves
5–10 cm across.
Flowers *2.5–4 cm*
across; epicalyx ⅔
as long as calyx;
petals 2–4× as
long as sepals.
Habitat
Roadsides,
banks, waste
ground,
on well-
drained soils.
Dist. Archaeophyte.
Common in most of BI
except N Scotland. (All Europe.)
Fls Jun–Sep.

Dwarf Mallow
Malva neglecta

Prostrate to erect, densely hairy annual
or biennial, to 60 cm. **Leaves** Basal leaves
4–7 cm across. **Flowers** *1.8–2.5 cm across,*
epicalyx ≤⅔ as long as calyx, petals ≥2×
as long as sepals. **Habitat** Grassy banks,
roadsides, rough ground, coastal drift
lines, on dry soils. **Dist**. Archaeophyte.
Throughout BI, but rare in Scotland,
Ireland. (Most of Europe.) **Fls** Jun–Sep.

Tree Mallow
Malva arborea

Tall, hairy shrub- or tree-like biennial to
300 cm. **Leaves** To 20 cm across. **Flowers**
3–4 cm across; *epicalyx joined to about*
halfway, longer than calyx, enlarging in
fruit; petals overlapping, 2–3× as long as
sepals. **Habitat** Cliffs, rocks, waste ground,
close to sea. **Dist**. Native in Ireland and W
coast of BI from N Wales to I of Wight;
introduced elsewhere except N Scotland.
(Mediterranean, SW Europe.) **Fls** Jul–Sep.

Marsh-mallow
Althaea officinalis

Erect, softly downy, velvety perennial to
120 cm. **Leaves** Lower leaves 3–8 cm across.
Flowers *2.5–4 cm across, stalks shorter than*
leaves; 6–9 epicalyx lobes; petals 2–3× as
long as sepals. **Habitat** Brackish marshes,
banks of coastal drainage dykes, ditches.
Dist. Native. Local, declining. S England
from Wash to S Wales. (Central and S
Europe.) **Fls** Aug–Sep.

MARSH-MALLOW

DROSERACEAE
Sundews

. . . .

Slender, insectivorous perennial bog plants. Leaves in a basal rosette, densely glandular and fringed with long glandular hairs. Flowers actinomorphic, bisexual; 4–8 sepals and petals; as many stamens as petals. Flowers of British species frequently don't open, but self-pollinate in bud.

Round-leaved Sundew
Drosera rotundifolia

Habitat Bare acid peat, among *Sphagnum*, wet heaths, bogs, moors, especially margins of bog pools; to 700 m. **Dist**. Native. Throughout BI where suitable habitats occur. (All Europe except Mediterranean.) **Fls** Jun–Aug.

Great Sundew
Drosera anglica

Habitat Wetter parts of acid *Sphagnum* bogs, stony lakeshores; lowland. **Dist**. Native. Widespread in W and NW Scotland, W Ireland; rare, scattered, declining elsewhere. (All Europe except Mediterranean.)

Oblong-leaved Sundew
Drosera intermedia

Habitat Wet heaths, bogs; drier habitats than *D. rotundifolia* and *D. anglica*, most often on bare peat. Lowland to 335 m.

Dist. Native. Local and declining. Scattered throughout BI in suitable habitats. (W and central Europe.) **Fls** Jun–Aug.

CISTACEAE
Rock-roses

Shrubs or herbs. Leaves simple, usually opposite. Flowers bisexual, actinomorphic; 5 sepals and petals, numerous stamens, ovary superior, 3 or 5 stigmas.

Common Rock-rose
Helianthemum nummularium *(R)

Creeping woody *perennial* to 30 cm. **Leaves** Sparsely hairy above, densely white-pubescent beneath; stipules narrow, 2× as long as petiole. **Flowers** 2–2.5 cm across; sepals unequal, petals *bright yellow*; style ± straight. **Habitat** Short, grazed calcareous grassland, cliffs, rocks, scree; to 640 m. **Dist**. Native. Throughout most of BI except extreme SW England, NW Scotland; very rare in Ireland. (Most of Europe.) **Fls** Jun–Sep.

VIOLACEAE
Violets and pansies

Annuals or perennials with alternate stalked leaves that have stipules. Flowers solitary, irregular; 5 sepals with short, backward-pointing lobes; 5 petals, the lower with a backward-pointing spur. Fruits are a 3-valved capsule.

Sweet Violet
Viola odorata

Perennial with long, creeping stolons, rooting at ends. *Leaves and flower stalks emerge from basal tuft.* **Leaves** Broadly ovate, deeply cordate, rounded at tip, blades thinly hairy, petioles with short reflexed hairs. **Flowers** *c*.15 mm, *sweet-scented; sepals blunt; petals rich violet or white, with lilac spur.* **Habitat** Wood margins, scrub, shady hedge banks, chiefly on calcareous soils. **Dist**. Native in England, Wales, SE Ireland; naturalised elsewhere. (Most of Europe.) **Fls** Feb–Apr.

Note Our only fragrant violet, with many garden cultivars, including ones with pink and apricot flowers.

Hairy Violet
Viola hirta *(R)

Perennial. Similar to *V. odorata*, but *without stolons*; leaves narrower, tips not rounded, hairs on petioles spreading; *flowers pale*

blue-violet, not fragrant.
Habitat Open
woodland, wood
margins, scrub,
grassland,
on
calcareous
soils. **Dist**.
Native.
N to central
Scotland; rare in
Ireland. (W, central
and E Europe.) **Fls** Apr–
May. **Note** Small plants
with narrow petals and short spurs are
sometimes separated as ssp. *calcarea* and are
confined to calcareous grassland.

Common Dog-violet
Viola riviniana

Glabrous or slightly pubescent perennial, to
20 cm when in flower, *with a central non-
flowering rosette and leafy flowering shoots.*
Our commonest violet. **Leaves** Cordate;
stipules narrow, fringed,
shorter than glabrous
petiole. **Flowers**
14–22 mm; *spur
white or yellowish,
paler than petals,
notched at tip;* sepals
7–12 mm, lobes
>1.5 mm. **Fruits**
Glabrous capsule.
Habitat Woodland,
hedge banks,
downland, grass
heaths, old
pasture,
mountain
grassland;
to 1020 m.
Dist. Native.
Common throughout
BI. (All Europe.)
Fls Apr–Jun.

Early Dog-violet
Viola reichenbachiana

Similar to *V. riviniana*, but *sepal lobes
smaller, <1.5 mm; spur darker than petals,
not notched at tip*. **Habitat** Hedge banks,
deciduous woodland, avoiding acid soils.
Dist. Native. Locally abundant as far N
as S Scotland. (All Europe except N.) **Fls**
Mar–May.

Marsh Violet
Viola palustris

*Perennial with long,
creeping rhizomes*
that produce
leaves and
flowers at nodes.
Stems No aerial
stems.
Leaves
*1–4 cm
wide,
rounded or
kidney-shaped,
cordate*. **Flowers**
10–15 mm, sepals blunt,
petals lilac with dark veins.
Fruits Glabrous capsule.

Habitat Acid bogs, marshes, wet woods, woodland flushes. **Dist**. Native. Throughout BI. (All Europe except Mediterranean.) **Fls** Apr–Jul. **Note** Ssp. *juressii*, with narrower leaves and hairy petioles, occurs in similar habitats in SW England and W Wales.

Mountain Pansy
Viola lutea

Perennial with creeping rhizomes. **Stems** Aerial stems to 20 cm. **Leaves** Stipules palmately lobed, terminal segment scarcely wider than others. **Flowers** *Large, 2–3.5 cm*; bright yellow or violet, or a combination of both; spur *2–3× as long as sepal lobes*; stalks long, to 9 cm. **Habitat** Short montane grassland, often on leached soils overlying limestone; to 1050 m. **Dist**. Native. Widespread in upland Britain; very rare in Ireland. (W and central Europe.) **Fls** May–Aug.

Wild Pansy
Viola tricolor

Much-branched, glabrous annual (ssp. *tricolor*) or tufted perennial (ssp. *curtisii*). **Leaves** *Stipules ± palmately lobed, middle lobe lanceolate, entire, not leaf-like*. **Flowers** *1.5–2.5 cm* (<2 cm in ssp. *curtisii*), flat; *petals longer than sepals*, yellow (ssp. *curtisii*), or blue-violet or a combination of both (ssp. *tricolor*); *spur longer than or as long as sepal*

lobes; stalks 2–8 cm. **Habitat** Ssp. *tricolor* on arable land, rough grassland, waste ground; ssp. *curtisii* on sand-dunes and coastal grassland. **Dist**. Native. Ssp. *tricolor* throughout BI; ssp. *curtisii* on N and W coasts, inland East Anglia. (Ssp. *tricolor* throughout Europe; ssp. *curtisii* on Baltic and North Sea coasts.) **Fls** Apr–Sep.

Field Pansy
Viola arvensis

Much-branched annual. Similar to *V. tricolor*, but *mid-lobe of stipules ovate, toothed and leaf-like*; flowers smaller, 8–20 mm, flat, *petals shorter than sepals*, usually yellow-cream. **Habitat** Arable fields, waste ground, on neutral and calcareous soils.

Dist. Archaeophyte. Common throughout most of BI but rare in N Scotland, W Ireland. (Most of Europe except E Mediterranean.) **Fls** Apr–Oct.

CUCURBITACEAE
Cucurbits

White Bryony
Bryonia dioica

Tendril-climbing, dioecious perennial to *c*.4 m. **Leaves** Palmately lobed. **Flowers** Actinomorphic; male flowers stalked, 12–18 mm across; female flowers sessile, 10–12 mm across; 5 sepals and petals; 5 stamens. **Fruits** Red berry. **Habitat** Hedgerows, scrub, wood margins, on well-drained calcareous or base-rich soils. **Dist**. Native. Widespread and frequent in lowland England. (W, central and S Europe.) **Fls** May–Sep. **Note** All parts of plant are poisonous.

BRASSICACEAE (CRUCIFERAE)
Crucifers

Annual or perennial herbs with alternate leaves that lack stipules, and with distinctive regular flowers that have 4 sepals in opposite pairs, 4 petals alternating with the sepals and 6 stamens (sometimes 4). The ovary is superior, usually with 2 cells and a single style with 2 stigmas. The fruit is usually a capsule opening from below by 2 valves or sometimes breaking transversely into 1-seeded segments.

Identification often depends on details of the ripe fruits, and a lens may be needed to examine the hairs on the stems and leaves. Many species are annuals of open habitats or weeds of cultivation.

Rockets and Hedge Mustard ▶
Sisymbrium

Eastern Rocket
Sisymbrium orientale

Erect, branched, pubescent annual to 80 cm. **Leaves** Upper stem leaves with narrow terminal lobe and 0–1 pairs of lateral lobes. **Flowers** *c*.7 mm across, petals 1.5–2× as long as sepals. **Fruits** *50–120 mm, pubescent when young*. **Habitat** Waste ground, roadsides, railways. **Dist**. Introduced. Casual and locally common throughout most of BI. (S Europe.) **Fls** Jun–Aug.

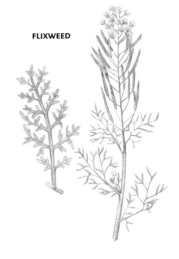

Hedge Mustard
Sisymbrium officinale

Erect, glabrous or sparsely hairy annual
or biennial to 100 cm. **Leaves** Deeply
divided, basal leaves in a rosette. **Flowers**
3 mm across, petals 1.5× as long as
sepals. **Fruits** *10–20 mm, held stiffly erect
and closely appressed to stem.* **Habitat**
Hedgerows, roadsides, cultivated ground,
waste places, usually close to habitation.
Dist. Archaeophyte. Throughout BI, but
rare in extreme N. (All Europe except N.)
Fls Jun–Jul.

Flixweed
Descurainia sophia

Erect, little-branched, pubescent annual
to 90 cm. **Leaves** *Greyish green, deeply
divided, with branched hairs.* **Flowers**
3 mm across, petals about as long as sepals.
Fruits 15–25 mm, stalks *c*.10 mm. **Habitat**
Cultivated land, road verges, waste ground,
on sandy soils. **Dist**. Archaeophyte. E
England; scattered throughout rest of BI.
(All Europe except extreme N.) **Fls** Jun–Aug.

Garlic Mustard
Alliaria petiolata

Erect, unbranched biennial to 120 cm.
Sparsely hairy below, glabrous above. *Roots
and leaves smelling of garlic when crushed.*
Leaves *Basal leaves in a rosette, stem leaves
stalked.* **Flowers** 6 mm across, petals *c*.2× as
long as sepals. **Fruits** 35–60 mm, 4-angled,
glabrous, standing ± erect. **Habitat** Wood

margins, hedgerows, roadsides, shady places, gardens, on fertile soils. **Dist**. Native. Common throughout BI except extreme N. (All Europe except N.) **Fls** Apr–Jun.

Thale Cress
Arabidopsis thaliana

Erect, sparsely hairy annual to 50 cm. **Leaves** Basal leaves hairy, in a rosette. **Flowers** *3 mm across*, petals *c*.2× as long as sepals. **Fruits** *10–18 mm glabrous, on slender, spreading stalks*. **Habitat** Dry, open stony ground, walls, waste places; common garden weed. **Dist**. Native. Throughout BI. (All Europe except extreme N.) **Fls** Apr–May, Sep–Oct.

Wallflower
Erysimum cheiri

Erect, branched, pubescent perennial to 60 cm. **Leaves** Rosette leaves to 10 cm. **Flowers** *c.2.5 cm across*, petals ≥2× as long as sepals. **Fruits** *25–70 mm, hairy*, ± erect, flattened, conspicuously 1-veined. **Habitat** Walls, cliffs, rocks. **Dist**. Archaeophyte. Cultivated since Middle Ages. Naturalised throughout BI except extreme N. (SE Europe.) **Fls** Apr–Jun.

Dame's-violet
Hesperis matronalis

Erect, *sparsely hairy*, branched perennial to 80 cm. **Stems** Very leafy. **Flowers** *Showy, pink, purple or white*, in crowded inflorescence; petals 15–30 mm, 2–3× as long as sepals. **Fruits** *Long, narrow, 50–115 mm, 'beaded'*. **Habitat** Hedgerows, roadsides, verges, usually near habitation. **Dist**. Introduced. Cultivated since Middle Ages. Naturalised throughout BI. (S and E Europe.) **Fls** May–Jul.

Hoary Stock
Matthiola incana

Densely hairy, erect grey-green perennial to 80 cm. **Stems** Woody, leafless below. **Leaves** *In rosettes, narrow, entire*, covered by short greyish hairs (hoary). **Flowers** *2.5–5 cm across*, purple, red or white. **Fruits** 45–130 mm, erect; valves downy, with distinct central vein. **Habitat** Sea cliffs. **Dist**. Introduced. Cultivated since sixteenth century. Rare. S and SW England; scattered in suitable habitats elsewhere. (Central Mediterranean.) **Fls** May–Jul.

Winter-cress
Barbarea vulgaris

Erect, branched, glabrous
biennial or
perennial to
90 cm. **Leaves**
Rosette leaves
pinnate,
with clasping
auricles; *upper
stem leaves
clasping, ovate, ±
simple*; all a deep,
shining green.
Flowers 7–9 mm
across, *buds glabrous*,
petals 2× as long as
sepals. **Fruits** ± erect,
15–32 mm, *persistent
style 2–3.5 mm.*
Habitat Stream banks, ditches, roadsides,
hedgerows; lowland to 380 m. **Dist**. Native.
Throughout BI except extreme N. (All
Europe except extreme SW.) **Fls** May–Aug.

Watercresses and yellow-cresses ►
Nasturtium and *Rorippa*

Watercress, Narrow-fruited
Watercress
Nasturtium officinale, N. microphyllum

Prostrate to erect, glabrous aquatic
perennials, to 60 cm, rooting at nodes.
Leaves Evergreen and remaining green
in autumn, leaflets entire or with remote
rounded teeth. **Flowers** 4–6 mm across,
petals *c*.2× as long as sepals. **Fruits** *N.
officinale* with *seeds in 2 distinct rows in
each cell*; seeds of *N. microphyllum* in 1
row in each cell. **Habitat** Shallow, clear,
unpolluted streams, ditches, spring-heads,
ponds, marshes. *N. microphyllum* tolerant of
slightly more acid conditions. **Dist**. Native.

WATERCRESS

**NARROW-FRUITED
WATERCRESS**

Common throughout BI. (Most of Europe
except Scandinavia and NE.) **Fls** May–Oct.

Marsh Yellow-cress
Rorippa palustris

Erect, glabrous
annual to 60 cm.
Leaves Stem leaves
with 2–6 pairs of
lateral lobes, leaflets
entire or coarsely
toothed. **Flowers**
*Sepals ≥1.6 mm,
petals about as long
as sepals.* **Fruits**
5–10 mm, *1–2× as
long as stalks* (rather
sausage-shaped), usually
arising from all round stem.

Habitat Bare mud of lake, reservoir and pond margins that dry out in summer. **Dist**. Native. Throughout BI except N Scotland. (All Europe except S and SW.) **Fls** Jun–Sep.

Creeping Yellow-cress
Rorippa sylvestris

Prostrate to erect, stoloniferous, ± glabrous perennial, to 60 cm. **Leaves** *Stem leaves deeply divided*, with 3–6 pairs of narrow lateral lobes, these without auricles. **Flowers** 5 mm across, *petals 1.5–2× as long as sepals.* **Fruits** 9–22 mm, slender, 2× as long as stalk, persistent style 0.5–2 mm. **Habitat** Margins of ponds, dykes, rivers and streams where water stands in winter; also garden weed on wet soils. **Dist**. Native. Throughout BI except extreme N Scotland. (All Europe except Scandinavia and extreme SW.) **Fls** Jun–Aug.

Great Yellow-cress
Rorippa amphibia

Tall, erect, ± glabrous, stoloniferous, branched perennial to 120 cm. **Leaves** *Stem*

leaves yellowish green, *simple, toothed or lobed.* **Flowers** *c.*6 mm across, *petals 1.5–2× as long as sepals.* **Fruits** 4.5–7.5 mm, *shorter than stalk,* persistent style 0.8– 1.8 mm. **Habitat** Marshy ground, marginal vegetation of rivers, lakes, ponds, streams. **Dist**. Native. England, Ireland; absent from Wales, Scotland, SW. (All Europe except Scandinavia and SW.) **Fls** Jun–Aug.

Honesty
Lunaria annua

Tall, pubescent biennial to 100 cm. **Leaves** Basal leaves long-stalked, stem leaves ± sessile. **Flowers** *c.30 mm across, deep purple,* sometimes white; petals about 2× as long as sepals. **Fruits** *Flattened, broadly ovate to almost circular*, rounded at apex. **Habitat** Naturalised in hedgerows, pathsides, waste ground, near habitation. **Dist**. Introduced. Cultivated since sixteenth century. Throughout BI, but rare in Scotland and Ireland. (Italy, SE Europe.) **Fls** Apr–Jun.

Bitter-cresses ▶ *Cardamine*

Cuckooflower/Lady's-smock
Cardamine pratensis

Erect, ± glabrous, unbranched perennial to 60 cm. Extremely variable. **Leaves** Rosette leaves pinnate, leaflets rounded, coarsely toothed, *terminal leaflet larger than laterals*; upper stem leaves with narrower entire leaflets. **Flowers** 12–18 mm across, petals *c*.3× as long as sepals, lilac; *anthers yellow*. **Fruits** 25–40 mm, valves without veins. **Habitat** Damp grassland, marshes, roadsides, hedgerows, stream sides; to 1080 m. **Dist**. Native. Common throughout BI. (All Europe except Mediterranean.) **Fls** Apr–Jun.

Large Bitter-cress
Cardamine amara

Prostrate to erect, glabrous winter-green perennial, to 60 cm. **Leaves** Pale green, with no basal rosette. **Flowers** 12–15 mm across; *petals c*.2× as long as sepals, *white; anthers dark violet*. **Fruits** 15–40 mm. **Habitat** Stream sides, marshes, fens, wet woodlands, on acid soils; shade-tolerant. To 640 m.

Dist. Native. Most of BI, but absent from SW England, most of Wales and Ireland, N Scotland. (All Europe except Mediterranean and extreme N.) **Fls** Apr–Jun.

Wavy Bitter-cress
Cardamine flexuosa

Erect, sparsely hairy annual to perennial, to 50 cm. **Leaves** Basal leaves in a loose rosette. **Flowers** Petals white, narrow, *c*.2× as long as sepals; *6 stamens*. **Fruits** 12–25 mm, valves without veins. **Habitat** Damp, shaded places, including woodland

Whitlowgrasses ▶ *Erophila*

Small, delicate, early-flowering annuals to 20 cm. Leaves are small, in a basal rosette; *stem leaves are absent.* Flowers are 3–6 mm across, *the petals deeply notched.* Fruits are 1.5–9 mm; *stalks are slender, longer than fruits.* Native. Throughout Europe except extreme N. Flowering occurs Mar–Jun. This is a complicated genus, now regarded as comprising 3 separate species in BI.

Common Whitlowgrass
Erophila verna

stream sides, marshes, gardens; to 830 m. **Dist**. Native. Common throughout BI. (Most of Europe except extreme N.) **Fls** Apr–Sep.

Hairy Bitter-cress
Cardamine hirsuta

Erect, sparsely hairy annual to 30 cm. **Leaves** Basal leaves in compact rosette. **Flowers** Petals white, narrow, *c.*2× as long as sepals; *4 stamens.* **Fruits** 10–25 mm, valves without veins. **Habitat** Garden weed; rocks and scree, especially on limestone. To 1190 m. **Dist**. Native. Common throughout BI. (W, central and S Europe.) **Fls** Most of year.

The commonest *Erophila*. **Habitat** Bare, open sandy areas, dunes, sandy heaths, rocks, walls, waste ground; also limestone rocks and pavement. **Dist**. Widespread and common throughout BI.

Scurvygrasses ▶ *Cochlearia*

English Scurvygrass
Cochlearia anglica

Erect, glabrous perennial to 35 cm. **Leaves** *Basal leaves in a rosette, leaf base tapering to long stalk; upper leaves sessile, usually clasping stem.* **Flowers** White or pale lilac, 10–14 mm across, petals 2–3× as long as sepals. **Fruits** 8–15 mm, rounded, flattened. **Habitat** Upper levels of salt marshes, muddy shores, tidal estuaries, brackish marshes. **Dist**. Native. Coasts of Britain and Ireland as far N as S Scotland. (Coast of Europe from S Sweden to S France.) **Fls** Apr–Jul.

ENGLISH SCURVYGRASS

Common Scurvygrass
Cochlearia officinalis

Prostrate to erect, glabrous biennial or perennial, to 40 cm. **Leaves** Fleshy; basal leaves in loose rosette, long-stalked, rounded and cordate at base, blades ≥2 cm; *upper stem leaves sessile and clasping stem*. **Flowers** *8–10 mm across*, usually white; petals 2–3× as long as sepals. **Fruits** *Globose*, 3–6 mm, *valves prominently veined*. **Habitat** Upper parts of salt marshes, sea cliffs, sea walls,

brackish marshes; occasional along salted roadsides inland. **Dist**. Native. All round coasts of BI, but rare in S and E. (Coasts of N Europe S to Brittany.) **Fls** May–Aug.

Danish Scurvygrass
Cochlearia danica

Mat-forming, prostrate to erect, glabrous annual, to 20 cm. **Leaves** Basal leaves long-stalked, shallowly lobed, cordate at base, often purplish; stem leaves distinctly lobed, *upper sessile but not clasping*. **Flowers** *Pale mauve, 4–5 mm across*. **Fruits** Ovoid, 3–5.5 mm, tapering at both ends; valves finely net-veined. **Habitat** Upper parts of sandy and shingly shores, cliffs, banks, walls. **Dist**. Native. Common all round coasts of BI; also rapidly spreading inland along salted road verges. (W coast of Europe N to S Finland.) **Fls** Jan–Jun.

Shepherd's-purse
Capsella bursa-pastoris

Erect, glabrous or sparsely hairy annual to 40 cm. **Leaves** Rosette leaves lobed; *stem leaves sessile, clasping*. **Flowers** 2.5 mm across, petals 2× as long as sepals. **Fruits** *Inverted triangle, notched at the top* (the

'shepherd's purse'),
6–9 mm. **Habitat**
Gardens, arable
fields, open areas,
disturbed ground
everywhere. **Dist**.
Archaeophyte.
Abundant
throughout BI.
(All Europe.)
Fls Year-round.

Shepherd's Cress
Teesdalia nudicaulis *(NI)

Erect, ± glabrous or sparsely pubescent,
branched annual to 45 cm. **Leaves** *Rosette
leaves deeply lobed*, stem leaves few. **Flowers**
Small, 2 mm across; *petals unequal*, inner
petals distinctly shorter than outer. **Fruits**
3–4 mm, narrowly orbicular,
notched at tip,
flattened on one
side; stalks spreading.
Habitat Open heaths,
disturbed ground, on
acid sandy
or gravelly
soils, coastal
sand, fine
shingle; lowland
to 455 m. **Dist**.
Native. Scattered
and declining
throughout
BI; very rare
in Ireland. (W
and central
Europe.) **Fls**
Apr–Jun.

Field Penny-cress
Thlaspi arvense

Erect, glabrous annual to
60 cm, with strong foetid
smell when crushed. **Stems**
Very leafy. **Leaves** No
basal rosette; stem leaves
oblong, sessile, with
clasping, pointed basal
lobes. **Flowers** 4–6 mm
across, petals *c*.2× as long as
sepals. **Fruits** *Almost circular,
10–20 mm across, flattened,
with very broad wings
and deep apical notch*;
stalks curving upwards.
Habitat Weed of arable
fields, gardens, disturbed
ground, on heavy, fertile
soils. **Dist**. Archaeophyte.
Throughout BI, but rare in
N Scotland, N Ireland.
(All Europe, but rare in
S.) **Fls** May–Jul.

Garlic Penny-cress
Thlaspi alliaceum

Erect, *pubescent* annual
to 60 cm. *Whole plant
smells of garlic.* **Stems**
Grooved. **Leaves** *Stem
leaves oblong, with
acute basal lobes.* **Fruits**
Ovate, narrowly winged,
5–10 mm, swollen;
persistent style shorter
than apical notch. **Habitat**
Rare casual or established
weed of arable fields.
Dist. Introduced. Scattered
throughout E and SE England.
(S and E Europe.) **Fls** May–Jun.

Field Pepperwort
Lepidium campestre

Erect, pubescent annual to 50 cm. **Stems** Flowering stem very leafy, branching above. **Leaves** Basal rosettes soon withering; *upper stem leaves narrow*, softly hairy, *basal lobes acute, clasping*. **Flowers** Small, 2–2.5 mm across, petals 1.5–2× as long as sepals; *anthers yellow*. **Fruits** Ovate, flattened, winged, 4.5–6.5 mm; *valves covered by small white vesicles (use lens); persistent style shorter than or just as long as notch.* **Habitat** Dry, open habitats, walls, waste ground, arable land. **Dist**. Archaeophyte. Throughout BI, but very rare in Scotland, Ireland. (In Europe S from S Sweden.) **Fls** May–Aug.

Smith's Pepperwort
Lepidium heterophyllum

Prostrate to erect, pubescent perennial, to 45 cm, branching from base as well as above. Similar to *L. campestre*, but flowers larger, 3–3.5 mm across, petals *c*.1.5× as long as sepals, *anthers reddish; valves of fruits without vesicles, persistent style distinctly longer than apical*

notch. **Habitat** Dry, open heathy areas, banks, shingle, arable land. **Dist**. Native. Throughout BI, but rare in N Scotland. (W and SW Europe.) **Fls** May–Aug.

Narrow-leaved Pepperwort
Lepidium ruderale

Erect, ± glabrous, much-branched annual to 40 cm. Whole plant has a foetid smell. **Leaves** Basal leaves deeply pinnate, with narrow lobes. **Flowers** Inconspicuous, greenish; *petals tiny or absent*; 2 stamens. **Fruits** 2–2.5 mm, flattened; persistent style shorter than apical notch. **Habitat** Dry upper end of salt marshes, sea walls, waste ground near sea; also waste places and salted road verges inland. **Dist.** Archaeophyte. Throughout BI, but rare in Scotland, Ireland. (W, central and E Europe.) **Fls** May–Jul.

Swine-cress
Lepidium coronopus

Prostrate, much-branched, glabrous annual.
Leaves Rosette and stem leaves deeply
divided. **Flowers** *c.*2.5 mm across, in dense
inflorescences arising opposite stem leaves;
petals longer than sepals. **Fruits** 2.5–3.5 mm,
longer than stalks, kidney-shaped, tapering
above to short persistent style, *valves
coarsely and irregularly ridged.* **Habitat**
Fertile trampled soil of paths, gateways,
pastures, waste ground. **Dist**. Archaeophyte.
Common in lowland England; scattered
elsewhere throughout BI. (All Europe except
N.) **Fls** Jun–Sep.

Hoary Cress
Lepidium draba

Erect, glabrous or pubescent, branched
perennial to 60 cm. Often forms extensive
patches. **Leaves** Basal leaves soon withering;
*stem leaves with basal lobes clasping
stem.* **Flowers** 5–6 mm across; in dense
inflorescence, petals 1.5–2× as long as
sepals. **Fruits** 4–6 mm, cordate, flattened,
unwinged; prominent persistent style to
>1.5 mm. **Habitat** Roadsides, railways,
arable land, waste ground, especially near
sea. **Dist**. Introduced. Common and
increasing throughout most of BI, but rare
in N Scotland, Ireland. (S and E Europe.)
Fls May–Jun.

Swine-cresses
Distinguished from all other white-flowered
crucifers by inflorescences that arise opposite
stem leaves (leaf-opposed) rather than in
their axils.

Lesser Swine-cress
Lepidium didymum

Prostrate, much-branched, ± glabrous
annual to 30 cm. Similar to *C. squamatus*,
but *petals tiny or absent*; fruits smaller,
1.3–1.7 mm, *shorter than stalks*, notched at
both base and apex, *valves smooth* (without
ridges). **Habitat** Weed of cultivated and
waste ground, paths, roadsides. **Dist**.
Introduced (native of South America).
Widespread in England, Wales; spreading to
N. (W, S and central Europe.) **Fls** Jul–Sep.

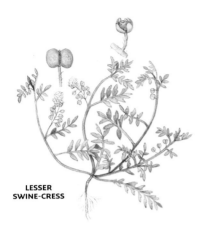

LESSER SWINE-CRESS

Awlwort
Subularia aquatica

Dwarf aquatic annual to 10 cm. The only aquatic crucifer with awl-shaped leaves and tiny white flowers. **Leaves** Glabrous, awl-shaped, in a basal rosette. **Flowers** In few-flowered inflorescence, *often submerged*; petals white, 2× as long as sepals. **Fruits** 2–5 mm, slightly compressed. **Habitat** Clear shallow margins of acidic upland pools, lakes; to 825 m. **Dist**. Native. Scotland, N England, W Wales, W Ireland. (N Europe, Pyrenees.) **Fls** Jun–Aug.

Wall-rockets ▶ *Diplotaxis*
Distinguished from other yellow-flowered crucifers with elongated fruits by having slightly compressed fruits, their valves with a single prominent vein and seeds in 2 rows in each cell. Two species with similar habitats. .

Perennial Wall-rocket
Diplotaxis tenuifolia

Erect, much-branched, glabrous, glaucous perennial to 80 cm. **Stems** Very leafy. **Leaves** *Foetid when crushed, rosette leaves absent.* **Flowers** *Petals pale yellow*, 8–15 mm, 2× as long as sepals. **Fruits** 20–50 mm, *with a distinct stalk above sepal scars*, valves with 1 distinct vein. **Habitat** Waste ground, especially around ports, industrial areas. **Dist**. Archaeophyte. Throughout BI, especially SE England, but very rare in Scotland, Ireland. (W, S and E Europe.) **Fls** May–Sep. **Comment** **Annual Wall-rocket** *D. muralis* similar, but an annual with *basal leaves in a rosette*, stem leaves few; *petals deep yellow*, ≤8 mm, *c*.1.5× as long as sepals; fruits *without stalk above sepal scars*. On dry, open areas, waste ground, especially on calcareous soils. Introduced and scattered throughout BI, rare in north and west. (Most of Europe except Scandinavia.) **Fls** Jun–Sep.

ANNUAL WALL-ROCKET

Rape, Turnip, mustards and Charlock
▶ *Brassica*, *Sinapis*, *Hirschfeldia*

Rape
Brassica napus

Erect, glaucous annual or biennial to 100 cm, *sparsely pubescent below*. **Leaves** Basal leaves long-stalked, glaucous; upper stem leaves sessile, simple, with rounded basal lobes clasping stem. **Flowers** In dense inflorescence, *buds overtopping open flowers*; sepals erect; *petals 11–15 mm, c.2× as long as sepals*. **Fruits** 35–95 mm, beak with 0–1 seeds. **Habitat** Common as weed of arable land, roadsides, disturbed ground. **Dist.** Introduced. Casual or naturalised throughout BI, but rare in NW Scotland, N Ireland. (Naturalised throughout Erope.) **Fls** Mar–Aug. **Note** Oil-seed Rape is ssp. *oleifera*.

Turnip
Brassica rapa

Erect annual or biennial to 100 cm. **Leaves** *Basal leaves coarsely hairy*, stalked, pinnate, *green*; upper stem leaves glabrous, sessile, basal lobes ± completely clasping stem. **Flowers** In dense inflorescence, *flowers overtopping buds; petals 6–13 mm, 1.5–2× as* long as sepals. **Fruits** 30–65 mm, beak without seed. **Habitat** Weed of cultivation, waste ground, roadsides, banks of streams and rivers. **Dist.** Archaeophyte. Established throughout BI, but rare in N Scotland. (All Europe, but rare in SW.) **Fls** May–Aug.

Black Mustard
Brassica nigra

Tall, much-branched annual to 200 cm, *bristly below, glabrous above*. **Stems** Wide-spreading. **Leaves** *All leaves stalked*, upper leaves rather glaucous. **Flowers** Petals 8–12 mm, 2× as long as sepals. **Fruits**

8–25 mm, *erect and held closely appressed to stem*; valves strongly keeled with fine lateral veins; beak seedless. **Habitat** Sea cliffs, shingle, riverbanks; also casual of waste ground and roadsides inland. Lowland to 380 m. **Dist**. Probably native. Widespread in England, Wales; rare in Scotland, Ireland. (Most of Europe except Scandinavia.) **Fls** May–Sep. **Similar spp**. Often confused with *Sinapis arvensis* or *Hirschfeldia incana* (below).

Charlock
Sinapis arvensis

Erect, branched or unbranched, sparsely hairy annual to 100 cm. **Leaves** Lower leaves stalked, with a large terminal lobe and few small laterals; *upper leaves sessile.* **Flowers** In dense inflorescence; *sepals narrow, inrolled, wide-spreading or reflexed;* petals 8–15 mm, *c.*2× as long as sepals. **Fruits** 25–50 mm; valves with 3–7 distinct veins; beak 7–16 mm, *c.* ½ as long as valves; usually 1-seeded. **Habitat** Common arable weed of roadsides, waste ground; lowland to 450 m. **Dist**. Archaeophyte. Abundant

throughout BI. (All Europe except NE.) **Fls** May–Jul.

White Mustard
Sinapis alba

Erect, branched or unbranched, sparsely hairy annual to 100 cm. Similar to *S. arvensis, but stem leaves stalked*, pinnate.

Fruits 20–40 mm, *with distinctive flat, often upward-curving beak, 10–24 mm, as long as valves.* **Habitat** Persistent arable weed, casual on waste ground, roadsides, usually on calcareous soils. **Dist**. Archaeophyte (origins unknown). Throughout BI, but rare and scattered outside England. **Fls** Jun–Aug. **Note** The original mustard of 'mustard and cress', now often replaced for this use by *Brassica napus*.

Hoary Mustard
Hirschfeldia incana

Erect, branched annual (or rarely perennial) to 120 cm. **Stems** *Lower part usually densely pubescent, with short, stiff white*

hairs. **Leaves** *Densely pubescent*, as lower stems. **Flowers** Petals 5.5–10 mm, *c.*2× as long as sepals. **Fruits** *Erect, closely appressed to stem, 7–15 mm; beak 3–6.5 mm, c. ½ as long as valves; 1(–2)-seeded*. **Habitat** Naturalised or casual of waste ground, roadsides, railways, docks, on well-drained soils. **Dist**. Introduced. Increasing. Widely distributed in England, Wales; rare further N. (S and SW Europe.) **Fls** May–Oct. **Similar** to *Brassica nigra* (p.79), from which it differs in shorter fruits, 1-seeded beak, and more hairy leaves and stems.

Sea Rocket
Cakile maritima

Prostrate to erect, *glabrous, succulent annual*, to 50 cm. **Leaves** Simple to pinnate. **Flowers** Sepals erect; **Petals** 6–10 mm, *mauve, pink or white, 2× as long as sepals*. **Fruits** *10–25 mm; comprising 2 unequal, 1-seeded joints that separate on ripening*. **Habitat** Fore dunes and drift line on sandy shores. **Dist**. Native. Frequent all round coasts of BI. (All round coasts of Europe.) **Fls** Jun–Aug.

Sea-kale
Crambe maritima

Large, glaucous, glabrous, much-branched *cabbage-like perennial* to 75 cm. Shoots and leaves dying back in winter. **Leaves** Lower leaves large, to 30 cm, ± lobed, with wavy margins. **Flowers** 10–15 mm across; petals white, green at base. **Fruits** *Large*, 10–14 mm; *2-jointed, the lower stalk-like, the terminal 1-seeded, ± spherical*. **Habitat** *Undisturbed shingle beaches*; rarely on cliffs and dunes. **Dist.** Native. Local, possibly declining. Coasts of BI N to Clyde. (Coasts of NW Europe to S Finland, Black Sea.) **Fls** Jun–Aug.

Wild Radish
Raphanus raphanistrum ssp. *raphanistrum*

Erect, roughly hairy or bristly annual to 60 cm. **Leaves** ± pinnate, with a large, rounded terminal lobe and 1–4 pairs of separated lateral lobes. **Flowers** *Petals*

WILD RADISH

with large *terminal lobe and 4–8 pairs of contiguous or overlapping lateral lobes*; petals yellow, sometimes white. **Fruits** 15–55 mm, *deeply constricted between the 1–5 seeds into ± spherical segments*. **Habitat** Open areas, rough maritime grassland, disturbed ground, cliffs, drift line on sand or shingle. **Dist.** Native. S and W coasts of BI; rare elsewhere. (Coasts of W and S Europe.) **Fls** Jun–Aug. **Note** Intermediates between the 2 subspecies occur in some parts of their ranges. The Garden Radish *R. sativus* also occasionally occurs as a casual; its origins are unknown and it does not occur as a wild plant.

yellow, lilac or white, usually with dark veins, 12–20 mm, 2× as long as sepals. **Fruits** *25–90 mm, constricted between the 3–8 seeds into ± oblong segments that separate on ripening.* **Habitat** Casual or persistent weed of cultivation, waste ground. **Dist.** Archaeophyte. Common throughout BI. (All Europe except extreme N.) **Fls** May–Sep.

Sea Radish
Raphanus raphanistrum ssp. *maritimus*

Tall, much-branched, roughly hairy or bristly biennial or perennial to 80 cm. Similar to ssp. *raphanistrum*, but basal leaves ± pinnate,

RESEDACEAE
Mignonettes
....

Annuals, biennials or perennials. Leaves simple or pinnate, with glandular stipules. Flowers irregular, small, in spike-like racemes; 4–7 sepals and petals; 7–40 stamens. Fruits are a capsule.

Weld
Reseda luteola

Robust, erect, little-branched, glabrous biennial to 150 cm. **Leaves** *Rosette and stem leaves simple, entire, margins wavy,* midrib pale. **Flowers** 4–5 mm across; 4 sepals and petals; back and side petals lobed, front entire; *20–25 stamens*. **Fruits** Almost spherical capsule, 5–6 mm, with 3 apical lobes. **Habitat** Disturbed and waste ground on calcareous soils, roadsides, field margins, abandoned quarries; lowland. **Dist.** Archaeophyte. Throughout BI, but rare in N Scotland, W Ireland. (Central and S Europe.) **Fls** Jun–Aug.

Wild Mignonette
Reseda lutea

Erect, much-branched,
± glabrous biennial or
perennial to 75 cm.
Leaves *Rosette leaves soon
withering; stem leaves
deeply lobed, with narrow
segments.* **Flowers** 6 mm
across; 6 sepals and petals;
back and side petals lobed,
front entire;
12–20 stamens.
Fruits Oblong
capsule, 10–18 mm,
with 3 apical lobes.
Habitat Disturbed
ground on calcareous
soils, road verges, field
margins; lowland. **Dist.**
Native. Throughout BI,
but rare in Scotland; introduced in Ireland.
(Central and S Europe.) **Fls** Jun–Aug.

ERICACEAE
Heaths, crowberries,
rhododendron and wintergreen
family
••••••••••••••••••••••••••••••••••••••

A family of trees or dwarf shrubs with
simple, usually evergreen, whorled, opposite
or alternate leaves. Flowers are regular or
slightly irregular; 4 or 5 sepals and petals,
petals usually fused; as many as, or 2× as
many, stamens as petals; ovary superior to
inferior, 1 style. Fruit is a capsule or berry.
Almost all members of the Ericaceae, except
for *Arbutus*, are plants of acid soils.

Crowberry
Empetrum nigrum

Low evergreen, heather-like shrub to
45 cm. **Leaves** *Alternate, entire, with
revolute margins.* **Flowers** Pink, bisexual or
dioecious; *3 sepals; 3 petals, free* (heathers

ssp. *hermaphroditum*

have 4–5 fused petals); *3 stamens.* **Fruits**
Black berry-like drupe. **Habitat** Mountains,
moorlands, blanket bog on dry, acid peat
in exposed places; open birch, pine
woodland. To 1270 m. **Dist.**
Native. Common in upland
Britain. (N Europe,
mts of central and S
Europe.) **Fls** May–Jun.
Note Ssp. *nigrum* has
prostrate, rooting stems,
± parallel-sided leaves,
3–4× as long as broad,
and dioecious flowers,
and is found throughout
species' range. Ssp.
hermaphroditum has
± erect stems, not rooting, leaves 2–3× as
long as broad, with ± convex margins, and
bisexual flowers, and is confined to exposed
sites at higher altitudes in N Scotland, Lake
District (rare), Snowdonia.

Bog-rosemary
Andromeda polifolia *(NI)

Low, straggling, glabrous, dwarf evergreen
shrub to 35 cm. **Leaves** 15–35 mm,

alternate, linear, revolute, *green above, glaucous beneath*. **Flowers** 5–7 mm across, *5 sepals and petals*, 10 stamens. **Habitat** Acid *Sphagnum* peat of raised and blanket bogs; to 735 m. **Dist**. Native. Local in upland Britain; common in central Ireland. (N and central Europe.) **Fls** May–Sep.

BOG-ROSEMARY

Bearberry
Arctostaphylos uva-ursi

Dwarf, mat-forming evergreen shrub to 150 cm, with prostrate rooting branches. **Leaves** 1–2.5 cm, alternate, rather leathery, *glabrous, entire, conspicuously net-veined beneath*. **Flowers** Corolla 4–6 mm across; 5 sepals and petals; 10 stamens. **Fruits** *Red* berry-like drupe. **Habitat** Exposed moorland on thin, stony or peaty soil; to 915 m. **Dist**. Native. Common in Scottish Highlands; scattered in W Ireland, N England. (N Europe, mts of S Europe.) **Fls** May–Jul.

Heather/Ling
Calluna vulgaris

Much-branched, prostrate to erect, dwarf evergreen shrub, to *c*.60 cm. **Leaves** *Small*, 1–3 mm, *opposite*, overlapping on young

shoots, linear, margins revolute. **Flowers** In raceme-like inflorescence, 3–15 cm; corolla 3–4.5 mm; 4 petals, fused at base only; *calyx same colour as, and larger than, corolla*; 8 stamens. **Habitat** Abundant and often dominant on heaths, moors, bogs, and open birch, pine and oak woodland, on acid soils and peat; to 1040 m. **Dist**. Native. Throughout BI. (Most of Europe, decreasing to E.) **Fls** Jul–Sep.

Heaths ▶ *Erica*

Cross-leaved Heath
Erica tetralix

Erect, much-branched, evergreen dwarf shrub to 60 cm. **Stems** Rooting at base,

twigs pubescent. **Leaves** 2–4 mm, *in whorls of 4; grey-green with dense, short hairs and long glandular hairs*; margins revolute, obscuring most of lower side of leaf. **Flowers** In umbel-like clusters; *sepals shortly pubescent and with long glandular hairs*; corolla 6–7 mm, pale pink; stamens not projecting, *anthers with an appendage.* **Habitat** Acid bogs, wet heaths, moorland; to 670 m. **Dist**. Native. Throughout BI, abundant in N and W. (W Europe.) **Fls** Jul–Sep.

Bell Heather
Erica cinerea

Erect, much-branched, evergreen dwarf shrub to 60 cm. **Stems** *With bunches of short leafy shoots in leaf axils.* **Leaves** 5–7 mm, in whorls of 3, linear, *glabrous*; dark, shining green. **Flowers** In short racemes; corolla 4–6 mm, dark reddish purple; stamens not projecting. **Habitat** Dry heathland, open woodland, maritime heaths, on acid, well-drained soils; to 930 m. **Dist**. Native. Throughout BI. (W Europe.) **Fls** Jul–Sep.

Cranberries and bilberries ▶ *Vaccinium*

Cranberry
Vaccinium oxycoccos

Prostrate, trailing, creeping perennial, with long, wiry stems. **Leaves** *Small, 4–8 mm,* alternate, widely spaced, ± oblong, green above, pale beneath, margins revolute. **Flowers** In groups of 1–4, *stalks minutely*

hairy; corolla lobed nearly to base, lobes strongly revolute. **Fruits** 6–8 mm, spherical to pear-shaped. **Habitat** Wet acid bogs and heaths, open boggy woodland, often creeping over *Sphagnum* moss; to 760 m. **Dist**. Native. Widespread in N and W Britain; very rare elsewhere. (N, central and E Europe.) **Fls** Jun–Aug.

Cowberry
Vaccinium vitis-idaea

Dwarf evergreen shrub to 30 cm, with numerous erect, much-branched stems. **Stems** Twigs smooth. **Leaves** 1–3 cm, glabrous; dark green and glossy above, paler below; margin entire, or obscurely and bluntly toothed. **Flowers** Corolla *c*.6 mm, *bell-shaped*. **Fruits** Red, 6–10 mm across, spherical. **Habitat** Moors, open woodland on acid soils; to 1095 m. **Dist**. Native. Common in upland and N Britain, Ireland. (N Europe, mts of central Europe.) **Fls** Jun–Aug.

Bilberry
Vaccinium myrtillus

Dwarf deciduous shrub to 60 cm, with numerous erect stems. **Stems** *Twigs conspicuously ridged*, green. **Leaves** 1–3 cm,

*bright green,
conspicuously net-
veined, margin
toothed.* **Flowers**
Corolla 4–6 mm.
Fruits Black, with
a bloom, *c.*8 mm
across, spherical.
Habitat Moors,
heathland, open acid
woodlands, drier
parts of peat bogs;
to 1300 m. **Dist.**
Native. Common in
N and W BI; local on heaths of S England.
(Most of Europe.) **Fls** Apr–Jun.

BILBERRY

Wintergreens ▶ *Pyrola*
Evergreen perennials with a creeping
rhizome. Flowers bisexual, regular, 5 petals
and sepals, petals free.

Common Wintergreen
Pyrola minor

Erect evergreen
perennial, flowering
stem to 30 cm.
Leaves 2.5–4 cm,
oval, light green,
petiole shorter than
blade. **Flowers**
*c.*6 mm, globose;
*style straight, 1–2 mm,
shorter than stamens, not
projecting beyond corolla,*
without a ring
below stigma.
Habitat
Moorland,
damp rock
ledges in N;
calcareous
woodland in
S. To 1130 m. **Dist.**
Native. Scattered throughout BI, but absent
in SW. (N and central Europe.) **Fls** Jun–Aug.

Yellow Bird's-nest
Hypopitys monotropa EN. *(NI)

Erect saprophytic
perennial to 30 cm.
*Whole plant white
to yellowish, without
chlorophyll.* Has
2 subspecies that
are genetically
different but difficult
to separate on morphological
characters. **Leaves** Scale-like.
Flowers Regular, in racemes; 4–5
sepals and petals; 8–10 stamens.
In ssp. *monotropa*, inside of petals,
stamens and carpels is pubescent;
in ssp. *hypophegea*, it is usually
glabrous. **Similar spp**. Unlikely
to be confused with any other
plant, except for the saprophytic
broomrapes (p.181), although
these have quite different flowers.
Habitat On leaf litter, usually
in pine, beech or hazel woods.
Dist. Native. Scattered, declining and very
local throughout BI; very rare in Scotland,
Ireland. (All Europe.) **Fls** Jun–Aug.

PRIMULACEAE
Primrose family
••

Superficially a very variable family of annuals
and herbaceous perennials with a single-
celled superior ovary. Leaves are simple or
pinnate, without stipules. Flowers are regular;
5 sepals; 5 petals (absent in *Glaux*), united at
least at base; 5 stamens; numerous ovules.
Fruit is a capsule.

Primrose
Primula vulgaris *(NI, against sale only)

Perennial. **Leaves** 8–15 cm, in a basal
rosette, sparsely hairy above, pubescent
below, tapering gradually to base (cf.
Cowslip). **Flowers** *c.*30 mm across, *arising*

singly from base of plant; stalks to *c.*10 cm, with long, shaggy hairs. **Habitat** Woodland clearings, coppice, hedge banks, old grassland, especially on heavy soils. **Dist**. Native. Throughout BI. (W, S and SE Europe.) **Fls** Dec–May.

Cowslip
Primula veris *(NI)

Glandular-pubescent perennial. **Leaves** 5–15 cm, in a basal rosette, finely pubescent on both surfaces, abruptly contracted towards base (cf. Primrose). **Flowers** *c.*10–15 mm across, *in umbels on scape* (stalk) to 30 cm; distinct *orange spots at base of petals; corolla with folds in throat; calyx uniformly green.* **Fruits** Capsule enclosed by enlarged calyx. **Habitat** Old meadows, grassland, hedge banks, woodland clearings, motorway verges, usually on calcareous soils. **Dist**. Native. Throughout BI, but very rare in N Scotland, N Ireland. (All Europe except extreme N.) **Fls** Apr–May.

Oxlip
Primula elatior

Pubescent perennial. **Leaves** In a basal rosette; similar to *P. veris.* **Flowers** 15–18 mm across, *in umbels*, scape to 30 cm; paler than *P. veris*, nodding and all turned to one side; *corolla without folds in throat; calyx with dark green midribs.* **Fruits** Capsule as long as calyx. **Habitat** Old coppice woodlands on chalky boulder clay. **Dist**. Native. Very local. E England (Cambridgeshire, Essex, Suffolk). (Central Europe.) **Fls** Apr–May.

Bird's-eye Primrose
Primula farinosa VU.

Perennial. **Leaves** 1–5 cm, in a basal rosette, *edges crinkly*, undersides mealy white. **Flowers** *c.*1 cm across; scape to 15 cm, mealy; *petals separated* from each other. **Fruits** Capsule much longer than calyx. **Habitat** Damp, grazed calcareous grassland, calcareous mires. **Dist**. Native. Very local. Carboniferous limestone areas of N England. (All Europe except SE.) **Fls** May–Jun.

Water-violet
Hottonia palustris *(NI)

Floating and rooting aquatic perennial.
Leaves *Submerged, whorled, pinnate with narrow lobes.* **Flowers** whorled, 20–25 mm across, *lilac with yellow throat*; in emergent inflorescence; scape erect, to 40 cm; calyx divided to base. **Fruits** Spherical capsule. **Habitat** Shallow, clear, unpolluted, still or slow-moving base-rich water, ditches, dykes, ponds; lowland. **Dist.** Native. Declining. Scattered throughout England; rare in Wales, Ireland; absent from Scotland. (N and central Europe.) **Fls** May–Jun.

YELLOW PIMPERNEL

Yellow loosestrifes ► *Lysimachia*

Yellow Pimpernel
Lysimachia nemorum

Slender, *evergreen, glabrous, prostrate* perennial to 40 cm. **Leaves** 1–3 cm, opposite, ovate, *acute*. **Flowers** In axils of leaves, 5–10 mm across, on slender stalks; *sepals narrow*. **Habitat** Damp woodland rides, woodland flushes, hedge banks, ditch sides, marshes, on acid soils. **Dist**. Native. Throughout BI. (W and central Europe.) **Fls** May–Sep.

Creeping-Jenny
Lysimachia nummularia

Creeping, evergreen, glabrous perennial to 60 cm. **Leaves** 1.5–3 cm, opposite, broadly ovate, *rounded at tip*. **Flowers** In axils of leaves, 15–25 mm across; *sepals ovate*; petals dotted with black glands, shortly fringed.

CREEPING-JENNY

Habitat Shaded river and stream margins, damp hedgerows, ditches, grassland. **Dist**. Native. Most of England, Wales, Ireland; introduced in SW England, Scotland. (Most of Europe.) **Fls** Jun–Aug.

Yellow Loosestrife
Lysimachia vulgaris

Tall, erect, pubescent, rhizomatous perennial to 150 cm, often forming large clumps. **Leaves** Opposite or in whorls, 3–10 cm, dotted with orange or black glands. **Flowers** In panicles, 8–15 mm across; *margins of sepals orange, hairy; margins of petals glabrous.* **Habitat** Marshes, fens, margins of rivers, lakes and ponds, on fertile soils. **Dist**. Native. Throughout BI except N Scotland. (All Europe.) **Fls** Jul–Aug.

Chickweed-wintergreen
Trientalis europaea

Erect, unbranched, glabrous, rhizomatous, deciduous perennial to 25 cm. **Leaves** Shining, with or without fine teeth, ±

sessile, *in a whorl of 5–6 at top of stem.* **Flowers** *Solitary*, 15–18 mm across; stalks long, 2–7 cm; *usually 7 sepals and petals.* **Habitat** Mossy pine, birch and oak woods, moorland, on damp acid soil; to 1100 m. **Dist**. Native. Local in N England, E and N Scotland (N Europe). **Fls** Jun–Jul.

Brookweed
Samolus valerandi

Glabrous, little-branched, deciduous perennial to 45 cm. **Leaves** Basal and cauline, alternate. **Flowers** *White, 2–4 mm across, in a leafy raceme*; 5 sepals, petals and stamens. **Habitat** Spring lines on sea cliffs, and open, seasonally wet ditches, lagoon and lake shores, on calcareous or brackish soils. **Dist**. Native. Local. Predominantly coastal, all round BI except N and NE Scotland; also inland East Anglia, Somerset, Ireland. (All Europe.) **Fls** Jun–Aug.

Bog Pimpernel
Anagallis tenella

Slender, creeping, glabrous, evergreen perennial to 15 cm, *rooting at nodes*. **Leaves** Opposite, entire, *c*.5 mm. **Flowers** *c*.10 mm across; stalks slender, much longer than leaves; *petals ≥×2 longer than sepals*. **Habitat** Mossy spring mires, edges of acid pools, woodland rides and wet pastures on acid soils, dune slacks; to 610 m. **Dist**. Native. Throughout BI. (W Europe.) **Fls** Jun–Aug.

Scarlet Pimpernel
Anagallis arvensis

Prostrate, glabrous annual or perennial to 30 cm. **Stems** *Square in section*, with glandular dots, *not rooting at nodes*. **Leaves**

ssp. *arvensis* (margin densely fringed)

ssp. *foemina*

Opposite, entire, 15–28 mm, with black glandular dots beneath. **Flowers** 5–7 mm across; stalks slender; *sepals not much shorter than petals*. Ssp. *arvensis* flowers red or pink, rarely blue or violet; petals densely fringed with glandular hairs (seen to consist of 3 cells under microscope). Ssp. *foemina*, Blue Pimpernel, flowers blue; petals sparsely fringed with glandular hairs (seen to consist of 4 cells under microscope). **Habitat** Ssp. *arvensis* common weed of arable crops, gardens, dunes, waste ground; ssp. *foemina* weed of arable land. **Dist**. Cosmopolitan. Ssp. *arvensis* native; throughout BI, but rare in Scotland. Ssp. *foemina* archaeophyte; local and scattered in lowland England. **Fls** Jun–Sep. **Note** Blue-flowered pimpernels are difficult to identify without examining the petal hairs under a microscope.

Chaffweed
Centunculus minimus

Small, erect, glabrous annual to 5 cm. **Leaves** Upper leaves alternate, 3–5 mm. **Flowers** Sessile, in axils of leaves; *tiny, c.1 mm across, petals much shorter than sepals*. **Habitat** Bare, damp, open ground on acid soils, heaths, woodland rides, dune slacks, sea cliffs. **Dist**. Native. Scattered throughout BI, mostly in S and W. (Most of Europe.) **Fls** Jun–Jul. **Similar spp**. Sometimes confused with *Radiola linoides* of similar stature, with which it often grows, but that species is more branched, and has opposite leaves, flowers in a branched inflorescence and 4 petals.

Sea-milkwort
Glaux maritima

Small, prostrate or sub-erect, glabrous, *succulent* perennial to 30 cm. **Leaves**

Opposite, in 4 rows, 4–12 mm. **Flowers** Sessile, in axils of leaves, *c.*5 mm across; *sepals white or pink; petals absent.* **Habitat** Drier parts of salt marshes, dune slacks, brackish grassland, rock crevices. **Dist.** Native. All round British coasts. (Coasts of N and W Europe.) **Fls** Jun–Aug.

CRASSULACEAE
Stonecrops

Easily recognised family, with usually succulent, simple and entire leaves. Flowers are regular, bisexual; usually 5 petals and sepals; as many as or 2× as many stamens as petals; as many carpels as petals, free.

New Zealand Pigmyweed
Crassula helmsii

Trailing or prostrate, glabrous perennial to 30 cm. **Leaves** 4–15 mm, in well-separated

opposite pairs. **Flowers** 1–2 mm across, *on long stalks in axils of leaves*; 4 petals, longer than sepals. **Habitat** Forms extensive mats in shallow water at edge of ponds, dykes, reservoirs. Competes aggressively with native vegetation. **Dist.** Introduced (native of Australia and New Zealand). Rapidly spreading, but still scarce in Scotland, Ireland. **Fls** Jun–Aug.

Navelwort/Pennywort
Umbilicus rupestris

Erect, glabrous, unbranched perennial to 40 cm. **Leaves** *Mostly basal, stalked, circular, peltate,* 1.5–7 cm across. **Flowers** *Drooping,* 8–10 mm, tubular, *in a many-flowered spike; 5 petals; 10 stamens.* **Habitat** Cliffs, rock crevices, walls, dry sandy hedge banks; to 550 m. **Dist.** Native. Common in W BI. (Mediterranean, W Europe.) **Fls** Jun–Sep.

Roseroot
Sedum rosea

Erect, glabrous, glaucous
perennial to 30 cm.
Rhizomes Thick,
fleshy. **Stems**
Several. **Leaves**
Flat, 1–4 cm,
alternate, dense,
increasing in size
up stem. **Flowers**
Dioecious, *4 petals,
greenish yellow.*
Habitat Mountain
rock ledges,
crevices, usually on
base-rich soils; to
1160 m. **Dist**. Native.
Upland Britain,
sea cliffs in W and N.
(Arctic Europe.)
Fls May–Aug.

Rock Stonecrop
Sedum forsterianum

Glabrous, evergreen, mat-forming
perennial to 30 cm.
Leaves Alternate,
linear, 10–20 mm,
upper surface flat,
*tips abruptly pointed;
in dense, rosette-like
clusters at tips of sterile
branches*, with persistent dead
leaves below. **Flowers** *Yellow*,
c.12 mm across, in umbel-
like inflorescence; 6–8 petals.
Habitat Rocks,
scree, rocky
hillsides; to
365 m.
Dist.
Native.
Wales,
SW England.

Widely cultivated and naturalised outside
native range. (W and SW Europe.)
Fls Jun–Jul.

Biting Stonecrop
Sedum acre

Glabrous, mat-forming, evergreen perennial
to 10 cm. **Leaves** Alternate, *overlapping*,
broadest near base, rounded in section,
3–5 mm; *hot and acrid to taste*. **Flowers**
Yellow, *c*.12 mm across, in few-flowered
inflorescence; 5 petals, 6–8 mm. **Habitat**
Sand-dunes, shingle beaches, cliff tops,
heaths, walls, motorway reservations, dry,
open grassland. **Dist**. Native. Throughout
BI, but scarce in N Scotland. (All Europe.)
Fls Jun–Jul.

English Stonecrop
Sedum anglicum

Creeping, mat-forming, glabrous, glaucous,
evergreen perennial to 5 cm. **Leaves**
Alternate, 3–5 mm, egg-shaped, spreading

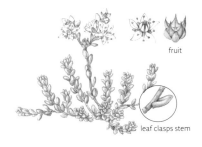

fruit

leaf clasps stem

and *clasping stem at base.* **Flowers** *White,* *c.*12 mm across, in *few-flowered inflorescence with 2 main branches*; scales at base of petals red. **Habitat** Rocks, dunes, shingle beaches; also rocky woodlands, walls, mine spoil, on acid soils. To 1080 m. **Dist**. Native. W Britain, Ireland; scattered elsewhere. (W Europe.) **Fls** Jun–Sep.

White Stonecrop
Sedum album

Creeping, mat-forming, glabrous, bright green perennial to 15 cm. **Leaves** *Alternate,* 6–12 mm, *not clasping at base.* **Flowers** *White,* 6–9 mm across, in *dense-flowered inflorescence with several branches*; scales at base of petals yellow. **Habitat** Rocks and old walls, shingle, churchyards; to 570 m. **Dist**. Archaeophyte, although may be native on limestone rocks in S Devon, Mendips. Throughout BI, but rare in N Scotland. (All Europe.) **Fls** Jun–Aug.

leaf not clasping

Orpine
Sedum telephium

Erect, glabrous, slightly glaucous perennial to 60 cm, with carrot-shaped root tubers. **Leaves** *Flat,* 2–8 cm, alternate, numerous. **Flowers** *Red, 5 petals,* 3–5 mm. **Habitat** Hedge banks, lanesides, woodland clearings, field borders, limestone pavement; to 455 m. **Dist**. Native; introduced in Ireland. Throughout BI except N Scotland. Native distribution obscured by frequent escapes

from cultivation. (N, W and central Europe.) **Fls** Jul–Sep.

SAXIFRAGACEAE
Saxifrages
••

Leaves are usually alternate or all basal. Flowers are bisexual, regular; usually 5 sepals and petals; 10 stamens; receptacle characteristically cup-shaped or flat; 2 carpels, fused at base. Fruit is a capsule. *Saxifraga* includes a number of cushion-forming alpines.

Starry Saxifrage
Saxifraga stellaris

Erect, stoloniferous perennial with basal leaf rosettes. **Stems** *Flowering stems leafless,* hairy, glandular, to 20 cm. **Leaves** 0.5–3 cm, ± *sessile.* **Flowers** *In open inflorescence; petals 4–6 mm, with 2 yellow spots near base.*

petal

**STARRY
SAXIFRAGE**

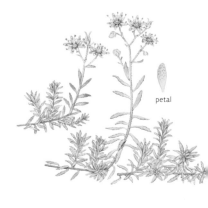

petal

Habitat Stream sides, springs, flushes, wet rock ledges, wet stony ground; to 1340 m. **Dist**. Native. Widespread in uplands. (N Europe, mts of central and S Europe.) **Fls** Jun–Aug.

Purple Saxifrage
Saxifraga oppositifolia *(NI)

Densely tufted, cushion- or mat-forming alpine perennial. **Leaves** Opposite, in 4 rows, overlapping, 2–6 mm, with marginal hairs. **Flowers** Purple, solitary, petals 5–10 mm. **Habitat** Damp rocks, ledges, stony ground, scree, steep slopes, on calcareous or basic rocks; to 1210 m. **Dist**. Native. Locally common in mts of N and W Britain. (Arctic Europe, mts of central and S Europe.) **Fls** Feb–May.

leaves
ciliate
margin

Yellow Saxifrage
Saxifraga aizoides *(NI)

Erect alpine perennial to 20 cm. **Stems** Non-flowering stems prostrate, densely leafy. **Leaves** 1–2 cm, narrow with fringe of marginal hairs. **Flowers** *Yellow, in open inflorescence of 1–10 flowers*; petals 4–7 mm with red dots. **Habitat** Rocks, boulders, in mountain streams; wet gravelly, stony ground. To 1175 m. **Dist**. Native. Locally common in mts of N England, Scotland, NW Ireland. (Arctic Europe, mts of central and S Europe.) **Fls** Jun–Sep.

Mossy Saxifrage
Saxifraga hypnoides
VU.

Mat-forming, stoloniferous perennial to 20 cm. **Stems** Non-flowering shoots numerous, prostrate; flowering stems ± glabrous. **Leaves** *c*.1 cm, with long non-glandular hairs, *lobes linear, terminal lobe with short hair point*. **Flowers** Petals 4–10 mm.

Habitat Sides of mountain streams, cliffs, screes, rocky slopes; rarely on sand-dunes. To 1215 m. **Dist.** Native. Widespread throughout British uplands. (NW Europe.) **Fls** May–Jul.

Meadow Saxifrage
Saxifraga granulata *(R)

Erect, pubescent, glandular perennial to 50 cm, *with brown bulbils in axils of basal rosette leaves.* **Stems** Flowering stems, solitary, unbranched. **Leaves** *Blades* 0.5–3 cm, *with lobes* long glandular and non-glandular hairs; petiole much longer than blade. **Flowers** White, pedicels 5–20 mm, densely glandular; *petals 10–17 mm.* **Habitat** Well-drained neutral or basic rough pastures, meadows, grassy banks, churchyards. **Dist**. Native. Local throughout most of BI except SW England, N Scotland, Ireland. (Most of Europe.) **Fls** Jun–Aug.

Rue-leaved Saxifrage
Saxifraga tridactylites

Erect, glandular-hairy, sparsely branched, often reddish *annual to c.10 cm.* **Leaves** *Basal leaves lobed, bulbils absent.* **Flowers** White, in sparse inflorescence, pedicels much longer than flowers, petals 2–3 mm. **Habitat** Dry,

glandular hairs
fruit

open areas, wall tops, sand-dunes, heath grassland, waste ground, limestone rocks; to 595 m. **Dist**. Native. Widespread in lowland S Britain; rare in Scotland. (Most of Europe.) **Fls** Apr–Jun.

Opposite-leaved Golden Saxifrage
Chrysosplenium oppositifolium

Sparsely hairy, stoloniferous perennial to 15cm. **Stems** Leafy; non-flowering shoots prostrate, flowering stems erect. **Leaves** *Opposite, not cordate, petiole as long as or shorter than blade.* **Flowers** 3–4 mm across; 4–5 sepals; petals absent. **Habitat** Woodland flushes, stream sides, springs, wet rocks, on acid soils; to 1100 m. **Dist**. Native. Common throughout BI. (W and central Europe.) **Fls** Apr–Jun.

fruit

Alternate-leaved Golden Saxifrage
Chrysosplenium alternifolium

Similar to *C. oppositifolium*, but more robust, stolons leafless; *basal leaves cordate, pedicels much longer than blade*; flowering stems taller, and with only 1 leaf; flowers 5–6 mm across. **Habitat** Similar to *C. oppositifolium*, with which it

fruit

**ALTERNATE-LEAVED
GOLDEN SAXIFRAGE**

often grows, but more local, ± restricted to base-rich moving ground water; also upland mossy flushes. To 915 m. **Dist**. Native. Widespread in N and W; rare in E and SW England; absent from Ireland. (Most of Europe except S.) **Fls** Apr–Jun.

Grass-of-Parnassus
Parnassia palustris

Distinctive, erect, glabrous perennial. **Stems** *Flowering stems to 30 cm, with single leaf near base.* **Leaves** Basal leaves cordate, 1–5 cm; petioles long. **Flowers** *Solitary,* with 5 large yellowish staminodes (sterile stamens); petals 7–12 mm. **Habitat** Base-rich fens, mires, wet grassland; machair, dune slacks. To 1005 m. **Dist**. Native. Widespread in N Britain, East Anglia; declining in S. (All Europe except extreme N.) **Fls** Jul–Oct.

ROSACEAE
Rose family

A large, diverse family of trees, shrubs and herbs with alternate leaves that almost always have stipules. Flowers are regular, sometimes with an epicalyx beneath the calyx looking like a second ring of sepals; usually 5 sepals and petals, petals free, sometimes absent; stamens numerous, usually 2–4× as many as petals; one to many carpels, usually free, or ovary inferior with carpels united to and enclosed by the receptacle. Fruits vary, usually an achene or follicle or, in trees and shrubs, a drupe. Flowers with numerous stamens and free carpels are sometimes mistaken for the Ranunculaceae, but the alternate leaves with stipules should almost always avoid confusion (although note that the water-crowfoots do have stipules).

Meadowsweet
Filipendula ulmaria

Tall perennial to 120 cm, sometimes forming dense stands. **Leaves** Basal ones 30–60 cm, with up to 5 large leaflets. **Flowers** *In dense inflorescence; 5 sepals; 5 petals*, 2–5 mm. **Habitat** Marshes, fens, wet woods, ditches; river, stream and lake margins; wet alpine meadows, rock ledges. To 880 m.

fruit

Dist. Native. Common throughout BI. (All Europe except Mediterranean.) **Fls** Jun–Sep.

Dropwort
Filipendula vulgaris

Erect, ± glabrous perennial to 80 cm. **Stems** *Flowering stems ± unbranched*. **Leaves** Basal ones numerous, 2–25 cm, with 8–20 pairs of leaflets; stem leaves few. **Flowers** *6 sepals; 6 petals*, 5–9 mm. **Habitat** Dry calcareous grassland; to 365 m. **Dist**. Native. Lowland England; scattered elsewhere. Planted in N Wales. (Most of Europe.) **Fls** May–Aug.

Cloudberry
Rubus chamaemorus *(NI)

Low, dioecious, *non-spiny*, rhizomatous perennial, with annual shoots. **Stems** Flowering stems erect, to 20 cm. **Flowers** *Solitary*; 5 sepals; 5 petals, 8–12 mm. **Fruits** *Orange when ripe*, with 4–20 drupelets.

Habitat Hummocks in blanket bogs, upland moorland; to 1160 m. **Dist**. Native. Locally abundant in upland Britain N from Pennines; very rare in Wales, Ireland. (N Europe, mts of S and E Europe.) **Fls** Jun–Aug.

Stone Bramble
Rubus saxatilis

Stoloniferous, deciduous perennial to 40 cm, pubescent and with weak prickles. **Stems** Flowering stems arising from base of plant. **Leaves** *With 3 leaflets*; stipules attached to stem, not petiole. **Flowers** *8–15 mm across, in few-flowered inflorescence*. **Fruits** *Red*. **Habitat** Open, damp rocky woodland, shaded rocks, scree, on calcareous or base-rich soils; to 975 m. **Dist**. Native. Widespread, but local in uplands. (N Europe, mts of S Europe.) **Fls** Jun–Aug.

Raspberry
Rubus idaeus

Erect shrub to 160 cm. **Stems** Usually biennial, with weak prickles. **Leaves** *Pinnate*; 3–7 leaflets, *white beneath*. **Flowers** *c*.10 mm across, in few-flowered cyme; petals as long as sepals. **Fruits** *Red*. **Habitat** Open woodland, heaths, commons, downland; also as an escape

RASPBERRY

from cultivation. To 745 m. **Dist.** Native.
Throughout BI. (Most of Europe.)
Fls Jun–Aug.

Dewberry
Rubus caesius

Deciduous shrub. **Stems** *Prostrate, rooting
at tip, glabrous, with bluish bloom*; prickles
weak. **Leaves** *With 3 overlapping leaflets.*
Flowers Large, 2–3 cm across. **Fruits**
*Large, black; few drupelets, these with bluish
bloom.* **Habitat** Hedges, scrub, rough,
dry grassland, on basic soils; fen carr,
dune slacks. **Dist.** Native. Widespread in
England, Wales; rare in Ireland; ± absent
from Scotland. (Most of Europe.) **Fls**
Jun–Sep.

Bramble/Blackberry
Rubus 'fruticosus'

Deciduous or semi-evergreen, intensely
prickly shrub, often forming dense patches.
Stems Rooting at tips. **Leaves** *Palmate.*
Fruits *Black, hardly pruinose* (with a
bloom). **Dist**. Native. Common throughout
BI. **Habitat** Woodlands, hedgerows, scrub,
commons, heaths, cliffs. (All Europe.)
Fls May–Sep. **Note** *Rubus 'fruticosus'* is
an aggregate name for a large number of
'apomictic' (producing viable seed without
fertilisation) 'micro-species'. Over 320
different 'micro-species' have been named
from the BI; no attempt is made to deal
with these individually here.

Cinquefoils ▶ *Potentilla*

Marsh Cinquefoil
Comarum palustre

Rhizomatous, ascending perennial to 45 cm.
Leaves With 5 or 7 leaflets, these 3–6 cm.
Flowers In few-flowered inflorescence, *all
parts of flowers purple, sepals enlarging after
flowering, petals shorter than sepals.* **Habitat**

Solitary, on long stalks; 5 sepals; 5 petals, *c.*10 mm. **Habitat** Roadsides, farm tracks, gateways, waste ground, abandoned arable land, dunes, upper levels of salt marshes. **Dist**. Native. Common throughout BI. (All Europe except S and SW.) **Fls** Jun–Aug.

Tormentil
Potentilla erecta

Perennial to 30 cm, with basal rosette of leaves that withers before flowering. **Stems** Not rooting. **Leaves** *Ternate*, basal leaves with long stalks, *stem leaves sessile*, stipules leaflet-like. **Flowers** *7–15 mm across, 4 petals; ≤20 carpels.* **Habitat** Grassland, heaths, moors, bogs, fens, open woodland, hedge banks, usually on mildly acid soils; to 1040 m. **Dist**. Native. Common throughout BI. (All Europe except extreme S.) **Fls** Jun–Sep.

Fens, marshes, flushed bogs, lake and pool margins; to 800 m. **Dist**. Native. Common and widespread in N and W Britain; local in S, East Anglia. (All Europe except S and SW.) **Fls** May–Jul.

Silverweed
Potentilla anserina

Stoloniferous perennial. **Leaves** *In basal rosettes, pinnate*, with 7–12 pairs of main leaflets, *densely silvery-silky beneath.* **Flowers**

Trailing Tormentil
Potentilla anglica

Perennial to 80 cm, with rooting prostrate stems and persistent basal rosette. **Leaves** *Basal leaves with 5 leaflets*, long-stalked; stem leaves ternate; stipules entire. **Flowers**

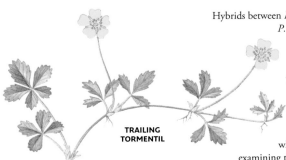

TRAILING TORMENTIL

Hybrids between *P. erecta, P. anglica* and *P. reptans* are common and identification of intermediate plants can be very difficult. The hybrids are always sterile so the only reliable character for good *P. anglica* is the presence of viable seeds, which can be checked by examining the fruiting heads to see whether the carpels are swollen.

Solitary, 14–18 mm across, 4 or 5 petals; 20–50 carpels. **Habitat** Field borders, woodland clearings, hedge banks, grass heaths, on well-drained acid soils. **Dist**. Native. Throughout BI except N Scotland; commoner in W. (Central and W Europe.) **Fls** Jun–Sep.

Creeping Cinquefoil
Potentilla reptans

Prostrate, stoloniferous perennial to 100 cm, with *persistent basal rosette*. **Leaves** *Palmate*, petioles long. **Flowers** Solitary; 5 sepals; *5 petals, 15–25 mm across, 2× as long as sepals; 60–120 carpels*. **Habitat** Grazed grassland, road verges, tracks, hedge banks, waste ground; lowland to 415 m. **Dist**. Native. BI as far N as Clyde. (Most of Europe.) **Fls** Jun–Sep.

Barren Strawberry
Potentilla sterilis

Pubescent, stoloniferous perennial to 15 cm. **Leaves** *Ternate, dull bluish green*; leaflets broadly obovate, toothed to base, apical tooth shorter than its neighbours. **Flowers** *White*, 10–15 mm across; *petals c.5 mm, not contiguous, about as long as sepals*. **Habitat** Hedge banks, dry grassland, walls, scrub, woodland clearings, on well-drained soils; to 790 m. **Dist**. Throughout BI except extreme N Scotland. (W and central Europe.) **Fls** Feb–May.

Wild Strawberry
Fragaria vesca

Pubescent, stoloniferous perennial to 30 cm. **Leaves** Ternate, bright green; leaflets sessile, apical tooth as long as or longer than its neighbours (cf. *P. sterilis*). **Flowers** 12–18 mm across; *petals contiguous or overlapping, longer than sepals.* **Habitat** Woodlands, scrub, hedge banks, rough grassland, on base-rich soils; to 640 m. **Dist**. Throughout BI. (Most of Europe.) **Fls** Apr–Jul.

Sibbaldia
Sibbaldia procumbens VU.

Short, tufted, pubescent alpine perennial, with basal rosette of leaves. **Leaves** *Ternate, apical tooth of leaflets smaller than its neighbours.* **Flowers** About 5 mm across, in compact heads; *petals tiny or absent.* **Habitat** Areas of late snow-lie, exposed ridges, summit detritus; to 1310 m. **Dist**. Native. Local and widespread in Scottish Highlands. (Arctic Europe, mts of central and S Europe.) **Fls** Jul–Aug.

Mountain Avens
Dryas octopetala *(NI)

Much-branched, prostrate, evergreen perennial, with woody base. **Leaves** 0.5–2.5 cm, *densely white-felted beneath.* **Flowers** *Solitary*, 2.5–4 cm across; stalks 2–8 cm; *usually 8 petals*; numerous carpels. **Fruits** Style persistent, covered by long, feathery hairs. **Habitat** Rock ledges, steep cliffs, calcareous grassland, limestone pavement (Ireland), on calcareous soils; coastal shell-sand (N Scotland). To 1035 m. **Dist**. Native. Very local in upland Britain. (Arctic Europe, mts of central and S Europe.) **Fls** Jun–Jul.

Water Avens
Geum rivale

Erect, pubescent perennial to 60 cm. **Leaves** Basal leaves with 3–6 pairs of lateral leaflets, *terminal leaflet rounded, 2–5 cm across; stipules small,*

carpel and awn

c.5 mm. **Flowers** *Nodding; petals purple* about as long as sepals, 10–15 mm, *with long, narrow basal segment (clawed), tip notched*; stamens and carpels numerous. **Fruits** Style persistent as awn on fruit tip. **Habitat** Wet meadows, marshes, fens, damp woodlands, stream sides, rock ledges, on base-rich soils; prefers shade. To 975 m. **Dist**. Native. Throughout BI but commoner in N. (Most of Europe except extreme N.) **Fls** May–Sep.

Wood Avens
Geum urbanum

Erect, pubescent perennial to 60 cm. **Leaves** Basal leaves with 2–3 pairs of lateral leaflets, *terminal leaflet large, 3-lobed; stipules large, leaf-like*. **Flowers** *Erect; petals yellow* about as long as sepals, 5–9 mm, *neither clawed nor notched at tip*. **Habitat** Shaded areas, woodlands, scrub, hedgerows, roadsides, gardens, on base-rich soils; lowland to 450 m. **Dist**. Native. Common throughout BI except extreme N. (All Europe except extreme N.) **Fls** Jun–Aug.

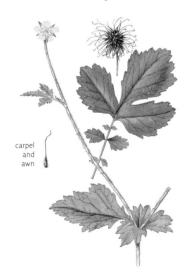

carpel
and
awn

Agrimony
Agrimonia eupatoria

Erect, pubescent, sparsely branched perennial to 100 cm. **Leaves** *Densely hairy but not usually glandular.* **Flowers** 5–8 mm across, in spike-like inflorescence; epicalyx absent; petals not notched. **Fruits** *Receptacle grooved throughout its length, lowest spines spreading horizontally or ascending.* **Habitat** Rough grassland, field borders, scrub, hedge banks, roadsides, woodland clearings; lowland to 365 m. **Dist**. Native. Common throughout BI except N Scotland. (All Europe except extreme N.) **Fls** Jun–Aug.

fruit

Great Burnet
Sanguisorba officinalis *(R)

Tall, erect, glabrous *perennial to 100 cm.* **Leaves** *Leaflets to 2–4 cm, stalked, cordate at base.* **Flowers** *10–20 mm, crimson, bisexual, in oblong heads*; 4 stamens. **Habitat** Wet meadows, pastures, marshes, lake shores; to 460 m. **Dist**. Native. Central, N and SW England, Wales. (W, central and E Europe.) **Fls** Jun–Sep.

♀ flower

♂ flower

underside leaf

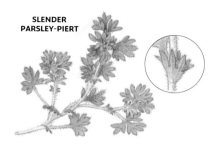

SLENDER PARSLEY-PIERT

Salad Burnet
Poterium sanguisorba ssp. *sanguisorba*

Erect, glabrous, rather glaucous perennial to 50 cm, smelling of cucumber when crushed. **Leaves** *Leaflets 0.5–2 cm, rounded at base, with short stalk*; few stem leaves or these absent. **Flowers** 7–12 mm, *green, in globular heads*; lower flowers male, middle bisexual, upper female; numerous stamens. **Fruits** *Receptacle* ridged but *not winged, faces reticulate*. **Habitat** Dry calcareous grassland; to 500 m. **Dist**. Native. Common in Britain as far N as S Scotland; rare in Ireland. (W, central and E Europe.) **Fls** May–Aug.

Parsley-piert, Slender Parsley-piert
Aphanes arvensis, Aphanes australis

Small, inconspicuous, prostrate to erect, pubescent annuals, to *c.*10 cm. **Flowers** Small, in dense clusters opposite leaves; stipules fused into a lobed leaf-like cup; fruiting inflorescence

PARSLEY-PIERT

partly enclosed by stipular cup; in *A. arvensis stipule lobes triangular, c. ½ length of entire portion, as long as or shorter than calyx; receptacle constricted below sepals; sepals erect*; in *A. australis stipule lobes ovate-oblong, about as long as entire portion, longer than calyx; outline of calyx and receptacle ± continuous; sepals convergent*. **Habitat** Arable fields, bare patches in permanent grassland, woodland rides, waste places, roadsides; *A. australis* less often on arable land than *A. arvensis*. **Dist**. Native. Throughout BI. (Most of Europe except N and SW.) **Fls** Apr–Oct. **Note** The 2 species of *Aphanes* can be difficult to separate. Stipule lobes and receptacle must be examined when plant is in fruit; sterile plants can't be distinguished.

Lady's-mantles ► *Alchemilla*
The Lady's-mantles are a group of distinctive perennials several of which are common plants of upland grasslands. With the exception of Alpine Lady's-mantle, *A. alpina*, they are all apomictic, that is they produce viable seed without fertilisation, and consequently are very difficult to identify.

Lady's-mantle
Alchemilla vulgaris agg.

Glabrous to densely pubescent decumbent to ascending perennials to 50 cm. **Leaves** Mostly basal, orbicular, palmately lobed <½ way to base, green on both sides.

LADY'S-MANTLE

Flowers Greenish, 3–4 mm across, epicalyx present, petals 0. **Habitat** Damp meadows, pastures, roadside verges, open woodland, rock ledges, to 1200 m. **Dist.** Native. Widespread and common in N and W, rare in S. **Fls** Jun–Sept.

Alpine Lady's-mantle
Alchemilla alpina

Perennial alpine to 20 cm. **Leaves** Most basal, 2.5–3.5 mm across, *palmately divided to base; green, glabrous above, densely silvery-silky beneath.* **Flowers** c.*3 mm across.* **Habitat** Mountain grassland, scree, rock ledges,

summit detritus; to 1270 m. Down to sea-level on W coast of Scotland. **Dist.** Native. Locally common in Lake District and Scottish Highlands. (N Europe, Alps, Pyrenees.) **Fls** Jun–Aug.

Roses ▶ *Rosa*
Some 12 species of wild rose are usually recognised as native in the British Isles, but the picture is complicated by the variability of the species and the frequency of hybrids. For this reason it is not always easy to name the plants. The leaves and ripe hips provide the most useful characters, but details of the prickles and bristles on the stems and the lobing of the sepals are also important. The colour of the flowers is more variable.

Burnet Rose
Rosa spinosissima

Low, erect, suckering deciduous *shrub* to 50 cm, *forming large patches.* **Stems** *Densely covered by slender prickles and stiff bristles* (acicles). **Leaves** *Glabrous*, leaflets small, 0.5–1.5 cm. **Flowers** 2–4 cm across, solitary; pedicels 1.5–2.5 cm, glandular or smooth, sepals entire. **Fruits** ± spherical, 1–1.5 cm, *purplish black.* **Habitat** Sand-dunes, dune slacks, sea cliffs, rough chalk grassland, limestone pavement; to 520 m. **Dist.** Native. Throughout BI, especially coastal; scattered inland. (W, central and E Europe.) **Fls** May–Jul.

HAIRY
DOG-ROSE

Field Rose
Rosa arvensis

Glabrous deciduous shrub with weak
trailing or scrambling stems, often climbing
over other shrubs. **Stems** Prickles hooked,
± equal. **Flowers** White, 3–5 cm across;
*pedicels 2–4 cm with stalked glands; sepals
short, ovate, lobes few or absent; styles united
into column as long as shorter stamens.*
Habitat Scrub, hedgerows, wood margins;
to 410 m. **Dist.** Native. Frequent in
England, Wales, E Ireland; absent from
Scotland. (W, central and SE Europe.)
Fls Jun–Jul.

Dog-rose
Rosa canina

Deciduous shrub with arching stems, to
3 m. The commonest British rose. **Stems**

DOG-ROSE

Prickles strongly hooked. **Leaves** *Leaflets
1.5–4 cm, glabrous, eglandular or with a
few glands on main veins beneath.* **Flowers**
4–6 cm across. Pedicels 0.5–2 cm, glabrous
or sparsely glandular-pubescent; *sepals
reflexed after flowering, falling before fruit
reddens, lobes ± entire; stigmas in conical
head that is narrower than disc.* **Fruits**
1.5–2 cm, *smooth.* **Habitat** Hedgerows,
scrub, thickets, cliffs, wood margins,
waste ground; to 550 m. **Dist.** Native.
Throughout BI, becoming less common
in Scotland. (Most of Europe except N
Scandinavia, W France.) **Fls** Jun–Jul.
Comment In northern England and
Scotland *R. canina* is largely replaced by
Hairy Dog-rose and **Glaucous Dog-rose**
R. caesia, distinguished from *R. canina* by
the *sepals persisting and becoming erect after
flowering.*

Sweet-briar
Rosa rubiginosa

Erect deciduous shrub to 2 m. **Stems**
*Prickles hooked, unequal in size, mixed
with stout bristles.* **Leaves** *Leaflets oval,*

SWEET-BRIAR

rounded at base; covered beneath with sweet-scented glands, smelling of apples when crushed. **Flowers** *Bright pink,* 2.5–4 cm across; *pedicels c.1 cm, glandular-hispid; sepals persistent, erect or spreading.* **Fruits** 1–1.5 cm, *glandular-hispid at base.* **Habitat** Calcareous grassland, scrub, hedges, quarries, waste ground. **Dist.** Native. Throughout most of BI. (W, central and E Europe.) **Fls** Jun–Jul.

FABACEAE
Peas, vetches and clovers (legumes)
•••

One of the largest families of flowering plants, with characteristic flowers like that of a Sweet Pea. Trees, shrubs or (in British Isles usually) herbs. Leaves are simple or, more usually, compound, often pinnate or trifoliate, alternate and usually with stipules. Flowers are strongly irregular; 5 sepals, joined into a tube at the base; 5 petals, consisting of an upper standard, 2 lateral wings, and a lower lip (keel) comprised of the 2 fused lower petals; 10 stamens, all united into a tube, or with 9 joined and 1 free and contained within the keel; ovary superior, 1 style. Fruit is basically a dehiscent pod (legume) with large seeds.

Purple Milk-vetch
Astragalus danicus EN. *(R)

Ascending, *pubescent* perennial to 35 cm. **Leaves** 3–7 cm, *stipules joined at base.* **Flowers** 15–18 mm, *blue-purple,* erect, tip of lower petal blunt, *peduncle longer than adjacent leaf.* **Fruits** Pod, 7–10 mm, with

white appressed hairs. **Habitat/ Dist.** Native. Very local. Old calcareous grassland in E England, Wiltshire; calcareous sand-dunes on E coast of Scotland. (Central and E Europe.) **Fls** May–Jul.

fruit

Sainfoin
Onobrychis viciifolia

Erect, *pubescent* perennial to 60 cm. **Leaves** Leaflets 1–3 cm, *6–12 pairs.* **Flowers** *Pink,* 10–12 mm, peduncle longer than leaves. **Fruits** Pubescent pod, 6–8 mm, with reticulated ridges. **Habitat** Unimproved chalk grassland, tracksides, road verges; to 335 m. **Dist**. Alien or native. Widely cultivated for fodder until the nineteenth century, natural distribution obscured by relic of cultivation. Locally frequent in lowland England; rare elsewhere. (Most of Europe except N.) **Fls** Jun–Aug.

fruit

Kidney Vetch
Anthyllis vulneraria

Prostrate to erect, pubescent perennial, to 60 cm. Very variable, with a number of named forms. **Leaves** To 14 cm, *pinnate, without tendrils*, lower leaves often reduced to single large terminal leaflet. **Flowers** 12–15 mm, *in paired umbels surrounded by leaf-like bracts; calyx inflated and covered by white woolly hairs*. **Fruits** Glabrous pod, *c*.3mm. **Habitat** Calcareous grassland, sea cliffs, rock ledges, maritime heath; to 945 m. **Dist**. Native. Common throughout BI. (All Europe.) **Fls** Jun–Sep.

Bird's-foot-trefoils ▶ *Lotus*

Common Bird's-foot-trefoil
Lotus corniculatus

Prostrate, ± glabrous perennial to 40 cm. **Stems** *Solid*. **Leaves** Leaflets 3–10 mm, *<3 × as long as wide*. **Flowers** 10–15 mm; calyx teeth erect in bud, sinus between upper 2 calyx teeth obtuse. **Fruits** Pod, 15–30 mm. **Habitat** Calcareous grassland, meadows, hill pastures, grass heaths, cliffs, shingle, sand-dunes; to 915 m. **Dist**. Native. Throughout BI. (All Europe.) **Fls** Jun–Sep.

COMMON BIRD'S-
FOOT-TREFOIL

fruit

Greater Bird's-foot-trefoil
Lotus pedunculatus

Erect, *usually pubescent perennial* to 75 cm. **Stems** *Hollow*. **Leaves** Leaflets 15–20 mm, those of upper leaves <3× as long as broad. **Flowers** 10–18 mm, calyx teeth spreading in bud. **Fruits** Pods, 15–35 mm. **Habitat** Marshes, wet pastures, ditches, woodland

fruit

paths, pond and river margins; lowland to 390 m. **Dist**. Native. Most of BI. (Most of Europe except extreme N and S.) **Fls** Jun–Aug.

Narrow-leaved Bird's-foot-trefoil
Lotus tenuis

Similar to *L. corniculatus*, but more slender; *leaflets narrower, those of upper leaves >4× as long as broad*; flowers 6–12 mm, *2 upper calyx teeth converging*; pod 15–30 mm. **Habitat** Coastal grazing marshes, sea walls; inland rough grassland, pits, road verges. **Dist**. Native. Local in England S of line from Humber to Severn. (All Europe except N.) **Fls** Jun–Aug.

rare in Ireland. (Most of Europe except extreme N and S.) **Fls** Apr–Aug.

Horseshoe Vetch
Hippocrepis comosa

fruit

Almost *glabrous*, prostrate perennial to 45 cm. **Leaves** 30–50 mm, *with 4–5 pairs leaflets plus a terminal leaflet*. **Flowers** *Yellow*, 5–10 mm, *in 5–8-flowered umbels*, peduncles longer than adjacent leaf. **Fruits** *Pods*, 10–30 mm, *constricted into horseshoe-shaped segments*. **Habitat** Short, dry turf, warm slopes, chalk and limestone grassland. **Dist**. Native. Local in England N to N Yorkshire. (S and SW Europe.) **Fls** May–Jul.

fruit

Bird's-foot
Ornithopus perpusillus *(R)

Tiny, prostrate, *pubescent annual* to 30 cm. **Leaves** 15–30 mm, *with 4–10 pairs of leaflets plus a terminal leaflet*. **Flowers** *White*, 3–4 mm, *in 3–6-flowered umbels, with pinnate bracts*. **Fruits** Curved pod, 10–20 mm, constricted between seeds. **Habitat** Short turf: grass heaths, dunes, lawns, road verges, on dry sandy soils. Lowland to 380 m. **Dist**. Native. Throughout most of BI except N Scotland;

Vetches, peas and vetchlings ▶ *Vicia* and *Lathyrus*

The vetches, *Vicia*, and peas and vetchlings, *Lathyrus*, are very similar, the technical difference between them relying on details of the stamen tube and stigmas, which are not easy to see. For the sake of simplicity and to avoid confusion, the two are treated together in the following key. In general, *Lathyrus* species have angled, flattened or winged stems with 0–2 pairs of leaflets with or without tendrils, whilst the stems of *Vicia* species are round in section and have two to many pairs of leaflets with tendrils. Exceptions include *V. bithynica*, which has winged stems and only 1–2 pairs of leaflets, and *V. orobus*, which has no tendrils.

Tufted Vetch
Vicia cracca

fruit

fruit

Tall, straggling, pubescent perennial to 200 cm. **Leaves** With 5–12 pairs of lanceolate leaflets, tendrils branched, stipules entire. **Flowers** 10–12 mm, 10–40 *forming 2–10 cm inflorescence; peduncles long, 2–10 cm.* **Fruits** *Glabrous*, pod, 10–25 mm. **Habitat** Rough grassland, old pasture, hedge banks, scrub, woodland edges, coastal shingle; to 550 m. **Dist**. Native. Common throughout BI. (All Europe.) **Fls** Jun–Aug.

Bush Vetch
Vicia sepium

Tall, scrambling ± glabrous perennial to 100 cm. **Leaves** *With 5–9 pairs* of ovate leaflets, tendrils branched; stipules not, or

only slightly, toothed. **Flowers** 12–15 mm, 2–6 forming *1–2 cm inflorescence*, ± sessile. **Fruits** Glabrous pod, 20–25 mm. **Habitat** Hedge banks, woodland clearings, scrub, rough grassland; to 820 m. **Dist**. Native. Common throughout BI. (All Europe, but rare in Mediterranean.) **Fls** May–Aug.

Wood Bitter-vetch
Vicia orobus *(R)

Erect, branched, ± pubescent perennial to 60 cm. **Leaves** *With 6–10 pairs of leaflets, tendrils absent*, stipules slightly toothed. **Flowers** *White, with purple veins*, 12–15 mm, drooping; 6–20 forming 1–3 cm inflorescence; peduncles about as long as leaves. **Fruits** Glabrous pod,

fruit

20–30 mm. **Habitat** Rocky woodlands, cliffs, shaded rocks; coastal in N Scotland. To 455 m. **Dist**. Native. Scattered, local, declining. W Britain, especially Wales. (W Europe.) **Fls** Jun–Sep.

Hairy Tare
Vicia hirsuta

Slender, scrambling, glabrous annual to 30 cm. **Leaves** With 4–10 pairs of narrow leaflets, *tendrils branched*, stipules 4-lobed. **Flowers** *3–5 mm, in 1–9-flowered inflorescence*, peduncles 1–3 cm. **Fruits** *Pubescent pod, 6–11 mm, 2-seeded.* **Habitat** Rough grassland, pastures, scrub, sea cliffs, shingle beaches, roadside verges; to 335 m. **Dist**. Native. Common throughout most of BI, but rare in NW Scotland, W Ireland. (All Europe.) **Fls** May–Aug.

Smooth Tare
Vicia tetrasperma

Slender, scrambling, ± glabrous annual to 60 cm. **Leaves** *With 4–6 pairs of narrow leaflets*, these 10–20 mm; *tendrils usually unbranched*. **Flowers** *4–8 mm, in 1–2-flowered inflorescence*; peduncle equalling or shorter than leaves. **Fruits**

Glabrous pod, 10–15 mm, *4-seeded, hilum of seed oblong*. **Habitat** Rough grassland, old pastures, scrub, roadsides, arable fields. **Dist**. Native. England, Wales, N to Yorkshire; casual further N. (All Europe except N.) **Fls** May–Aug.

Common Vetch
Vicia sativa

Sparsely hairy, scrambling annual to 120 cm. Very variable; 3 ssp. usually recognised. **Leaves** With 4–8 pairs of leaflets, these 10–20 mm; tendrils branched; *stipules often with black blotch*. **Flowers** *1–2, ± sessile*, 10–30 mm. **Fruits** Glabrous

to sparsely pubescent pods, 25–80 mm, 4–12-seeded, seeds smooth. **Habitat** Ssp. *nigra* on dry grassland, dunes, shingle, sea cliffs; ssp. *segetalis* and ssp. *sativa* on field borders, roadside verges, waste and cultivated ground. **Dist**. Ssp. *nigra* native throughout BI, but rare in N Scotland, Ireland; ssp. *segetalis* archaeophyte, originally a fodder crop and now naturalised, common throughout BI N to S Scotland, but rare in Ireland; ssp. *sativa* originally a fodder crop, now local, declining, throughout BI. (All Europe.) **Fls** May–Sep.

Sea Pea
Lathyrus japonicus *(R)

fruit

Prostrate, glabrous, glaucous perennial to 90 cm. **Stems** *Angled, not winged*. **Leaves** *With 3–5 pairs of leaflets*, these 20–40 mm; *tendrils simple or branched*; stipules ovate. **Flowers** 15–25 mm, in 2–10-flowered inflorescence, peduncles shorter than leaves. **Fruits** Glabrous pod, 3–5 cm. **Habitat** Forms conspicuous patches on *shingle beaches*. **Dist**. Native. Very local. Scattered around coasts of BI, principally in East Anglia and SE. (W and N Europe.) **Fls** Jun–Aug.

Bitter-vetch
Lathyrus linifolius

Erect, glabrous perennial to 40 cm. **Stems** *Winged*. **Leaves** *With 2–4 pairs of leaflets*, these 10–30 mm; *tendrils absent*; stipules

linear, entire. **Flowers** 10–15 mm; *peduncles glabrous*, with 2–6 flowers. **Fruits** Glabrous pod, 3–4 cm. **Habitat** Hill grassland, hedge banks, rocky woodlands, wood borders, on dry acid soils; to 760 m. **Dist**. Native. Throughout BI except East Anglia. (S, W and central Europe.) **Fls** Apr–Jul.

fruit

Narrow-leaved Everlasting-pea
Lathyrus sylvestris

Glabrous, scrambling perennial to 200 cm. **Stems** Broadly winged. **Leaves** With *1 pair of leaflets*, these 70–150 mm; *tendrils much branched; stipules < ½ as wide as stem*. **Flowers** *15–17 mm, pale pink*, in 3–8-flowered inflorescence, calyx teeth shorter than tube. **Fruits** Glabrous pod, 5–7 cm. **Habitat** Wood margins, scrub, hedgerows, sea cliffs. **Dist**. Native. Local in England, Wales; scattered and naturalised elsewhere, but absent from Ireland. (Most of Europe except extreme N and S.) **Fls** Jun–Aug.

fruit

Broad-leaved Everlasting-pea
Lathyrus latifolius

Vigorous, scrambling perennial. Similar
to *L. sylvestris*, but more robust, to 3 m;
leaflets broader, *stipules > ½ as wide as stem;
flowers larger, 20–30 mm, brighter coloured*,
in 5–15-flowered inflorescence, lowest calyx
tooth as long as or longer than tube; pod
5–11 cm. **Habitat** Persistent escape from
cultivation on roadside and railway banks,
sea cliffs, waste ground. **Dist**. Introduced.
Naturalised and common throughout
England; scattered elsewhere. (S and central
Europe.) **Fls** Jun–Aug.

MEADOW VETCHLING

fruit

fruit

Note The garden Sweet Pea is *L. odoratus*
while the Garden Pea is *Pisum sativum*
(*Pisum* differs from *Lathyrus* in having
smooth, not angled, stems).

Meadow Vetchling
Lathyrus pratensis

Sparsely pubescent, scrambling perennial to
120 cm. **Stems** *Angled, not winged*. **Leaves**
With 1 pair of leaflets, these 10–30 mm;
tendrils simple or branched. **Flowers**
Yellow, 10–18 mm; peduncles longer
than leaves, with 5–12 flowers. **Fruits**
Glabrous or sparsely pubescent, *flattened
pod*, 25–35 mm. **Habitat** Rough grassland,
meadows, hedge banks, rough ground close
to sea; lowland to 450 m. **Dist**. Native.
Common throughout BI. (All Europe.)
Fls May–Aug.

Grass Vetchling
Lathyrus nissolia

Erect, ± glabrous
annual to 90 cm.
Leaves *Grass-
like*, to 15 cm;
tendrils absent.
Flowers *Pink*,
8–18 mm; peduncles
equalling or shorter
than leaves, with 1–2
flowers. **Fruits** Pod,
30–60 mm. **Habitat**
Rough grassland,
roadside verges,
woodland rides,
coastal grassland,
shingle. **Dist**.
Native. Local in
central and S England, E Wales; scattered
casual further N; absent from Ireland.
(W, central and S Europe.) **Fls** May–Jul.

fruit

Restharrows ▶ *Ononis*

Common Restharrow
Ononis repens

Prostrate, glandular-pubescent, *woody
perennial* to 60 cm. **Stems** Rooting at

base, green, sometimes tinged red, *equally hairy all round*. **Leaves** Stipules clasping stem, toothed; leaflets <2.5× as long as wide, blunt. **Flowers** 10–20 mm, *wings as long as keel*. **Fruits** Pod, 5–8 mm, shorter than calyx. **Habitat** Well-drained, usually calcareous soils; rough grassland, tracksides, roadside verges, sand-dunes, shingle. Lowland to 365 m. **Dist**. Native. Most of BI except N Scotland, W Ireland. (W and central Europe.) **Fls** Jun–Sep.

Melilots ▶ *Melilotus*

Common Melilot, Tall Melilot
Melilotus officinalis, Melilotus altissimus

Tall, erect branched biennials to 150 cm; **Flowers** 5–6 mm in racemes. *M. altissimus:* all petals same length; pods black, pubescent. *M. officinalis*: keel shorter than wings and standard; pods brown, wrinkled, glabrous. **Habitat** Waste ground, roadsides, field borders, coastal habitats. **Dist**. Archaeophyte. Widespread SE of a line from Tyne to Severn, scattered elsewhere, rare in Ireland, N Scotland. **Fls** July–Sept.

fruit

TALL MELILOT

White Melilot
Melilotus albus

Erect, branched annual or biennial to 150 cm. **Flowers** *White*, 4–5 mm. **Fruits** Ridged, glabrous pod, 4–5 mm, brown when ripe. **Habitat** Weed of arable land, waste ground, roadsides. **Dist**. Introduced. Casual or naturalised, N to central Scotland; commonest in SE. (Most of Europe.) **Fls** Jul–Aug.

fruit

Medicks ▶ *Medicago*

Leaves of medicks can usually be distinguished from those of clovers (*Trifolium*; pp.114–18) by the tooth in the apical notch of the middle leaflet.

Lucerne/Alfalfa
Medicago sativa sativa

Erect, pubescent perennial to 90 cm. **Leaves** Leaflets narrow. **Flowers** *Purple*, 8–11 mm, in compact racemes to 40 mm. **Fruits** Pubescent or glabrous pod, spiralled 2–3 turns. **Habitat** Field borders, roadsides, waste ground. **Dist**. Introduced (origins obscure, probably SW Asia). First cultivated as fodder crop in the seventeenth century.

fruit

Widely naturalised SE of a line from Tyne to Severn; scattered elsewhere; very rare in N Scotland, Ireland. (Throughout Europe.) **Fls** Aug–Sep.

Black Medick
Medicago lupulina

Prostrate or ascending, pubescent annual or perennial to 50 cm. **Leaves** Leaflets 3–20 mm. **Flowers** *2–3 mm*, in compact 3–8 mm inflorescence. **Fruits** *Spineless pod*, 1.5–3 mm, *black when ripe.* **Habitat** Short calcareous grassland, well-drained soils, road verges, lawns; lowland to 440 m. **Dist**. Native. Common throughout BI except for N Scotland. (All Europe except extreme N.) **Fls** May–Sep.

fruit

Spotted Medick
Medicago arabica

Prostrate, ± glabrous annual to 60 cm. **Leaves** *Leaflets to 25 mm, each with black blotch* (may fade); stipules toothed. **Flowers** 4–6 mm, in 1–5-flowered inflorescence. **Fruits** *Spiny, glabrous pods*, 4–6 mm across, with 3–5 coils. **Habitat** Light soils; grassy habitats, lawns, waste ground, especially near coast.

Dist. Native. SE of a line from Wash to Severn; casual elsewhere. (S Europe, NW to Netherlands.) **Fls** May–Sep.

Clovers and trefoils ▶ *Trifolium*

Bird's-foot Clover/Fenugreek
Trifolium ornithopodioides

Slender, ± *glabrous*, prostrate annual to 20 cm. **Leaves** *Petioles to 25 mm, >2× as long as leaflet*; stipules with long, fine points. **Flowers** *Pink*, 6–8 mm, in *1–4-flowered inflorescence*; peduncles shorter than petioles. **Fruits** Slightly curved pod, 5–7 mm, *longer than calyx*. **Habitat** Short, compacted sandy turf close to sea. **Dist**. Native. Coastal areas of England, Wales, N to Lancashire, I of Man; very rare in W Ireland. (W Europe.) **Fls** May–Sep.

White Clover/Dutch Clover
Trifolium repens

Creeping, *glabrous* perennial to 50 cm, *rooting at nodes*. Extremely variable species with many cultivated varieties. **Leaves** *Leaflets 10–25 mm, usually with inverted white V-shaped mark*, lateral veins straight; *stipules green*, sometimes with red veins. **Flowers** 7–12 mm, *white (to pale pink)*, standards with rounded tip; in

15–20-flowered inflorescence; peduncles erect, glabrous, to 20 cm; *calyx green with white veins.* **Habitat** Meadows, pastures, calcareous grassland, lawns, tracks; to 800 m. **Dist**. Abundant throughout BI. (All Europe.) **Fls** Jun–Sep.

Alsike Clover
Trifolium hybridum

Erect to ± prostrate, almost glabrous perennial to 60 cm. **Leaves** Stipules entire, tapering to fine point. **Flowers** 7–10 mm, *white and pink, in axillary inflorescence; peduncles to 15 cm.* **Habitat** Meadows, pastures, roadside verges. **Dist**. Introduced. Formerly much cultivated as a forage crop. Widely distributed throughout BI, but scarce in most of Scotland, Ireland. (Most of Europe.) **Fls** Jun–Sep.

Strawberry Clover
Trifolium fragiferum

Creeping, stoloniferous, ± glabrous perennial to 30 cm, *rooting at nodes.* **Leaves** *Leaflets 10–15 mm, unmarked, lateral veins thickened, recurved at margin* (cf. *T. repens*, p.114).

Flowers 5–7 mm; peduncles shorter than petioles; *calyx strongly inflated, densely hairy.* **Fruits** Pod, enclosed in persistent calyx. **Habitat** Old pasture, grazed commons, on heavy clay soils; brackish grazing marsh, sea walls near coast. **Dist**. Native. Widespread SE of a line from Humber to Severn; coastal further N to central Scotland, Ireland. (Most of Europe except extreme N.) **Fls** Jul–Sep.

Red Clover
Trifolium pratense

Prostrate to erect, *pubescent perennial*, to 60 cm. Very variable. **Leaves** Leaflets 10–30 mm, often with inverted white V-shaped mark; free part of stipules ovate, with fine brown bristle-like point. **Flowers** *Red, in terminal, ± sessile inflorescence*; corolla 15–18 mm, longer than calyx. **Habitat** Pastures, meadows, rough grassland, verges. **Dist**. Native. Abundant throughout BI. Widely cultivated. (All Europe.) **Fls** May–Sep.

Hop Trefoil
Trifolium campestre

Erect, ± pubescent annual to 30 cm.
Leaves Leaflets 8–10 mm, *stalk of terminal
leaflet >5 mm*; stipules acute. **Flowers**
4–7 mm, *pale yellow, turning brownish*;
in 10–26-flowered inflorescence; *standard
rather broad, not folded, becoming pleated;
pedicels c. ½ as long as calyx tube*. **Habitat**
Rough grassland, road verges, sand-dunes,
waste ground. **Dist**. Native. Frequent
throughout BI, becoming
rarer to N. (Most of
Europe except extreme
N.) **Fls** Jun–Sep.

Lesser Trefoil
Trifolium dubium

Slender, prostrate, sparsely pubescent
annual to 25 cm. **Leaves** Leaflets to 11 mm,
terminal leaflet with short stalk; petiole
<2× length of leaflet. **Flowers** 3–4 mm,
in 10–26-flowered inflorescence; *standard
folded; pedicels shorter than calyx tube*.
Habitat Short, open grassland, roadside
verges, lawns, commons. **Dist**. Native.
Common throughout BI. (Most of Europe
except extreme N.) **Fls** May–Oct. **Note**
Often grows with *T. micranthum* and
Medicago lupulina (p.114), with which it is
frequently confused.

Slender Trefoil
Trifolium micranthum

Slender, prostrate, sparsely pubescent
annual to 10 cm. **Leaves** Leaflets *c*.5 mm,
terminal leaflet sessile. **Flowers** 2.5–3 mm, *in
2–6-flowered inflorescence*; peduncles as long
as, or longer than, leaves; standard notched,
folded; *pedicels about as long as calyx tube*
(cf. *T. dubium*). **Habitat** Short, open
grassland, garden lawns, road verges, waste

ground. **Dist**. Native. Widely distributed in England, Wales (more common in SE), coastal Ireland; scattered elsewhere; casual in Scotland. (W and S Europe.) **Fls** Jun–Jul.

Zigzag Clover
Trifolium medium

Straggling, prostrate to erect, thinly pubescent, rhizomatous perennial to 50 cm. **Leaves** Leaflets narrow, 10–15 mm; *free part of stipules awl-shaped, green.* **Flowers** *Pink, in terminal inflorescence, with pair of leaves beneath*; corolla 12–20 mm, 2–3× as long as calyx. **Habitat** Meadows, pastures, roadsides, on heavy soils; upland grasslands rich in tall herbs. To 610 m. **Dist**. Native. Local throughout BI, but scarce in N Scotland, Ireland. (All Europe except extreme N and S.) **Fls** Jun–Sep.

Knotted Clover
Trifolium striatum

Prostrate to erect, *softly pubescent annual*, to 30 cm. **Leaves** Leaflets 5–15 mm, *lateral veins straight*; stipules triangular, finely pointed, with red or green veins. **Flowers** Pink, 4–7 mm; *in terminal and axillary, sessile heads, ± enclosed in enlarged stipule of adjacent leaf.* **Habitat** Grassy banks, heath grassland, dune turf, on dry sandy soils. **Dist**. Native. Local. Scattered throughout BI N to central Scotland; very rare in Ireland. (W Europe, Mediterranean.) **Fls** May–Jul.

Rough Clover
Trifolium scabrum

Prostrate or erect, *pubescent annual* to 25 cm. **Leaves** *Leaflets 5–8 mm, pubescent on both surfaces, lateral veins curving backwards and thickened towards margins* (visible when held up to light). **Flowers**

flower

fruit

White, 4–7 mm; in *mostly axillary, sessile heads*, 5–12 mm. **Habitat** Similar to *T. striatum* (p.117): open dune turf, banks, tracksides, on dry sandy or gravelly soils. **Dist**. Native. Local and predominantly coastal throughout BI to central Scotland; inland East Anglia; very rare in Ireland. (S and W Europe.) **Fls** May–Jul.

Hare's-foot Clover
Trifolium arvense

Softly pubescent, rather *grey-green erect*, branched annual to 20 cm. **Leaves** *Leaflets* 10–15 mm, *narrow*, oblong, terminal leaflet longer than petiole; stipules with long, fine points.

Flowers White or pink, 3–6 mm; *in terminal, axillary, softly downy, cylindrical heads*, to 20 mm; corolla much shorter than calyx. **Habitat** Sand-dunes, sea cliffs, road verges, grassy heaths, waste ground, on dry sandy soils. **Dist**. Native. Local throughout BI except N Scotland and most of Ireland. (Most of Europe except extreme N.) **Fls** Jun–Sep.

Subterranean Clover
Trifolium subterraneum *(R)

Pubescent, prostrate annual to 20 cm. **Leaves** Leaflets 5–12 mm, cordate; petioles long, 2–5 cm; stipules ovate, acute. **Flowers** *In axillary heads with a mix of 2–5 fertile and several sterile flowers*; fertile flowers cream, 8–12 mm; *sterile flowers with lobed calyx teeth*. **Fruits** Spherical pod, 2.5 mm, *becoming buried*. **Habitat** Grassland on sandy soils, walls, cliff tops near coast;

calcareous grassland inland. **Dist**. Native. Local and mostly coastal. S England, Wales. (S and W Europe.) **Fls** May–Jun.

Gorses ▶ *Ulex*
Densely spiny shrubs, with branched green spines. Mature plants lack leaves, young plants have trifoliate leaves.

Gorse/Furze
Ulex europaeus

Densely spiny, evergreen *shrub to 2 m*. **Stems** Sparsely pubescent, hairs black; *main spines* 1.5–2.5 cm, *very rigid, deeply furrowed*. **Flowers** Smell of coconut; *bracteoles 2–4.5 mm, ≥2× as wide as pedicels*; calyx ⅔ length of corolla, with spreading hairs. **Habitat** Heathland, commons, roadsides, sea cliffs, waste ground, on well-drained, usually acid soils, but also calcareous soils near coast; to 640 m. **Dist**. Native. Widespread and locally abundant throughout BI except Scottish islands. (W Europe.) **Fls** Dec–Jun.

Western Gorse, Dwarf Gorse
Ulex gallii, Ulex minor

U. gallii similar to **WESTERN GORSE** *U. europaeus*, but smaller in stature, 1.5–2 m, and *U. minor* smaller again, prostrate to 1 m. **Stems** Pubescent, hairs brown; *U. gallii* main spines rigid, faintly furrowed to striate whereas those of *U. minor* weak, 0.8–1.5 cm, striate or smooth, not furrowed, slightly curved. **Flowers** Bracteoles 0.5–0.8 mm; *U. gallii calyx 9–13 mm,* ⅔–¾ length of corolla, with appressed hairs, *teeth convergent,* wings longer than keel, *U. minor calyx 5–9 mm,* almost as long as corolla, teeth divergent, wings about as long as keel. **Habitat** *U. gallii:* heaths, cliff tops, abandoned pasture, coastal shingle, to 670 m; *U. minor:*

DWARF GORSE

dry to damp acid sandy heaths. **Dist.** Native. *U. gallii:* W Britain, N to Solway, E to Dorset; also East Anglia; *U. minor:* Very local. SE England. (W Europe.) **Fls** Jul–Sep.

Broom
Cytisus scoparius

Erect, much-branched, non-spiny shrub to 2 m. **Stems** *Twigs green, deeply grooved, glabrous.* **Leaves** *Trifoliate.* **Flowers** 15–20 mm. **Fruits** Black pod, 2.5–4 cm,

pubescent on margins. **Habitat** Heathlands, open woodland, roadside verges, railway embankments, on light sandy soils. **Dist.** Native. Widespread throughout BI except Scottish islands. (W, central and S Europe.) **Fls** May–Jun. **Note** Ssp. *maritimus* is a rare prostrate plant with silky twigs, found on sea cliffs in SW England, Wales, Channel Is.

fruit

Petty Whin/Needle Furze
Genista anglica

Spiny, erect shrub to 100 cm. **Stems** Twigs brown; *spines curved, unbranched,* 1–2 cm. **Leaves** Simple, 2–8 mm, glabrous. **Flowers** 7–10 mm, glabrous. **Fruits** Glabrous pod, 12–15 mm, inflated. **Habitat** Heaths, moors; *fruit* to 730 m. **Dist.** Native. Local, declining. Throughout Britain except extreme N Scotland; absent from Ireland. (W Europe.) **Fls** May–Jun.

HALORAGACEAE
Water-milfoils
••

Submerged aquatic or sub-aquatic perennials. Leaves in whorls of 3–6, pinnate, with hair-like segments. Flowers tiny and inconspicuous, in terminal emergent spikes; 4 sepals and petals, or these absent; 8 stamens. Fruits separating into up to 4 nutlets. Identification of non-flowering shoots is not always possible with confidence, as some vegetative characters overlap.

Water-milfoils ▶ *Myriophyllum*

Alternate Water-milfoil
Myriophyllum alterniflorum

Submerged aquatic to 120 cm.
Leaves With 6–18 segments, usually 4 in a whorl, *about equalling internodes.*
Flowers *Opposite or alternate. Flowering spike drooping in bud*; basal flowers female, with leaf-like bracts; upper flowers male, with small, entire bracts, petals yellow and red. **Habitat** Lakes, ponds, streams, dykes, in peaty, acid waters; to 780 m.
Dist. Native. Widely distributed; common in N and W of BI, scarce in lowlands. (Most of Europe except extreme N.) **Fls** May–Aug.

Spiked Water-milfoil
Myriophyllum spicatum

Submerged aquatic to 250 cm, *with distinct reddish tinge.* **Leaves** *Rather rigid,* not collapsing when removed from water, usually *4 in a whorl*, 0.5–1.5× as long as internodes, with 13–35 segments. **Flowers** Flowering spikes erect in bud; flowers in whorls of 4, all but lowest bracts *entire and shorter than flowers*, petals red. **Habitat**

Ponds, lakes, ditches, streams, in clear, eutrophic, usually calcareous waters; will tolerate brackish conditions.
Dist. Native. Widespread throughout BI, but becoming scarcer in N and W. (All Europe.) **Fls** Jun–Jul.

ELEAGNACEAE
Sea-buckthorn family
••••••••••••••••••••••••••••••

Sea-buckthorn
Hippophae rhamnoides

Much-branched, thorny, suckering deciduous shrub to 3 m. **Leaves** Alternate, silvery, 1–8 cm. **Flowers** Dioecious, 2 sepals, petals absent. **Fruits** *Berry-like, bright orange*, 6–8 mm. **Habitat** Fixed coastal dunes, forming dense thickets. **Dist**. Native.

E coast N to Scottish border; widely planted in coastal areas and along roadsides throughout BI. (W coast of Europe; inland central and E Europe.) **Fls** Mar–Apr, before leaves.

LYTHRACEAE
Loosestrifes

Purple Loosestrife
Lythrum salicaria

Tall, pubescent perennial to 120 cm. **Leaves** 4–7 cm, opposite or in whorls of 3. **Flowers** Regular, 10–15 mm across with epicalyx, in dense, many-flowered inflorescence spike; 6 sepals and petals; 12 stamens. **Habitat** Tall fens, fen carr, reed swamp, marginal vegetation of lakes, rivers, ponds, canals. **Dist**. Native. Widespread and locally common throughout BI, but rare in N Scotland. (All Europe except extreme N.) **Fls** Jun–Aug.

Water Purslane
Lythrum portula

Glabrous, creeping annual to 25 cm, *rooting at nodes*. **Leaves** *c*.1 cm, opposite. **Flowers** *Tiny, c.1 mm across, in axils of leaves*; 6 sepals and petals; 6 or 12 stamens. **Habitat** Seasonally flooded, open habitats, woodland rides, pool and reservoir margins, on acid soils. **Dist**. Native. Throughout BI, especially S and W; rare in N Scotland. (All Europe except extreme N.) **Fls** Jun–Oct.

WATER PURSLANE

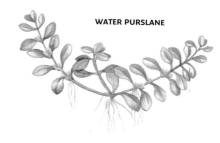

THYMELAEACEAE
Daphnes

Spurge-laurel
Daphne laureola

Small, glabrous evergreen shrub. **Leaves** Dark, glossy green, 5–12 cm, crowded towards top of stem. **Flowers** 8–12 mm across, green, forming inflorescence of 5–10 flowers in axillary groups; 4 sepals; petals absent. **Fruits** Black, berry-like. **Habitat** Deciduous woodland on heavy and calcareous soils; shade-tolerant. **Dist**. Native in England, Wales, N to Scottish border; planted elsewhere as game cover. (W, S and S-central Europe.) **Fls** Feb–Mar.

fruit

ONAGRACEAE
Willowherbs and evening-primroses
••••••••••••••••••••••••••••••••••

A rather varied family, characterised by the combination of regular flowers with an inferior ovary; 2 or 4(5) free sepals; 2 or 4(5) petals and 2, 4 or 8(10) stamens; fruit is a capsule or berry. Annuals or perennials with simple opposite or alternate leaves; flowers sometimes with a hypanthium (elongated part of flower between top of ovary and base of calyx, an extension of the receptacle).

Willowherbs ► *Epilobium*

Great Willowherb/Codlins and Cream
Epilobium hirsutum

Tall, erect, pubescent, rhizomatous perennial to 180 cm, with *dense glandular, spreading hairs*. **Leaves** Sessile, *opposite, weakly clasping and decurrent*, 6–12 cm. **Flowers** *15–23 mm across, stigma 4-lobed*. **Fruits** Capsule, 5–8 cm. **Habitat** River, stream, lake and pond margins, fens, marshes, on fertile soils; to 665 m. **Dist**. Native.

Common throughout BI N to central Scotland; rare further N. (All Europe except extreme N.) **Fls** Jul–Aug.

Hoary Willowherb
Epilobium parviflorum

Erect, *pubescent, stoloniferous perennial to 60 cm, with dense glandular, spreading hairs*. **Leaves** *Sessile, opposite, not clasping or decurrent*, 3–7 cm. **Flowers** 6–9 mm *across*, pale pink; *stigma 4-lobed*. **Fruits** Capsule, 3.5–6.5 cm. **Habitat** Disturbed and waste ground, marshes, stream banks; to 365 m. **Dist**. Native. Common throughout BI, but becoming scarce in N Scotland. (All Europe except extreme N.) **Fls** Jul–Aug.

Broad-leaved Willowherb
Epilobium montanum

Erect, ± glabrous, stoloniferous perennial to 60 cm. **Stems** Smooth. **Leaves** *Ovate, opposite*, 4–7 cm, *rounded at base*; petiole short, 2–6 mm. **Flowers** 6–9 mm across, *stigma 4-lobed*. **Fruits** Capsule, 4–8 cm. **Habitat** Woodland, waste ground, walls, hedge banks, ditches; also a garden weed. To 845 m. **Dist**. Native. Common throughout BI. (All Europe.) **Fls** Jun–Aug.

Square-stalked Willowherb
Epilobium tetragonum

Erect, stoloniferous perennial to 60 cm, *producing overwintering leaf rosettes in autumn*. **Stems** *4-angled*, glabrous below, pubescent above. **Leaves** 2–7.5 cm, *narrow, strap-shaped*; lower leaves opposite, middle ones alternate. **Flowers** 6–8 mm across, *calyx tube without glandular hairs*, stigma entire. **Fruits** *Long capsule, 6.5–10 cm*. **Habitat** Cultivated and waste ground, roadsides, hedge banks, stream sides; lowland. **Dist**. Native. Widespread in England, Wales, N to Yorkshire. (All Europe except extreme N.) **Fls** Jul–Aug.

Short-fruited Willowherb
Epilobium obscurum

Erect perennial to 75 cm, *producing leafy stolons*. **Stems** With 4 raised lines, glabrous below, pubescent above. **Leaves** 3–7 cm, *ovate-lanceolate*, sessile, decurrent. **Flowers** 7–9 mm across; *calyx tube with sparse, spreading glandular hairs*; stigma entire. **Fruits** *Capsule, 4–6 cm*. **Habitat** Damp woodland, stream sides, ditches, marshes, cultivated ground; to 775 m. **Dist**. Native. Widespread throughout BI. (All Europe except extreme N and E.) **Fls** Jul–Aug.

Pale Willowherb
Epilobium roseum

Erect, stoloniferous perennial to 75 cm, *producing overwintering leaf rosettes*. **Stems** Glabrous below, with crisped non-glandular and spreading glandular hairs above. **Leaves** 3–8 cm, mostly alternate; *distinctly stalked*, petiole 4–15 mm. **Flowers** 4–6 mm across, *petals pale pink*, stigma club-shaped. **Fruits** Capsule, 4–7 cm. **Habitat** Waste ground on damp soils, moist woodland, hedgerows, gardens; lowland to 560 m. **Dist**. Native. Scattered and local throughout BI, but rare in Scotland, Ireland. (Most of Europe except extreme N.) **Fls** Jul–Aug.

American Willowherb
Epilobium ciliatum

Tall, much-branched, often reddish *non-stoloniferous* perennial to 75 cm. **Stems** With 4 raised lines; crisped hairs and *numerous spreading glandular hairs above*. **Leaves** Opposite, ± glabrous, 3–10 cm. **Flowers** 4–6 mm across, *petals deeply notched*, stigma club-shaped. **Fruits** Capsule, 4–6.5 cm, with glandular hairs.

Habitat Gardens, waste ground, roadsides, walls, stream sides, damp woodland. **Dist**. Introduced (native of North America); first recorded in BI in 1891. Common throughout much of lowland BI, still spreading N and W. (Most of Europe especially NW.) **Fls** Jun–Aug.

AMERICAN WILLOWHERB

Marsh Willowherb
Epilobium palustre

Erect, sub-glabrous, stoloniferous perennial to 60 cm. **Stems** *Stolons long and producing bulbil-like buds at tips in autumn; stems smooth, without raised lines.* **Leaves** Lanceolate, rather glaucous, 0.5–1.0 cm, opposite, ± sessile. **Flowers** 4–6 mm across, petals pale pink, stigma club-shaped. **Fruits** Capsule, 5–8 cm. **Habitat** Fens, marshes, valley bogs, woodland flushes, on mildly acid soils; to 845 m. **Dist**. Native. Frequent throughout BI. (All Europe except extreme S.) **Fls** Jul–Aug.

Chickweed Willowherb
Epilobium alsinifolium *(R)

Prostrate to erect, ± glabrous, stoloniferous alpine perennial to 20 cm. **Stems** *Stolons below ground, with pairs of yellowish scale-leaves.* **Leaves** *Rather glaucous, distinctly toothed*, opposite, 1.5–4 cm, ovate-lanceolate. **Flowers** 8–9 mm across. **Fruits** Capsule, 3–5 cm. **Habitat** Mossy mountain flushes, springs, stream sides, on acid or basic soils; to 1140 m. **Dist**. Native. N England, N Wales (rare), Scotland. (Arctic and montane Europe.) **Fls** Jul–Aug. **Note Alpine Willowherb** *E. anagallidifolium*, with above ground stolons, smaller lanceolate leaves and smaller drooping flowers 4–5 mm across, grows in similar alpine habitats in Scotland.

CHICKWEED WILLOWHERB

ALPINE WILLOW-HERB

Rosebay Willowherb
Chamerion angustifolium

Tall perennial to 150 cm. **Leaves** *5–15 cm, all spirally arranged.* **Flowers** *2–3 cm across, slightly zygomorphic, held horizontally*; in long, spike-like inflorescence; stigma 4-lobed. **Fruits** Capsule, 2.5–8 cm. **Habitat**

Forms dense stands on waste ground, roadsides, railways, heathland, woodland clearings, disturbed and burnt ground, upland scree; to 975 m. **Dist**. Native. Common throughout BI. (All Europe, but rare in S.) **Fls** Jul–Sep.

Evening-primroses ▶
Oenothera

Common Evening-primrose
Oenothera biennis

Tall, erect biennial to 150 cm; *green parts of stems and capsules without red-based hairs.* **Flowers** In erect inflorescence; *sepals green; petals 15–30 mm,* wider than long. **Fruits** Capsule, 2–3 cm, *all glandular-hairy.* **Habitat** Waste ground, roadsides, railways, sand-dunes. **Dist**. Introduced (native of North America). Established throughout lowland England; rare elsewhere. (Most of Europe except extreme N and S.) **Fls** Jun–Sep.

Enchanter's-nightshade
Circaea lutetiana

Erect, stoloniferous perennial to 70 cm. **Leaves** 4–10 cm, *obscurely toothed, rounded at base; petiole furrowed above,* pubescent. **Flowers** *Open flowers distributed along inflorescence; flower stalks and sepals (2) glandular-pubescent;* 2 petals, 2–4 mm, notched to at least halfway. **Fruits** *c.*3 mm, densely covered by stiff, hooked bristles. **Habitat** Woodlands, hedgerows, stream banks; also a garden weed. **Dist**. Native. Common throughout BI N to central Scotland. (Most of Europe except NE.) **Fls** Jun–Aug.

CORNACEAE
Dogwoods
• •

Dwarf Cornel
Cornus suecica

Erect perennial to 20 cm. **Leaves** 1–3 cm, pubescent above, glabrous beneath. **Flowers**

Inflorescence appearing flower-like, an umbel of 8–25 flowers surrounded by 4 white ovate bracts, 5–8 mm. **Fruits** Red, c.5 mm. **Habitat** Among dwarf shrubs and mosses on acid mountain moorland; to 915 m. **Dist.** Native. Scottish Highlands; very rare in N England. (N Europe.) **Fls** Jul–Aug.

SANTALACEAE
Bastard-toadflax and sandalwood family

Bastard-toadflax
Thesium humifusum

Prostrate, semi-parasitic yellowish-green perennial to 45 cm. **Leaves** Alternate, 5–15 mm. **Flowers** *Small, c.*3 mm across; *5 greenish* perianth segments. **Habitat** Short turf on dry, thin calcareous soils on warm slopes. **Dist**. Native. Rare. Chalk areas of S England. (W Europe.) **Fls** Jun–Aug.

fruit

VISCACEAE
Mistletoes

Mistletoe
Viscum album

Woody evergreen partial parasite on branches of trees. **Stems** To 100 cm, green, much branched. **Leaves** 5–8 cm. **Flowers** Dioecious, in compact 3–5-flowered inflorescence; sepals small or absent, 4 petals. **Fruits** White berry, c.10 mm. **Habitat** Orchards, hedgerows, parks, gardens, on apples, limes, hawthorn, poplars; also on maples, willows. **Dist**.

Native. Local in England, Wales; rare in Scotland, Ireland. (Most of Europe.) **Fls** Feb–Mar.

EUPHORBIACEAE
Spurges

A varied family consisting of 2 herbaceous genera in Britain: *Euphorbia*, the spurges; and *Mercurialis*, mercuries. Leaves are simple, alternate. Inflorescence is complex; flowers are unisexual, monoecious or dioecious; 3 or 5 sepals and petals, or these absent; 1 to many stamens; ovary superior. Fruit is a capsule separating into 3 parts.

Dog's Mercury
Mercurialis perennis

Erect, rhizomatous, pubescent, unbranched perennial to 40 cm. Dioecious. **Leaves** 3–8 cm, opposite. **Flowers** 4–5 mm across; 3 tepals, sepal-like; *female flowers long-stalked*, in axillary clusters; male flowers on pendulous, catkin-like spikes. **Fruits** Capsule, 6–8 mm. **Habitat** Deciduous woodland, old hedgerows, hillside scree, limestone pavement, on calcareous or base-rich soils; to 1005 m. **Dist**. Native.

Common throughout Britain except N Scotland; very rare in Ireland (Burren only). (Most of Europe except extreme N.) **Fls** Feb–Apr.

Annual Mercury
Mercurialis annua

Erect, ± glabrous, branched annual to 50 cm. Dioecious. **Leaves** 1.5–5 cm. **Flowers** *Female flowers axillary, sessile.* **Habitat** Gardens, allotments, waste ground, on light, fertile soils. **Dist**. Archaeophyte. Common in S England, SE of line from Wash to Severn; scattered further N; absent from Scotland. (Most of Europe.) **Fls** Jul–Oct.

Sun Spurge
Euphorbia helioscopia

Erect, glabrous, unbranched annual to 50 cm. **Leaves** 1.5–3 cm, *obovate,* toothed; umbel 5-rayed; *all bracts similar to leaves*; glands rounded, green. **Fruits** Smooth, glabrous capsule, 3–5 mm. **Habitat** Arable land, waste ground, roadsides, gardens; lowland to 450 m. **Dist**. Archaeophyte. Common throughout most of BI, but rare in N Scotland, W Ireland. (All Europe.) **Fls** May–Oct.

Dwarf Spurge
Euphorbia exigua

Erect, glabrous, glaucous *annual* to 20 cm. **Leaves** *Linear, sessile*; umbel 3-rayed; *bracts similar to leaves, glands horned*. **Fruits** Smooth, glabrous capsule, 2 mm. **Habitat** Arable weed on light calcareous soils. **Dist**. Archaeophyte. Widespread but declining. Local SE of line from Humber to Wash; rare elsewhere; absent from Scotland, rare in Ireland. (Most of Europe except extreme N.) **Fls** Jun–Oct.

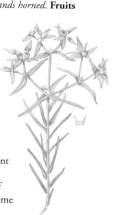

Petty Spurge
Euphorbia peplus

Erect, glabrous green annual to 30 cm. **Leaves** *Ovate-obovate, short-stalked*; umbel 3-rayed; *bracts similar to leaves*, glands horned. **Fruits** Glabrous, winged capsule, 2 mm. **Habitat** Weed of gardens, cultivated land, waste ground, on fertile soils. **Dist**. Archaeophyte. Common throughout most of BI, but scarce in extreme N. (Most of Europe except extreme N.) **Fls** Apr–Nov.

Sea Spurge
Euphorbia paralias

Prostrate to erect, glabrous, glaucous perennial to 40 cm, with unbranched sterile and flowering stems. Bracts and leaves markedly different. **Leaves** *Ovate-oblong*, sessile, fleshy, *blunt*, 0.5–2 cm, crowded and overlapping, *midrib obscure beneath*; umbel 3–6-rayed; glands horned. **Fruits** Capsule, 4 mm, rough all over; *seeds smooth*. **Habitat** Sandy shores, sand-dunes, fine shingle. **Dist**. Native. Local on coasts of Britain, Ireland, N to Solway. (Coasts of W and S Europe.) **Fls** Jul–Oct.

Portland Spurge
Euphorbia portlandica

Erect, glabrous biennial or perennial to 40 cm, most stems flowering. Bracts and leaves different. **Leaves** *Obovate, widest above middle*, somewhat fleshy, *blunt with sharp point*, 0.5–2 cm, *midrib prominent beneath*; umbel 3–6-rayed; glands horned. **Fruits** Capsule, 3 mm, rough near midline; *seeds pitted*. **Habitat** Sandy shores, limestone cliffs. **Dist.** Native. W coast of BI, N to Clyde and E to I of Wight. (W Europe.) **Fls** May–Sep.

Wood Spurge
Euphorbia amygdaloides

Erect, *pubescent* perennial to 90 cm, *flowering in 2nd year from top of previous year's stem*. **Leaves** 3–8 cm; umbel 5–10-rayed; *bracts yellow, fused at base*; glands horned. **Fruits** Rough capsule, 4 mm. **Habitat** Old woods, coppice, hedge banks, on mildly acid soils. **Dist**. Native. Local in lowland Britain, N to N Wales; absent from Ireland. (NW, central and S Europe.) **Fls** Mar–May. **Note** Ssp. *robbiae*, with shiny, glabrous, dark green leaves, is widely cultivated and occasionally becomes naturalised.

WOOD SPURGE

Cypress Spurge
Euphorbia cyparissias

Glabrous, rhizomatous perennial to 50 cm, with numerous erect flowering and non-flowering stems. **Leaves** *Narrow, ≤2 mm wide, linear, numerous, those on non-flowering shoots crowded;* umbel 9–15-rayed; umbel bracts markedly different from those above, which become reddish; glands horned. **Habitat** Commonly cultivated, occurring as garden escape on roadsides, tracksides, banks, walls, calcareous grassland. **Dist**. Introduced. Naturalised throughout BI, but rare in Scotland, Ireland. (Most of Europe except extreme N and S.) **Fls** May–Aug.

LINACEAE
Flaxes
••

Annuals or perennials, with simple, entire leaves that lack stipules. Flowers bisexual, regular; 4–5 sepals and petals, free; 4–5 stamens; ovary superior. Fruits are an 8–10-valved capsule.

Pale Flax
Linum bienne

Erect, glabrous annual or perennial, with several stems, to 60 cm. **Leaves** Alternate, 10–25 mm × *0.5–1.5 mm,* with 1–3 veins. **Flowers** Pale blue; *sepals as long as capsule, tapering to tip,* inner ones with glandular hairs; petals 8–12 mm; *stigmas club-shaped.* **Fruits** Capsule, 4–6 mm. **Habitat** Dry, well-drained, permanent pastures near sea; lowland. **Dist**. Native. S and SW England, Wales, SE Ireland. (W and S Europe.) **Fls** May–Sep.

Fairy Flax
Linum catharticum

Slender, erect, unbranched, glabrous annual to 25 cm. **Leaves** *Opposite,* ovate,

FAIRY FLAX

5–12 mm, with 1 vein. **Flowers** In loose, open cyme; *pedicels slender, 5–10 mm; petals white, 4–6 mm.* **Habitat** Grazed calcareous grassland, mires, flushes, limestone cliffs, calcareous dunes; to 840 m. **Dist**. Native. Common throughout BI. (Most of Europe except extreme N.) **Fls** Jun–Sep.

POLYGALACEAE
Milkworts
....

Common Milkwort
Polygala vulgaris

Prostrate to erect, much-branched perennial, to 30 cm. Very variable. **Leaves** *All leaves alternate,* ± acute; lower leaves 5–10 mm, upper ones longer. **Flowers** *5–8 mm,* blue, pink or white, in inflorescence of >10 flowers; *inner sepals c.6 mm, veins much branched.* **Habitat** Short calcareous grassland, heaths, commons, sand-dunes; to 730 m. **Dist**. Native. Frequent throughout BI. (Most of Europe.) **Fls** May–Sep.

pink form

pale form

Heath Milkwort
Polygala serpyllifolia

Similar to *P. vulgaris*, but smaller, ± prostrate, to 25 cm; *lower stem leaves opposite* (if withered, check leaf scars); *flowers 5–6 mm,* usually deep blue, rarely white or pink, in shorter *inflorescence of 3–8 flowers; inner sepals c.4.5–5.5 mm, veins much branched.* **Habitat** Heaths, moors, acid and mountain grassland; to 1035 m. **Dist**. Native. Throughout BI, common in N and W. (W and central Europe.) **Fls** Apr–Aug.

pale form

OXALIDACEAE
Wood-sorrels
....

Perennial herbs with trifoliate (or palmate) leaves. Flowers bisexual, regular, with 5 free petals and sepals, and 10 stamens; ovary superior; 5 styles. Fruit is a capsule. Most of the introduced *Oxalis* species occur as casuals or are naturalised as relics of cultivation. They rarely set seed, but spread by means of bulbils or stem fragments, frequently becoming weeds of gardens or nurseries, or establishing on waste ground or hedge banks near habitation.

Wood-sorrel
Oxalis acetosella

Slender, rhizomatous perennial. **Leaves** Trifoliate, pubescent. **Flowers** Solitary; petals 8–15 mm, white with lilac veins.

GERANIACEAE
Crane's-bills and stork's-bills
••

A distinctive family of annual and perennial herbs, often with large, showy flowers. Leaves are alternate, usually palmate or pinnate, and with stipules. Flowers are regular or slightly irregular; 5 free petals and sepals; 5 or 10 stamens; ovary superior with 5 cells, each of which is elongated into a beak; 5 stigmas. Fruit is dry, with each cell containing 1 seed. The shape of the leaves, hairiness of the stems, leaves and carpels, and the shape of the petals are important identification characters. Garden ivy-leaved 'geraniums' belong to the genus *Pelargonium*.

Habitat Shaded woodlands, hedge-rows, banks, rough upland grassland, grikes in limestone pavement; to 1160 m. **Dist**. Native. Common throughout BI. (Most of Europe, but rare in S.) **Fls** Apr–May.

Procumbent Yellow-sorrel
Oxalis corniculata

Habitat Cosmopolitan weed, persistent in gardens and nurseries. **Dist**. Introduced in C17th (native distribution unknown). Most widely distributed of the introduced *Oxalis*. **Fls** Jun–Sep.

Meadow Crane's-bill
Geranium pratense

Tall, erect, rhizomatous, glandular-pubescent perennial to 80 cm. **Leaves** 7–15 cm across. **Flowers** Axillary, in pairs; petals 15–18 mm, apex rounded. **Similar spp.** *Leaves are more deeply divided than those of* G. sylvaticum; *flowers are violet-blue, while those of* G. sylvaticum *are pinkish mauve.* **Habitat** Lowland hay meadows, permanent pastures, roadsides, on base-rich or calcareous soils; to *c*.550 m. **Dist**. Native.

Widespread throughout much of Britain, but scarce in Scotland, East Anglia, SW; absent from Ireland. Commonly cultivated, and widely naturalised outside its native range. (Most of Europe, but rare in N and Mediterranean.) **Fls** Jun–Sep.

Wood Crane's-bill
Geranium sylvaticum *(NI)

Erect, rhizomatous, glandular perennial to 80 cm. **Leaves** 7–12 cm across. **Flowers** Axillary, in pairs; petals 12–18 mm across, apex rounded. **Similar spp.** For separation details from *G. pratense*, *see* that species. **Habitat** Damp woodlands, hay meadows, permanent pastures, verges, stream banks, damp mountain rock ledges, on base-rich or calcareous soils; to *c*.1000 m. **Dist**. Native; also commonly cultivated. Widely distributed and often common in N Britain from S Yorkshire to central Scotland; very rare in Ireland. (Most of Europe; restricted to mts in S.) **Fls** Jun–Jul.

Round-leaved Crane's-bill
Geranium rotundifolium

Much-branched, trailing to erect, glandular-hairy annual, to 40 cm. **Leaves** 3–6 cm across. **Flowers** Numerous; petals 5–7 mm, rounded to slightly emarginated. **Similar spp.** *Distinguished from similar species by*

rounded, not notched, tips to petals and relatively shallowly lobed leaves. **Habitat** Usually dry hedge banks, wall tops; occasionally an arable weed on both sandy and calcareous soils. **Dist**. Native. Local in S Britain, S Wales, S Ireland. (Most of Europe except extreme N.) **Fls** Apr–Sep.

Long-stalked Crane's-bill
Geranium columbinum

Erect or scrambling, sparsely hairy annual to 60 cm. **Leaves** 2–5 cm across, deeply lobed. **Flowers** *Stalks long, to 6 cm*; petals 7–9 mm across. **Similar spp.** *The long flower stalks are characteristic and distinguish it from other small-flowered species with deeply divided leaves.* **Habitat** Open grassland, field margins, scrub, rocky hillsides, sand-dunes,

quarries, chiefly on dry calcareous or base-rich soils. Occasionally an arable weed. **Dist**. Native. Rather local, most frequent in S and SW England, becoming increasingly scarce to N. (All Europe except extreme N.) **Fls** Jun–Sep.

Bloody Crane's-bill
Geranium sanguineum

Much-branched perennial to 40 cm. **Leaves** Deeply divided, 2–6 cm across. **Flowers** Solitary, peduncles long, petals 12–18 mm across. **Similar spp.** *Distinguished from other large-flowered species by solitary crimson flowers.* **Habitat** Limestone rocks, coastal cliffs, open woodland, scree, grassland; also fixed calcareous coastal sand-dunes. To *c*.370 m. **Dist.** Native. Scattered throughout much of N and W Britain. (Most of Europe except extreme N.) **Fls** May–Aug.

Cut-leaved Crane's-bill
Geranium dissectum

Straggling, pubescent annual to 60 cm. **Leaves** *Divided almost to base, 2–7 cm.* **Flowers** Stalks 0.5–1.5 cm, petals 4.5–6 mm across, carpels pubescent. **Habitat** Waste ground, gardens, rough grassland, waysides, especially on fertile soils; to 380 m. **Dist**. Archaeophyte. Widespread and common throughout BI, becoming scarcer N from central Scotland. (Most of Europe except extreme N.) **Fls** May–Aug.

CUT-LEAVED CRANE'S-BILL

Hedgerow Crane's-bill
Geranium pyrenaicum

Erect, glandular-pubescent perennial to 60 cm. **Leaves** 5–8 cm, lobes widened towards tip. **Flowers** In pairs; *petals 7–10 mm, deeply notched*; carpels pubescent. **Habitat** Hedgerows, field margins, waste ground, on well-drained soils. **Dist**. Introduced. Frequent in S and E England; scarce elsewhere. (Native of the mts of S Europe and SW Asia.) **Fls** Jun–Aug.

Dove's-foot Crane's-bill
Geranium molle

Glandular-pubescent annual to 40 cm. **Leaves** 1–5 cm across. **Flowers** Pedicels *with mix of long and short eglandular and* *short glandular hairs; petals 3–6 mm*, deeply notched; *all stamens with anthers; carpels glabrous.* **Habitat** Dry grassland, lawns, arable, cultivated and waste ground, sand-dunes, on both calcareous and sandy soils. **Dist**. Native. Widespread and common throughout BI, but less frequent in Scotland and Ireland. (All Europe except extreme N.) **Fls** Apr–Oct.

DOVE'S-FOOT CRANE'S-BILL

Small-flowered Crane's-bill
Geranium pusillum

Pubescent annual to 40 cm. **Leaves** 1–4 cm across. **Flowers** *Pedicels with uniformly short eglandular hairs (glandular hairs present or not); petals 2–4 mm, deeply notched; 5 stamens without anthers; carpels pubescent.* **Similar spp**. Easily overlooked for *G. molle*, but the hairs on the stem are uniformly short; flowers are smaller (petals 2–4 mm) and a paler, dull pink; carpels are hairy; and only 5 stamens have anthers. **Habitat** Short grassland, arable, cultivated and waste

ground, roadsides, on dry, well-drained soils. **Dist**. Native. Widespread in England except SW; rare, scattered and usually coastal elsewhere. (Most of Europe except N.) **Fls** Jun–Sep.

Shining Crane's-bill
Geranium lucidum

Much-branched, leafy annual to 40 cm. **Leaves** *± glabrous, shallowly lobed, bright glossy green*, 2–6 cm across. **Flowers** Petals 8–9 mm; carpels reticulate, glabrous. **Habitat** Shaded rocks, walls, hedge banks, waste ground, especially on calcareous soils. Occasionally as a garden weed. **Dist**. Native. Widespread throughout most of BI except N Scotland. (Most of Europe except NE.) **Fls** May–Aug.

Herb-Robert
Geranium robertianum

Much-branched, pubescent annual or biennial to 50 cm, with *distinctive unpleasant smell.* **Stems** *Often reddish.* **Leaves** *Bright dark green.* **Flowers** *Sepals erect, petals 9–14 mm, anthers orange or purple.* **Habitat** Woodlands, hedge banks, scree, limestone pavement, old walls, coastal shingle, avoiding the most acid soils and preferring shaded habitats. **Dist**. Native. Widespread and common throughout BI. (All Europe except extreme N.) **Fls** May–Sep. **Note** The prostrate plant of coastal shingle, with small flowers and glabrous fruits, is spp. *maritimum.*

HERB-ROBERT

Common Stork's-bill
Erodium cicutarium

Much-branched, glandular or eglandular annual to 60 cm. **Flowers** 12–14 mm across, in 3–7-flowered inflorescence. **Fruits** *carpels 5–6.5 mm, pit at apex not glandular, separated from rest of fruit by ridge and furrow* (need to use a lens). **Habitat** Dry heaths, commons, sandy grassland, sand-dunes; to 420 m. **Dist**. Native. Throughout BI, mostly coastal in W, Ireland. (All Europe.) **Fls** Jun–Sep.

Sea Stork's-bill
Erodium maritimum

Small, prostrate annual to 30 cm. **Leaves** *5–15 mm, simple, pinnately lobed*. **Flowers** 1–2, peduncles about as long as leaves; sepals *c*.4 mm; *petals as long as sepals or absent*; carpels pubescent. **Habitat** Open areas, cliff tops, mature dunes, walls, seabird colonies. **Dist**. Native. Coasts of SW England, Wales, N to Solway Firth; E Ireland, Channel Is, I of Man. (NW Europe.) **Fls** May–Jul.

BALSAMINACEAE
Balsams
••

Glabrous, somewhat succulent annuals. Leaves simple, alternate, opposite or whorled. Flowers strongly irregular, ovary superior; 5 or 3 petal-like sepals, the lower large and spurred; 5 petals, the upper large, the lower united in pairs; 5 stamens. Fruit is a capsule.

Balsams ▶ *Impatiens*

Indian Balsam
Impatiens glandulifera

Tall, erect, glabrous annual to 200 cm. **Leaves** Opposite or in whorls of 3, 6–15 cm. **Flowers** Large, 2.5–4 cm, deep or pale pink or white. **Habitat** River sides, ditches, wet woodlands; very invasive, forming dense

INDIAN BALSAM

Orange Balsam
Impatiens capensis

Erect, glabrous annual to 150 cm. Vegetatively similar to *I. noli-tangere*, but leaves smaller, 3–8 cm, with <10 teeth on each side; flowers 2–3 cm, orange with brown spots inside. **Habitat** Banks of rivers, canals, reservoirs. **Dist**. Introduced (native of E North America). Naturalised in scattered localities throughout England. (France.) **Fls** Jun–Aug.

stands. **Dist**. Introduced in 1839 (native of Himalayas). Naturalised throughout BI. (Most of Europe.) **Fls** Jul–Oct.

Small Balsam
Impatiens parviflora

Erect, glabrous annual to 100 cm. **Leaves** Alternate, 5–15 cm, with >20 teeth on each side. **Flowers** Small, 5–15 mm, pale yellow, 4–10 forming axillary inflorescence. **Habitat** Woodland, parks, plantations, tracksides, shaded riverbanks. **Dist**. Introduced (native of Siberia, Turkestan). Naturalised throughout Britain, but rare in SW and Scotland. (Naturalised throughout Europe.) **Fls** Jul–Nov.

HYDROCOTYLACEAE
Pennnyworts
•••

Marsh Pennywort
Hydrocotyle vulgaris

Slender, creeping perennial, rooting at nodes. **Leaves** *Peltate*, 1–5 cm across, circular, *shallowly lobed*; petioles 1–25 cm, erect. **Flowers** Tiny, about 1 mm across, in 2–5-flowered umbels; peduncles shorter than petioles. **Habitat** Bogs, fens, marshes, wet meadows, dune slacks, pond and stream margins; to 530 m. **Dist**. Native. Throughout BI. (W, central and S Europe.) **Fls** Jun–Aug.

MARSH
PENNYWORT

APIACEAE (UMBELLIFERAE)
Umbellifers
•••

Most umbellifers are readily recognised
when in flower by the characteristic umbel
inflorescence, in which all the branches
arise from the same point like the ribs of
an umbrella. Umbellifers are annual or
perennial herbs (rarely shrubs, none of which
are native to BI); the leaves are alternate,
without stipules (except for *Hydrocotyle*),
and usually much divided with sheathing
petioles. The umbels are usually compound
with bracts and bracteoles; the flowers are
regular (except that the outer petals of the
outer flowers of the umbel may be enlarged);
5 small calyx teeth, or these absent; 5 petals;
5 stamens; ovary inferior, with 2 stigmas that
usually have a swollen base (stylopodium).
The fruit consists of 2, usually compressed,
ribbed carpels separated by a septum. When
ripe, the 2 carpels separate, held together by
the split stalk, the carpophore.

Details of the fruit are very important in
identification and should be checked with the
illustrations and descriptions in the text. In
addition, the leaves, degree of hairiness of the
plant and numbers of bracts and bracteoles
should be carefully examined.

Sanicle
Sanicula europaea

Erect, glabrous perennial to 60 cm. **Leaves**
Most basal, palmately lobed, 2–6 cm across;
petioles long, 5–25 cm. **Flowers** *In few
simple umbels; bracts small*, 2–5, simple or
branched; bracteoles several, simple. **Fruits**
c.3 mm, with hooked bristles. **Habitat**
Deciduous woodland, hedge banks, on
calcareous or base-rich soils; lowland to
500 m. **Dist**. Native. Throughout BI. (Most
of Europe except NE.) **Fls** May–Sep.

Sea-holly
Eryngium maritimum

Intensely glaucous, spiny, glabrous perennial
to 60 cm. **Leaves** All spiny; *basal leaves
5–12 cm, suborbicular*; stem leaves palmate.
Flowers 8 mm across, in 1.5–2.5 cm heads;
bracts spiny; bracteoles longer than flowers.
Habitat Coastal sand-dunes, fine shingle.
Dist. Native. All round coasts of BI except
N and E Scotland, NE England. (Coasts of
Europe to S Scandinavia.) **Fls** Jul–Aug.

Fruits *6–10 mm, smooth*, with short beak. **Habitat** Hedgerows, roadsides, railway banks, wood borders; to 760 m. **Dist**. Native. Throughout BI. (Most of Europe, but rare in Mediterranean.) **Fls** Apr–Jun.

Bur Parsley
Anthriscus caucalis

Spreading, sparsely pubescent annual to 70 cm. **Stems** *Hollow, glabrous*. **Leaves** 2–3-pinnate. **Flowers** In *umbels 2–4 cm across, leaf-opposed*, with short peduncle; 0–1 bracts; several bracteoles. **Fruits** *3 mm, with hooked bristles*. **Similar spp**. Garden Chervil *Anthriscus cerefolium* is an erect, pubescent annual that occasionally occurs as a casual on waste ground. It has pubescent rays, and smooth fruits, 7–10 mm, with a long, slender beak. **Habitat** Hedge banks, rough grassland, waste ground, sea walls, on sandy or gravelly soils. **Dist**. Native.

SEA HOLLY

Cow Parsley
Anthriscus sylvestris

Tall, erect, pubescent perennial to 150 cm. Commonest early flowering umbellifer. **Stems** *Hollow*. **Leaves** 3-pinnate. **Flowers** In umbels 2–6 cm across, terminal, rays glabrous; *bracts absent; several bracteoles*.

Local, scattered throughout BI, especially East Anglia. (W, S and central Europe.) **Fls** May–Jun.

Rough Chervil
Chaerophyllum temulum

Tall, erect, pubescent biennial to 100 cm. **Stems** *Solid, purple or purple-spotted*, with short, stiff hairs. **Leaves** *2–3-pinnate, pubescent on both surfaces.* **Flowers** 0–2 bracts; 5–8 bracteoles, shorter than pedicels. **Fruits** 4–6.5 mm. **Habitat** Roadsides, hedge banks, rough grassland, woodland borders, usually on dry basic soils; lowland to 350 m. **Dist**. Native throughout Britain, but rare or absent in N Scotland; introduced and rare in Ireland. (Most of Europe, but rare in Mediterranean; absent from extreme N.) **Fls** Jun–Jul, after *Anthriscus sylvestris*.

Pignut
Conopodium majus

Slender, erect, *glabrous perennial* to 50 cm. **Stems** *Hollow*, with underground tuber. **Leaves** *2–3-pinnate, lobes linear; basal leaves*

soon withering, stem leaves with sheathing base. **Flowers** In umbels, nodding in bud; 0–2 bracts; several bracteoles. **Fruits** 3–4.5 mm, *styles ± erect.* **Habitat** Open woodlands, rough grassland, grass heaths, upland hay meadows, hedge banks, on mildly acid soils; to 700 m. **Dist**. Native. Throughout BI. (W Europe.) **Fls** May–Jun.

Burnet-saxifrage
Pimpinella saxifraga

Erect, thinly pubescent, slender perennial to 100 cm. **Stems** Slightly ridged. **Leaves** Very variable, *basal leaves simply pinnate, stem leaves 2-pinnate.* **Flowers** *Bracts and bracteoles absent*; sepals absent; *petals with long, incurved point.* **Fruits** 2–3 mm. **Habitat** Dry, rough or grazed grassland, woodland edges, hedge banks, usually on base-rich or calcareous soils; to 810 m. **Dist**. Native. Throughout BI, but rare in N Scotland, N and W Ireland. (Most of Europe except extreme S.) **Fls** Jul–Aug.

Greater Burnet-saxifrage
Pimpinella major

Tall, erect, ± glabrous perennial to 120 cm. **Stems** *Strongly ridged.* **Leaves** *All simply pinnate*; segments of basal leaves shortly stalked, all coarsely toothed. **Flowers** *Bracts and bracteoles absent; sepals absent; petals with long, incurved points.* **Fruits** *3–4 mm.* **Habitat** Hedge banks, grassy roadsides,

GREATER BURNET-SAXIFRAGE

wood borders, on basic or calcareous soils; to 320 m. **Dist**. Native. Lowland England, SW Ireland; ± absent from Wales, Scotland. (Most of Europe except extreme N, S and SE.) **Fls** Jun–Jul.

Alexanders
Smyrnium olusatrum

Robust, glabrous biennial to 150 cm. **Stems** Solid, becoming hollow. **Leaves** Dark, glossy green, 2–3-pinnate or ternate, segments broad, petioles of stem leaves sheathing. **Flowers** Yellow-green; few bracts and bracteoles. **Fruits** Broad, 6.5–8 mm, black. **Habitat** Hedge banks, roadsides, cliffs, rough grassland, usually close to sea. **Dist**. Archaeophyte.

Locally common in most of BI, but rare in N England, Scotland. (S and SW Europe.) **Fls** Mar–Jun.

Water-dropworts ▶ *Oenanthe*

Hemlock Water-dropwort
Oenanthe crocata

Tall, robust, erect perennial to 150 cm. **Leaves** 3–4-pinnate; segments ovate, lobed or toothed; petioles sheathing. **Flowers** In terminal umbels, 5–10 cm across; several bracts and bracteoles. **Fruits** 4.5–5 mm, styles *c.* ½ as long as fruits. **Habitat** Wet woodlands, ditches, and stream, river and lake margins, on acid soils; lowland to 320 m. **Dist**. Native. Throughout BI, but commonest in S and W. (W Mediterranean, W and SW Europe.) **Fls** Jun–Sep. **Note** *Whole plant is extremely toxic.*

Tubular Water-dropwort
Oenanthe fistulosa VU.

Erect perennial to 60 cm. **Leaves** 1-pinnate; petioles long, cylindrical, hollow, longer than pinnate part of leaf. **Flowers** 3–4 forming partial umbels; bracts absent, several bracteoles. **Fruits** 3–4 mm, umbels becoming rounded, styles as long as fruit. **Habitat** Wet meadows, pastures, margins of drainage ditches, dykes, ponds, canals, on fertile soils. **Dist**. Native. Throughout lowland England, declining; rare and local in rest of BI. (W, central and S Europe.) **Fls** Jul–Sep.

Parsley Water-dropwort
Oenanthe lachenalii

Erect perennial to 100 cm. **Stems** Solid. **Leaves** 2-pinnate; lobes paddle-shaped, blunt; lower leaves soon withering. **Flowers** Up to 10 forming partial umbels; 5 bracts, several bracteoles. **Fruits** 2.5–3 mm, pedicels not thickening, styles shorter than fruit. **Habitat** Grazing marshes, margins of brackish dykes, estuarine rivers, rough coastal grassland; inland calcareous fens, marshes, wet meadows. **Dist**. Native. Coastal areas of BI except N Scotland; very local inland. (W and central Europe.) **Fls** Jun–Sep.

Hemlock
Conium maculatum

Tall, robust, much-branched, foetid, glabrous biennial to 250 cm. **Stems** Hollow, smooth, *purple-spotted*, glaucous. **Leaves** 2–3-pinnate; segments wedge-shaped, toothed. **Flowers** In terminal axillary umbels; *several bracts and bracteoles.*

Fruits *2–3.5 mm, rounded.* **Habitat** Riverbanks, ditches, roadsides, sea walls, waste ground; lowland to 305 m. **Dist**. Throughout BI, but rare in N Scotland. (All Europe except extreme N.) **Fls** Jun–Jul. **Note** *All parts of plant are poisonous.*

Wild Angelica
Angelica sylvestris

Tall, robust, ± *glabrous* perennial to 200 cm. **Stems** Hollow. **Leaves** 2–3-pinnate; *leaflets ovate, finely toothed; petioles strongly inflated.* **Flowers** Bracts absent, several bracteoles.

WILD ANGELICA

Leaves *1-pinnate*; leaflets large, ovate, toothed. **Flowers** Yellow; 0–2 bracts and bracteoles, soon falling. Fruits 4–7 mm. **Habitat** Rough grassland, roadside verges, hedge banks, waste ground, on calcareous soils. **Dist.** Native. England (common in S and SE), Wales; casual elsewhere. (Most of Europe except extreme N.) **Fls** Jul–Aug. **Note** The cultivated Parsnip, with its swollen root, is var. *hortensis* and occasionally occurs as a casual escape. *Juice of Parsnip can cause serious blisters in direct sunlight.*

Sweet Cicely
Myrrhis odorata

Robust, erect, sparsely pubescent perennial to 180 cm, *smelling strongly of aniseed.* **Stems** Hollow. **Leaves** 2–4-pinnate; lobes coarsely toothed, acute*; petioles of stem leaves sheathing.* **Flowers** Bracts absent, *c.5 bracteoles.* **Fruits** 15–25 mm, strongly ridged. **Habitat** Road verges, hedge banks, riverbanks, wood margins, often near buildings. **Dist.** Introduced. Naturalised and common in N England, Wales, Scotland, N Ireland. (Mts of S Europe.) **Fls** May–Jun.

Fruits 4–5 mm. **Habitat** Wet meadows, marshes, fens, wet woodlands, ditches; stream, river and lake margins. To 855 m. **Dist.** Native. Common throughout BI. (All Europe.) **Fls** Jul–Sep.

Wild Parsnip
Pastinaca sativa

Erect, thinly pubescent, *strong-smelling* biennial to 150 cm. **Stems** Hollow.

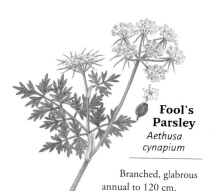

Fool's Parsley
Aethusa cynapium

Branched, glabrous annual to 120 cm. **Stems** Hollow. **Leaves** 2–3-pinnate. **Flowers** In terminal, leaf-opposed umbels; bracts absent; *3–4 bracteoles, strongly reflexed, on outer side of partial umbels.* **Fruits** 3–4 mm, glabrous, keeled. **Habitat** Weed of waste ground, arable fields, gardens. **Dist.** Native in Britain, N to Solway Firth; naturalised in Ireland. (Most of Europe, but rare in Mediterranean.) **Fls** Jul–Aug.

Fennel
Foeniculum vulgare

Tall, glabrous, glaucous, perennial to 250 cm. **Leaves** 3–4-pinnate; *segments long, filiform, not all in one plane.* **Flowers**

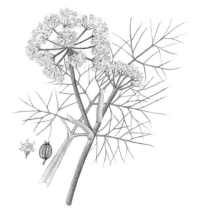

Yellow; bracts and bracteoles absent. **Fruits** 4–5 mm, glabrous, ribbed. **Habitat** Cliffs, waste ground, rough grassland, roadsides, especially close to sea. **Dist.** Archaeophyte. Widely distributed in England, Wales; scarce elsewhere. (Most of Europe except N; native of S and SW.) **Fls** Jul–Oct.

Spignel
Meum athamanticum

Tufted, branched, glabrous, aromatic perennial to 60 cm. *Base of plant with fibrous remains of old petioles.* **Stems** Hollow. **Leaves** *Most basal, 3–4-pinnate; segments filiform, whorled.* **Flowers** 0–few bracts; several bracteoles, linear. **Fruits** 5–7 mm, ridged. **Habitat** Rough grassland, pastures, hay meadows, in upland areas; to 610 m. **Dist.** Native. N England, Scotland. (Mts of W and central Europe.) **Fls** Jun–Jul.

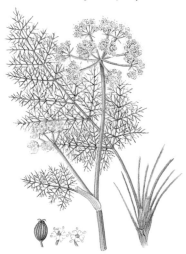

Ground-elder
Aegopodium podagraria

Erect, glabrous, rhizomatous perennial to 100 cm, with *far-creeping rhizomes.* **Leaves** *1–2-ternate; leaflets broad,* toothed. **Flowers**

GROUND-ELDER

Bracts and bracteoles absent. **Fruits** 3–4 mm, glabrous. **Habitat** Hedgerows, road verges, wood margins; persistent and troublesome garden weed. To 450 m. **Dist**. Archaeophyte. Common throughout BI. (Most of Europe, but rare in S.) **Fls** May–Jul.

Lesser Water-parsnip
Berula erecta

Decumbent or erect, glabrous, submerged or emergent, stoloniferous aquatic perennial to 100 cm. **Leaves** Simply pinnate; *5–10 pairs of leaflets*, 2–6 cm, sessile, coarsely toothed or slightly lobed; *lower petioles with ring-like mark towards base.* **Flowers** *In leaf-opposed*

umbels; *several bracts and bracteoles*. **Fruits** 1.5–2 mm, ridges not prominent, *almost circular*. **Habitat** Margins of ponds, ditches, dykes, canals, slow-moving rivers and marshes with fertile, calcareous water. **Dist**. Native. Frequent throughout lowland BI, but rare in Scotland and SW. (All Europe except extreme N.) **Fls** Jul–Sep.

Marshworts ▶ *Apium*

Fool's Watercress
Apium nodiflorum

Prostrate to erect, glabrous perennial to 100 cm. **Stems** Rooting at lower nodes. **Leaves** Simply pinnate; *2–4 pairs of leaflets*, ovate, longer than wide, weakly toothed; *lower petioles without ring-like mark.* **Flowers** *In leaf-opposed umbels*; peduncles shorter than rays; *bracts absent,* bracteoles as long as flowers. **Fruits** 1.5–2.5 mm, longer than wide, ridged. **Habitat** Shallow water of dykes, ditches, streams, ponds, on fertile or calcareous soils. **Dist**. Native. Widespread and common in England, Wales, Ireland; rare in Scotland. (Most of Europe.) **Fls** Jul–Aug.

Note Often confused with *Berula erecta* (p.144), but distinguished from this in the vegetative state by absence of ring-like mark on petiole, and, when flowering, by absence of bracts. Also mistaken for *Nasturtium officinale* (p.70).

Wild Celery
Apium graveolens

Tall, erect, glabrous biennial to 100 cm, *smelling strongly of celery*. **Stems** Solid, grooved. **Leaves** *Basal leaves pinnate, basal leaflets stalked*. **Flowers** *Greenish white*; in terminal, axillary umbels; *bracts and bracteoles absent*. **Fruits** 1–1.5 mm.

Habitat Usually in brackish water of river, stream, ditch and dyke margins, sea walls. **Dist**. Native. Coastal areas of BI N to Solway Firth; rare inland. (Coasts of Europe N to Denmark.) **Fls** Jun–Aug.

Rock Samphire
Crithmum maritimum

Much-branched, *glabrous, fleshy perennial* to 30 cm. **Stems** ± woody at base. **Leaves** *Succulent, 2–3-pinnate*; leaflets smooth, rounded in section, acute; petioles sheathing.

Flowers *Yellowish green*; several bracts and bracteoles. **Fruits** 3.5–5 mm, glabrous, ridged. **Habitat** Maritime rocks, cliffs, stabilised shingle, sea defences. **Dist**. Native. S and W coasts of Britain from Suffolk on E to Ayr on W; all round coasts of Ireland. (W and Mediterranean coasts of Europe.) **Fls** Jun–Aug.

Pepper-saxifrage
Silaum silaus

Erect, branched, glabrous perennial to 100 cm. **Leaves** *2–3-pinnate; leaflets lanceolate, finely toothed*. **Flowers** *Yellowish*, in umbels with long peduncles; 0–3 bracts, several bracteoles. **Fruits** 4–5 mm. **Habitat** Old meadows and grassy commons, rough grassland, roadsides, on heavy soils. **Dist**. Native. Widely distributed S and E of line from Tees to Exe; absent from Ireland. (W, central and E Europe.) **Fls** Jun–Aug.

Corn Parsley
Petroselinum segetum

Erect, glabrous, *slightly glaucous* biennial
to 100 cm. **Stems** *Branching at wide angle.*
Leaves *Narrowly oblong*; lowest leaves
simply pinnate, with *4–12 pairs of leaflets*;
leaflets coarsely toothed, matt. **Flowers** *In
uneven umbels*; 2–5 bracts and bracteoles,
longest bracts >½ as long as rays. **Fruits**
2.5–4 mm.

Habitat
Brackish
grassland, sea
walls, riverbanks,
roadsides, field
margins, on fertile
or calcareous
soils. **Dist.**
Native. Local.
Widely
distributed S
and E of line
from Humber
to Severn. (W
Europe.) **Fls**
Aug–Sep.

Cowbane
Cicuta virosa

Robust, erect, glabrous perennial to
150 cm. **Leaves** *2–3-pinnate; leaflets linear-
lanceolate, sharply toothed*; petioles hollow,
base sheathing. **Flowers** In terminal, leaf-
opposed, *dense-flowered* umbels; *bracts*

Stone Parsley
Sison amomum

Erect, glabrous, branching biennial to
100 cm, with *characteristic unpleasant
petrol-like smell*. **Leaves** Lowest leaves simply
pinnate, with *2–5 pairs of leaflets*; leaflets
broad, coarsely toothed or lobed. **Flowers**
In terminal, axillary umbels; 2–4 bracts and
bracteoles, *bracts < ½ as long as rays*. **Fruits**
1.5–3 mm. **Habitat** Hedgerows, grassy
banks, roadside verges, on heavy soils. Dist.
Locally frequent. Native. Widely distributed
S and E of line from Humber to Severn, N
Wales. (S and W Europe.) **Fls** Jul–Sep.

absent; several bracteoles, longer than pedicels.
Fruits 1.2–2 mm. **Habitat** Shallow water
of marshes, pond margins, ditches, drainage
dykes, carr woodland. **Dist.** Native. Very
local. Norfolk Broads, Shropshire, Cheshire,
central Ireland; scattered elsewhere. (Most of
Europe, but rare in S.) **Fls** Jul–Aug.

Whorled Caraway
Carum verticillatum

Erect, glabrous perennial to 60 cm. **Stems**
Base with dense tuft of fibrous remains of
old petioles. **Leaves** *Mostly basal, narrow
in outline, simply
pinnate; each
leaflet repeatedly
lobed into
fine segments,
appearing as
if whorled.*
Flowers Several
bracts and
bracteoles. **Fruits**
2–3 mm. **Habitat**
Damp marshes, rushy
pastures, steam
sides, on acid soils.
Dist. Native. W
England, Wales,
Scotland,
Ireland.
(W Europe.)
Fls Jul–Aug.

Hogweed
Heracleum sphondylium

Tall, robust, pubescent biennial to 200 cm.
The commonest late-summer-flowering
wayside umbellifer. **Stems** Hollow. **Leaves**
*Simply pinnate, roughly hairy on both
surfaces, leaflets lobed.* **Flowers** Bracts absent
or few; several bracteoles, reflexed; *petals
deeply notched.* **Fruits** 7–8 mm. **Habitat**
Hedgerows, roadside verges, woodland
clearings, rough grassland. **Dist.** Native.

Common throughout BI. (All Europe
except N Scandinavia.) **Fls** Jun–Sep.

Giant Hogweed
Heracleum mantegazzianum

*Enormous pubescent biennial or perennial
to 550 cm.* **Stems** Hollow, red-spotted.

Leaves Pinnate to ternate, up to 250 cm; *leaflets toothed or lobed, lobes acute.* **Flowers** In umbels to 50 cm across; several bracts and bracteoles. **Fruits** 9–14 mm. **Habitat** Banks of streams and rivers, waste ground, derelict gardens, roadsides. **Dist**. Introduced in 1820 (native of SW Asia). Naturalised, spreading throughout BI. (Most of Europe.) **Fls** Jun–Jul. **Note** *Causes dermatitis on contact with skin in sunlight.*

Upright Hedge-parsley
Torilis japonica

Erect, roughly hairy annual to 120 cm. **Stems** Solid. **Leaves** 1–3-pinnate, *lanceolate in outline.* **Flowers** *In umbels with 5–12 rays; 4–6 bracts;* several bracteoles; petals hairy beneath. **Fruits** 4–6 mm, with hooked spines. **Habitat** Hedgerows, road verges, woodland margins, rough grassland; to 410 m. **Dist**. Native. Common throughout most of BI, but rare or absent in N Scotland. (Most of Europe.) **Fls** Jul–Aug, after *Chaerophyllum temulum* (p.138).

Knotted Hedge-parsley
Torilis nodosa

Prostrate, sparsely pubescent annual to 35 cm. **Leaves** 1–2-pinnate; leaflets lanceolate, deeply lobed. **Flowers** Pinkish, *in sessile, leaf-opposed umbels, 0.5–1 cm across*; 2–3 rays, very short; bracts absent; bracteoles longer than flowers. **Fruits** 2–3 mm, very spiny. **Habitat** Dry, open areas, banks, sea walls, cliff tops, arable fields, waste ground. **Dist**. Native. Local, declining. Scattered throughout lowland Britain; very rare and mostly coastal in Scotland, Ireland. (S and W Europe.) **Fls** May–Jul.

Wild Carrot
Daucus carota ssp. *carota*

Erect, thinly pubescent or hispid biennial with characteristic smell, to 100 cm. **Stems** Solid. **Leaves** 3-pinnate; leaflets branched, lobes lanceolate-ovate. **Flowers** White, in umbels with numerous glabrous or thinly pubescent rays, *central flower often dark purple; 7–13 bracts, branched, about as long as pedicels.* **Fruits** 2.5–4 mm, spiny. **Habitat** Broken turf, rough grassland, roadsides, waste ground, on dry calcareous soils. **Dist.** Native. Widespread throughout BI; mostly coastal in Scotland. (Most of Europe.) **Fls** Jun–Aug. **Note** The cultivated carrot, with its fleshy orange taproot, is *D. carota* ssp. *sativus*; it occasionally occurs as a casual escape of cultivation.

Sea Carrot
Daucus carota ssp. *gummifer*

Similar to *Daucus carota* ssp. *carota*, but rays with spreading or reflexed hairs; umbels flat or convex in fruit. **Habitat** Maritime grassland, cliffs, stable sand-dunes. **Dist.** Native. Local on coasts of S and SW England, Wales, SE Ireland, Channel Is, Scilly Is. (Coasts of France, N Spain.) **Fls** Jun–Aug.

GENTIANACEAE
Gentians and centauries
••••••••••••••••••••••••••••••••••••••

Glabrous annuals or perennials with opposite, entire, sessile leaves. Flowers regular; sepals 4–5, fused; petals 4–5 fused into a corolla tube; stamens 4–5; ovary superior.

Marsh Gentian
Gentiana pneumonanthe

Erect glabrous perennial to 40 cm. **Leaves** *Stem leaves linear,* 1.5–4 cm. **Flowers** In 1–15-flowered inflorescence; *corolla tube 25–50 mm,* with 5 green lines on outside. **Habitat** Wet heaths, damp acidic grassland. **Dist.** Native. Very local, declining. Scattered throughout lowland England, N Wales, especially New Forest, Dorset. (Most of Europe except extreme N and S.) **Fls** Aug–Sep.

Centauries ►
Centaurium

Common Centaury
Centaurium erythraea

Erect, glabrous annual to 50 cm. **Stems** Usually solitary, branched. **Leaves** *Basal leaves 1–5 cm, in a rosette, ovate, prominently 3–7-veined beneath, apex acute.* **Flowers** *Sessile,* clustered; 1–2 bracts at base of calyx; corolla lobes 4.5–5.5 mm; *stigmas conical.* **Habitat** Permanent grassland, woodland rides, scrub, grassy heaths, dunes, road verges, on well-drained soils. **Dist**. Native. Throughout most of BI; rare, local and mostly coastal in Scotland. (Most of Europe except N Scandinavia.) **Fls** Jun–Oct.

Lesser Centaury
Centaurium pulchellum *(R)

Slender, erect annual to 15 cm. **Stems** Simple or much branched; *basal rosette absent; 2–4 stem internodes.* **Leaves** 2–15 mm, ovate. **Flowers** Deep pink; corolla lobes 2–4 mm; *bracts 1–4 mm below base of calyx; flower stalks 1–4 mm.* **Habitat** Dry, open areas, woodland rides, grassland, heaths, sand-dunes, on sandy or calcareous soils. **Dist**. Native. Widespread in S England; coastal further N; rare or absent in Scotland, Ireland. (Most of Europe except extreme N.) **Fls** Jun–Sep.

Gentians ▶ *Gentianella*

Autumn Gentian/ Felwort
Gentianella amarella

Erect, branched biennial to 30 cm. **Stems** *5–9 internodes,* all ± equal or upper ones shorter. **Leaves** Stem leaves 10–20 mm. **Flowers** *Calyx teeth ± equal;* corolla 14–20 mm, ≤2× as long as calyx. **Habitat** Short calcareous grassland,

calcareous dunes, dune slacks, machair; to 750 m. **Dist**. Native. Throughout BI. (N and central Europe.) **Fls** Aug–Oct.

Field Gentian
Gentianella campestris VU.

Erect annual or biennial to 30 cm. **Stems** Simple or branched. **Leaves** Stem leaves 20–30 mm. **Flowers** *4 calyx and corolla lobes; 2 outer calyx lobes much larger than, and hiding, 2 inner lobes;* corolla 15–25 mm, corolla tube as long as or longer than calyx. **Habitat** Pastures, hill grassland, grass heaths, sand-dunes, machair, on acid soils; to 915 m. **Dist**. Native. Declining. Widely distributed in N and upland Britain; rare elsewhere. (N and central Europe.) **Fls** Jul–Oct.

Yellow-wort
Blackstonia perfoliata

Erect, glaucous annual to 45 cm. **Leaves** Basal leaves 1–2 cm, in a rosette, obovate, with strong mid-vein and weaker laterals beneath; *stem leaves broad, fused across stem at base.* **Flowers** Corolla 10–15 mm across; *6–8 petals, yellow.* **Habitat** Herb-rich calcareous grassland, quarries, fixed coastal dunes. **Dist**. Native. Britain N to Humber; central and S Ireland. (W, S and central Europe.) **Fls** Jun–Oct.

APOCYNACEAE
Periwinkles

Lesser Periwinkle
Vinca minor

Evergreen, glabrous, trailing, slightly woody perennial to 60 cm. **Stems** Rooting. **Leaves** Opposite, 25–40 mm, *short-stalked.* **Flowers** Solitary in axils of leaves, 25–30 mm across; *5 sepals, glabrous*; 5 petals. **Habitat** Woodlands, roadside banks, waste ground; lowland to 380 m. **Dist.** Archaeophyte. Most of BI, but rare in N Scotland, Ireland. (S, W and central Europe.) **Fls** Mar–May.

Greater Periwinkle
Vinca major

Similar to *V. minor*, but stems ascending to 150 cm; leaves 20–70 mm, *leaf stalks c.10 mm*; flowers 40–50 mm across, *margins of sepals with fringe of hairs.* **Habitat** Woodland, hedge banks, roadside verges, waste ground. **Dist.** Introduced. Naturalised throughout most of England, Wales; scattered in Scotland, Ireland. (W and central Mediterranean.) **Fls** May–Jun.

SOLANACEAE
Nightshades

A rather varied family of herbs, shrubs and climbers often with large showy flowers. The leaves are almost always alternate and without stipules. The flowers are regular with a 5-lobed calyx and corolla; stamens 5; ovary superior with a single style with 1 or 2 stigmas. The fruit is a berry or capsule. Many members of the family contain poisonous alkaloids.

Deadly Nightshade
Atropa belladonna

Tall, much-branched, glabrous or pubescent, glandular perennial to 150 cm. *Poisonous.* **Leaves** To 8–20 cm, alternate. **Flowers** *Solitary, axillary, pendulous, 25–30 mm*; 5 sepals and petals; *calyx deeply 5-lobed.* **Fruits** *Black berry, 15–20 mm.* **Habitat** Open woodland, scrub, hedgerows, disturbed ground, on calcareous soils. **Dist.** Native. Scattered throughout lowland England; rare and naturalised elsewhere. (S, W and central Europe.) **Fls** Jun–Aug.

Duke of Argyll's Teaplant
Lycium barbarum

Suckering, scrambling, spiny deciduous shrub to 2.5 m. **Leaves** Simple, entire, glabrous, widest at middle. **Flowers** Axillary; calyx and corolla 5-lobed; corolla <17 mm across, dark veins of corolla lobes mostly unbranched; stamens protruding. **Fruits** Red berry. **Similar spp**. Chinese Teaplant *Lycium chinense* is similar, but leaves are widest below middle; corolla is >17 mm across, and dark veins of corolla lobes are branched. **Habitat** Both species are used for hedging, particularly in coastal areas; also naturalised on hedge banks, walls, waste ground, shingle. **Dist**. Introduced (native of China). (Naturalised over much of Europe.) **Fls** Jun–Sep.

Nightshades ▶ *Solanum*

Bittersweet/Woody Nightshade
Solanum dulcamara

Glabrous or pubescent, scrambling woody perennial to 300 cm. **Leaves** To *c*.8 cm, simple, entire or lobed. **Flowers** *c*.10 mm across, in leaf-opposed inflorescence; petals purple. **Fruits** Red berry, 8–12 mm. **Habitat** Hedgerows, scrub, wood borders, tall-herb fens, fen carr, shingle beaches (var. *marinum*).

Dist. Native. Common throughout BI, but rare in N Scotland. (Most of Europe except extreme N.) **Fls** Jun–Sep.

Black Nightshade
Solanum nigrum

Glabrous or pubescent, erect annual to 60 cm. **Leaves** Ovate, entire or toothed. **Flowers** White, in 5–10-flowered inflorescence. **Fruits** Black berry, 6–10 mm. **Habitat** Common weed of cultivation and disturbed and waste ground, especially on fertile soils. **Dist**. Native and widespread in England, Wales; naturalised further N. (Most of Europe.) **Fls** Jul–Sep.

CONVOLVULACEAE
Bindweeds and Dodder

Field Bindweed
Convolvulus arvensis

Trailing and climbing perennial to 75 cm. **Leaves** 2–5 cm. **Flowers** 0–3, 10–30 mm across, white or pink; peduncles longer than leaves; pedicels with 2 narrow bracteoles below and not overlapping sepals. **Fruits** Capsule, *c.*3 mm across. **Habitat** Arable fields, roadsides, rough grassland, waste ground. **Dist**. Native. Common throughout BI, but scarce in N Scotland, W Ireland. (All Europe except extreme N.) **Fls** Jun–Sep.

Hedge Bindweed
Calystegia sepium

Climbing, rhizomatous perennial to 200 cm. **Flowers** Solitary, 3.5–7 cm

across, white; bracteoles 10–18 mm wide, flattened against calyx, not or only slightly overlapping, not completely hiding sepals. **Habitat** Hedgerows, scrub, wood margins, fen carr, riverbanks, waste ground, gardens. **Dist**. Native. Abundant throughout most of BI, but scarce in N Scotland. (Most of Europe except extreme N.) **Fls** Jul–Sep.

Large Bindweed
Calystegia silvatica

Similar to *C. sepium*, but flowers 6–9 cm across; bracteoles 18–45 mm wide, strongly inflated at base, strongly overlapping at edges, almost completely hiding sepals; pedicels glabrous. **Habitat** Hedgerows, gardens, waste ground; less often in semi-natural habitats. **Dist**. Introduced. Established and common throughout BI, but scarce in N Scotland, Ireland. (S Europe.) **Fls** Jul–Sep.

Sea Bindweed
Calystegia soldanella

Prostrate, rhizomatous, glabrous perennial to 60 cm, with far-creeping rhizomes. **Stems** Not climbing. **Leaves** 1–4 cm, kidney-shaped. **Flowers** Solitary, 2.5–4 cm across, pink with white stripes; bracteoles shorter than calyx. **Habitat** Sand-dunes, sandy and fine shingly beaches. **Dist**. Native. All round

SEA BINDWEED

coasts of BI except N Scotland. (Coasts of S and W Europe N to Denmark.) **Fls** Jun–Aug.

Dodders ▶ *Cuscuta*
Rootless annual or perennial parasites without chlorophyll. Stems twining, attached to host plant by suckers. Leaves alternate, minute. Flowers in dense sessile heads; 4–5 calyx and corolla lobes; 4–5 stamens; corolla with ring of small scales below base of stamens; stigmas linear or capitate.

Dodder
Cuscuta epithymum

Annual. **Stems** Red. **Flowers** 5 calyx and corolla lobes; sepals acute; *corolla scales not lobed, large, ± closing corolla tube; stamens longer than corolla*; styles longer than ovary, stigmas linear. **Habitat** Heathlands, downland, dune grassland; parasitic on

gorses, heathers, Wild Thyme; casual on crops further N. **Dist**. Native. Local in S and SW England; rare elsewhere; absent from Scotland. (All Europe except extreme N.) **Fls** Jul–Sep.

MENYANTHACEAE
Bogbeans
•••

Bogbean
Menyanthes trifoliata

Glabrous, aquatic, perennial, rhizomatous *bog plant*, with leaves and flowering stems raised above water. **Stems** Flowering stems 12–30 cm. **Leaves** Trifoliate. **Flowers** *White*, 15–20 mm across, *in 10–20-flowered inflorescence*; 5 sepals and petals, *inner surface of petals fringed*. **Habitat** Shallow margins of acid pools, lakes, dykes, streams, wet bogs, fens; to 1005 m. **Dist**. Native. Widely distributed throughout BI. (Most of Europe, but rare in Mediterranean.) **Fls** May–Jul.

Fringed Water-lily
Nymphoides peltata

Glabrous, aquatic perennial, with *floating leaves and flowers*. **Leaves** *3–12 cm, orbicular*, deeply cordate at base, margins sinuate. **Flowers** *Yellow, 3–4 cm across*, in 2–5-flowered inflorescence; calyx and corolla 5-lobed; *petals fringed*. **Habitat** Shallow, slow-moving water in drains, dykes, canals, lakes, ponds. **Dist**. Native.

± restricted to East Anglian fens, but naturalised throughout most of rest of lowland Britain; rare in Scotland, Ireland. (Most of Europe.) **Fls** Jul–Aug.

BORAGINACEAE
Borage family

A distinctive family of usually roughly hairy annual or perennial herbs. Leaves are alternate, entire, without stipules. Flowers are regular (except *Echium*); inflorescence is often a spiralled cyme; calyx is 5-toothed; corolla is often funnel-shaped, 5-lobed; 5 stamens; ovary is superior, 4-celled and deeply 4-lobed. Fruit is a cluster of 4 nutlets.

Common Gromwell
Lithospermum officinale

Erect, much-branched, pubescent perennial to 80 cm. **Leaves** To 7 cm, *lateral nerves conspicuous beneath*. **Flowers** *Corolla* 3–6 mm across, not much longer than calyx, *yellowish*. **Fruits** *Shining white nutlets*. **Habitat** Wood margins, scrub, hedgerows, on base-rich or calcareous soils. **Dist**. Native. Local. Throughout lowland England; rare elsewhere. (Most of Europe, but rare in N and W.) **Fls** Jun–Jul.

Viper's-bugloss
Echium vulgare

Erect, *very hispid* biennial to 90 cm. **Leaves** Basal leaves to 15 cm, stalked, with prominent midrib and no apparent lateral veins. **Flowers** 10–18 mm, pink in bud turning bright blue; *corolla lobes unequal, uniformly pubescent on outside; 5 stamens, unequal, 4 longer than corolla.* **Fruits** *Ridged nutlets*. **Habitat** Open, disturbed ground, rough grassland, cliffs, dunes, shingle, waste ground, roadsides, on light calcareous or sandy soils; lowland to 365 m. **Dist**. Native. Widespread in Britain N to central Scotland; rare and coastal in Ireland. (All Europe.) **Fls** Jun–Sep.

Lungwort
Pulmonaria officinalis

Pubescent, rhizomatous perennial to 30 cm. **Leaves** *Basal leaves winter green, ovate,*

cordate; lamina longer than petiole, abruptly narrowed at base, with large white spots. **Flowers** *In glandular inflorescence*; calyx lobes sub-acute; corolla *c*.10 mm across. **Habitat** Woods, hedge banks, rough ground; lowland to 385 m. **Dist**. Introduced. Commonly grown in gardens, and naturalised throughout Britain; rare in Ireland. (Central and E Europe.) **Fls** Mar–May.

Comfreys ▶ *Symphytum*

Common Comfrey
Symphytum officinale

Erect, hispid, branched perennial to 150 cm. **Stems** With long, deflexed, conical hairs. **Leaves** Strongly and broadly decurrent, wings longer than 1 inter-node; stem leaves sessile. **Flowers** Calyx 7–8 mm, teeth acute, 2–3× as long as tube; corolla 15–17 mm, yellowish white (to pinkish). **Habitat** Fens, marshes, wet ditches, banks of rivers, streams and canals; lowland to 320 m. **Dist**. Native. Locally frequent throughout BI, but rare in W Wales, N Scotland. (Most of Europe, but rare in S.) **Fls** May–Jun.

Russian Comfrey
Symphytum × uplandicum

Tall, erect, branched perennial to 140 cm. Similar to *S. officinale*, but more hispid; upper stem leaves sessile and shortly decurrent, wings not extending >halfway to leaf below; calyx 5–7 mm; corolla pinkish blue, purplish or violet. **Habitat** Roadsides, hedge banks, wood margins, waste ground; to 365 m. **Dist**. Introduced as forage plant in 1870. Frequent throughout most of BI, but rare in N Scotland, Ireland. (Naturalised in W and central Europe.) **Fls** Jun–Aug.

Tuberous Comfrey
Symphytum tuberosum

Erect, hispid, sparsely branched, rhizomatous perennial to 60 cm. **Stems** Bristly. **Leaves** Stem leaves sessile, middle leaves considerably larger than lower. **Flowers** Calyx 7–8 mm, divided almost to base; corolla 12–16 mm, pale yellow. **Habitat** Damp woodland, hedge banks, margins of streams and rivers; to 335 m. **Dist**. Native in N England, Scotland; naturalised further S. Local. (W, central and S Europe.) **Fls** Jun–Jul.

TUBEROUS COMFREY

White Comfrey
Symphytum orientale

Erect, little-branched, softly pubescent perennial to 70 cm. **Leaves** Lower leaves to 14 cm, stalked, ovate, cordate at base.

Flowers Calyx 7–9 mm, teeth ½ length of tube; corolla 15–17 mm, white. **Habitat** Naturalised on hedge banks, lanesides, road verges, waste ground. **Dist.** Introduced. Frequent in SE England; scattered further N. (Native of Caucasus, S Russia, NW Turkey.) **Fls** Apr–May.

Bugloss
Anchusa arvensis

Erect, hispid annual to 50 cm. **Leaves** To *c.*15 cm, linear-oblong, margins undulate, toothed. **Flowers** ± sessile; bracts leaf-like, 4–7 mm across; calyx deeply divided; corolla tube curved, lobes slightly unequal. **Habitat** Arable weed on well-drained soils, sandy heaths, dunes near sea; to 420 m. **Dist**. Archaeophyte. Declining. Throughout BI, but rare in Ireland. (Most of Europe.) **Fls** Jun–Sep.

Green Alkanet
Pentaglottis sempervirens

Erect, branched, hispid perennial to 100 cm. **Leaves** To 30 cm, ovate, lower leaves stalked. **Flowers** ± sessile, in terminal, axillary, long-stalked inflorescence; calyx divided >¾ way to base; corolla bright blue, 8–10 mm across. **Habitat** Hedgerows, roadsides, woodland margins, usually near buildings; to 380 m. **Dist**. Introduced. Naturalised throughout BI, but rare in N Scotland, Ireland. (SW Europe.) **Fls** May–Jun.

**GREEN
ALKANET**

Forget-me-nots ▶ *Myosotis*

Water Forget-me-not
Myosotis scorpioides

Ascending to erect, pubescent, rhizomatous
or stoloniferous perennial, to 45 cm. **Leaves**
Lower leaves to 7 cm. **Flowers** In
inflorescence without bracts,
*c.*20 cm long; calyx
divided to <halfway,
teeth forming an equal-
sided triangle, hairs
appressed; corolla to
8–13 mm across; tips
of petals emarginate;
style longer than calyx
tube at flowering.
Habitat Margins of
ponds, rivers, ditches,
canals, streams; to
600 m. **Dist**. Native.
Common throughout
BI; introduced in
Orkney, Shetland.
(Central and N
Europe.) **Fls** May–Sep.

Tufted Forget-me-not
Myosotis laxa

Ascending to erect,
pubescent annual to
biennial. Similar to
M. scorpioides, with
which it often
grows, but without
rhizomes or stolons.
Flowers Inflorescence
*c.*15 cm long; calyx
divided to ≥halfway,
teeth forming isosceles
triangle (sides longer
than base); corolla
3.5–4 mm across; tips
of petals rounded; style
shorter than calyx tube
at flowering. **Habitat**
Marshes, fens, margins of
streams, rivers, dykes, canals,
ponds and pools; lowland
to 550 m. **Dist**. Native.
Frequent throughout
BI. (Most of Europe, but
rare in S.) **Fls** May–Aug.

Creeping Forget-me-not
Myosotis secunda

Decumbent to erect,
pubescent,
stoloniferous
perennial to 60 cm.
Stems Lower part
with spreading hairs.
Leaves Rather pale.
Flowers Lower part
of inflorescence with
leafy bracts; fruiting
pedicels 3–5× as long
as calyx, reflexed;
corolla 4–6 mm across;
style shorter than calyx
tube at flowering.

Habitat Streams, springs, pools, woodland flushes, wet pastures, in acid water; to 805 m. **Dist**. Native. Widespread in N, W and S BI. (W Europe.) **Fls** May–Aug.

Early Forget-me-not
Myosotis ramosissima

Slender, often tiny, prostrate to erect annual, to 25 cm. **Leaves** Lower ones ovate, forming rosette. **Flowers** Inflorescence without bracts, longer than leafy part of stem in fruit; pedicels shorter than or as long as calyx at fruiting; calyx with spreading hooked hairs; corolla blue, *c*.3 mm across; corolla tube shorter than calyx. **Habitat** Open habitats on dry, infertile soils, heath grassland, mature sand-dunes. **Dist**. Native. Frequent throughout most of BI, but rare and coastal in N Scotland, Ireland. (Most of Europe except extreme N.) **Fls** Apr–Jun.

Field Forget-me-not
Myosotis arvensis

Erect, pubescent annual to 30 cm. **Leaves** Lower leaves broadly ovate, forming rosette. **Flowers** In inflorescence without bracts, about as long as leafy stem at fruiting; pedicels to 2× as long as calyx at fruiting; calyx with crisped hairs; corolla blue, ≤5 mm across,

lobes concave; corolla tube shorter than calyx. **Habitat** Arable soils, roadsides, woodland rides, grassy heaths, disturbed ground; to 610 m. **Dist**. Archaeophyte. Common throughout BI. (All Europe.) **Fls** Apr–Sep.

Wood Forget-me-not
Myosotis sylvatica

Erect, pubescent perennial to 45 cm. **Stems** With spreading hairs. **Flowers** In inflorescence without bracts, elongated after flowering; pedicels 1.5–2× as long as calyx at fruiting; calyx densely pubescent with both curved and hooked hairs; corolla 6–10 mm across, lobes flat. **Fruits** Brown nutlet, acute at apex. **Habitat** Damp woodlands on fertile soils, rocky grassland; to 485 m. **Dist**. Native. Rather local. Throughout BI, but rare in N Scotland, Ireland. (Most of Europe except SW and extreme N.) **Fls** May–Jun.

Changing Forget-me-not
Myosotis discolor

Erect, slender, pubescent annual to 26 cm. **Flowers** In inflorescence without bracts; calyx teeth oblong-lanceolate; corolla to 2 mm across, at first yellow then pink to blue; corolla tube longer than calyx.

Fruits Pedicels shorter than calyx. **Habitat** Open and disturbed ground, grass heaths, arable land, woodland rides, road verges, banks, walls, on dry soils; to 610 m. **Dist**. Native. Throughout BI. (Most of Europe.) **Fls** May–Sep.

Borage
Borago officinalis

Robust, erect, hispid annual to 60 cm. **Leaves** 10– 20 cm; lower leaves stalked, upper ones sessile. **Flowers** 20 mm across, in few-flowered inflorescence with leaf-like bracts; pedicels 2–4 cm; calyx hispid, divided to base, lobes narrow; petals spreading; filaments glabrous, shorter than anthers; anthers united, dark purple, exserted. **Habitat** Roadsides, waste ground, near habitation. **Dist**. Throughout BI as casual garden escape. (S Europe.) **Fls** Jun–Aug.

Hound's-tongue
Cynoglossum officinale

Erect, softly pubescent grey-green biennial to 90 cm. **Leaves** Basal leaves softly silky on both surfaces, lanceolate-ovate, to *c.*30 cm. **Flowers** In elongated, spiralled, branched inflorescence; pedicels *c.*5 mm; calyx divided almost to base; corolla 6–10 mm across. **Fruits** Large nutlet covered

by hooked bristles, with distinct thickened border. **Habitat** Wood margins, rough open grassland, on dry, well-drained soils, coastal dunes, shingle; to 400 m. **Dist**. Native. Scattered throughout most of lowland England, Wales; coastal in the SW, Scotland, Ireland. (Most of Europe except extreme N and S.) **Fls** Jun–Aug.

LAMIACEAE (LABIATAE)
Labiates
••

A distinctive family of annuals, perennials or dwarf shrubs with square stems and pairs of opposite leaves that lack stipules. Inflorescences are often whorl-like or terminal and spike or head-like; flowers are irregular; calyx 5-toothed, often 2-lipped; corolla with well-developed tube, and 5-lobed with the 2 upper lobes forming a distinct lip and the 3 others forming a 3-lobed lower lip; 4 stamens, 2 long and 2 short; ovary superior and deeply 4-lobed. Fruit is a cluster of 4 nutlets. Some members of the Orobanchaceae, such as *Rhinanthus* (p.179), are similar to the labiates but these have a quite different ovary. The family contains many familiar culinary and aromatic herbs such as lavender, mint, thyme and rosemary.

Woundworts ▶ *Betonica* and *Stachys*

Betony
Betonica officinalis *(NI)

Sparsely pubescent, erect, rhizomatous perennial to 60 cm. **Leaves** Basal leaves long-stalked, forming persistent rosette; leaf blades 3–7 cm, cordate, crenate; few stem leaves. **Flowers** In inflorescence with bracteoles; corolla 12–18 mm, tube longer than calyx. **Habitat** Rough grassland, heaths, hedge banks, woodland clearings, cliff-top grassland, on dry, mildly acid soils; to 460 m. **Dist**. Native. Widespread in England, Wales; rare in Scotland, Ireland. (Most of Europe except N.) **Fls** Jun–Sep.

Hedge Woundwort
Stachys sylvatica

Erect, rhizomatous, roughly hairy, strong-smelling perennial to 100 cm. **Leaves** All leaves stalked, ovate, cordate; leaf blades 4–9 cm. **Flowers** In whorls in interrupted inflorescence; bracteoles very small; corolla reddish purple, 13–15 mm. **Habitat** Hedge banks, woodlands, shaded gardens; to 500 m. **Dist**. Native. Common throughout BI. (Most of Europe, but rare in S.) **Fls** Jul–Aug.

Marsh Woundwort
Stachys palustris

Erect, pubescent, rhizomatous perennial to 100 cm, slightly glandular above. **Leaves**

Stem leaves sessile, oblong-lanceolate, 5–12 cm. **Flowers** In inflorescence, interrupted below; bracteoles very small; corolla pinkish purple, 12–15 mm. **Habitat** Pond, lake, river, stream, dyke and canal margins, fens, marshes; to 540 m. **Dist**. Native. Frequent throughout almost all BI. (Most of Europe, but rare in S.) **Fls** Jul–Sep. **Note** The hybrid between *S. sylvatica* and *S. palustris*, *S. × ambigua*, is not infrequent, occurring in any of the parents' habitats.

Yellow Archangel
Lamiastrum galeobdolon

Erect, sparsely pubescent, stoloniferous perennial to 60 cm. **Stems** Stolons long, leafy. **Leaves** 40–70 mm, stalked. **Flowers** In dense axillary whorls; bracts leaf-like; corolla 2-lipped, *c*.20 cm, tube longer than calyx, yellow. **Habitat** Woodlands on heavy, neutral or calcareous soils; to 425 m. **Dist**. Native. Frequent. Widespread in England, Wales; naturalised in Scotland, Ireland. (Most of Europe, but rare in N and S.) **Fls** May–Jun. **Note** The widespread British plant is ssp. *montanum*, with stems that are pubescent on faces as well as angles, and ≥10 flowers per whorl. Ssp. *galeobdolon*, with stems that are hairy on angles only, and ≤8 flowers per whorl, is a rare plant of a few Lincolnshire woods and hedgerows. Ssp. *argentatum* VU. has large, conspicuous white blotches on the leaves; it is much grown in gardens and is spreading rapidly in hedgerows, roadsides and woodland edges.

MARSH WOUNDWORT

HEDGE WOUNDWORT

White Dead-nettle
Lamium album

Erect, pubescent,
rhizomatous or
stoloniferous perennial
to 60 cm. **Leaves** Blades
cordate, 30–70 mm,
stalked. **Flowers**
Bracts leaf-like; corolla
18–25 mm, white.
Habitat Hedgerows,
roadsides, waste ground,
gardens, farmyards, on
fertile soils close to habitation;
to 345 m. **Dist**.
Archaeophyte.
Common
throughout BI
except N and
W Scotland, W
Ireland. (Most of
Europe, but
rare in S.) **Fls** May–Dec.

Red Dead-nettle
Lamium purpureum

Erect, branched, pubescent annual to
45 cm. **Leaves** Blades
10–50 mm; *all leaves
and bracts stalked,
regularly crenate-serrate.*
Flowers Corolla
10–15 mm; corolla
tube longer than
calyx, with ring
of hairs near base.
Habitat Gardens,
arable fields, waste
places, road verges, on
fertile soils. **Dist**.
Archaeophyte.
Common
throughout most

of BI, but scarce in N Scotland, W Ireland.
(Most of Europe.) **Fls** Mar–Oct.

Cut-leaved Dead-nettle
Lamium hybridum

Similar to *L. purpureum*,
but *leaves and bracts deeply,
irregularly toothed*; corolla
tube with or without faint
ring of hairs towards base.
Habitat Similar to *L.
purpureum*: arable
weed on well-
drained, fertilised
soils, waste and
disturbed ground.
Dist. Archaeophyte.
Throughout BI, but
scarce in N and W.
(Most of Europe
except SE.)
Fls Mar–Oct.

Henbit Dead-nettle
Lamium amplexicaule

Sparsely pubescent, branched annual to
25 cm. **Leaves** Blades 10–25 mm, *orbicular,
rounded or cordate at base, crenate or shallowly
lobed, upper leaves sessile.* **Flowers** Sometimes
not opening; *bracts sessile,
clasping stem; calyx 5–7 mm* at
flowering, densely pubescent
with spreading white
hairs, *teeth erect or
connivent at fruiting*;
*corolla with long,
exserted tube, lower
lip <3 mm.* **Habitat**
Weed of cultivation
on light, dry soils.
Dist. Archaeophyte.
Most of BI; locally frequent
in S and E, but rare or
absent elsewhere. (All
Europe.) **Fls** Apr–Aug.

Common Hemp-nettle
Galeopsis tetrahit

Erect, branched, hispid annual to 100 cm. **Stems** With red-tipped glandular hairs below nodes. **Leaves** 2.5–10 cm. **Flowers** Calyx with prominent veins; corolla 15–20 mm, tube not much longer than calyx, *lower lip ± flat, without notch at tip, dark markings restricted to centre and base of lip, leaving clear, unmarked border.* **Habitat** Field borders, arable crops, fens, marshes, woodland clearings; to 450 m. **Dist.** Native. Throughout BI, but scarce in N Scotland, Ireland. (Most of Europe, but rare in SE.) **Fls** Jul–Sep. **Comment Bifid Hemp-nettle** *G. bifida*, grows in similar places and differs from *G. tetrahit* in the distinctly notched tip, revolute margins and more extensive dark markings of the lower lip.

G. bifida   G. tetrahit

Black Horehound
Ballota nigra

Erect, branched, pubescent perennial to 100 cm, with unpleasant smell. **Leaves** Stalked, leaf blades 2–5 cm. **Flowers** In many-flowered inflorescence with numerous whorls; bracts leaf-like; calyx funnel-shaped, with 5 broad, ± equal teeth; corolla reddish mauve, 10–15 mm, hairy. **Habitat** Hedge banks, tracksides, waste places, on well-drained, usually calcareous soils, often near habitation; to 480 m. **Dist.** Archaeophyte. Widespread in England N to Humber; scarce or absent in much of Scotland, W Wales, Ireland. (Most of Europe except extreme N.) **Fls** Jun–Oct.

Wood Sage
Teucrium scorodonia

Erect, pubescent, branched, rhizomatous perennial to 30 cm. **Leaves** 30–70 mm, stalked, wrinkled. **Flowers** *Pale yellowish green*; bracts shorter than flowers. **Habitat** Woodlands, rough grassland, hedgerows, scrub, heaths, rocky hillsides, limestone pavement, sand-dunes, shingle; to 550 m. **Dist.** Native. Widespread throughout almost all BI. (S, W and central Europe.) **Fls** Jul–Sep.

Bugle
Ajuga reptans

Erect, slightly pubescent, *stoloniferous* perennial to 30 cm. **Stems** Simple, *upper part with 2 sides hairy*. **Leaves** Basal leaves forming a rosette, stalked, *scarcely toothed*, ± glabrous, blades 4–7 cm. **Flowers** Upper bracts shorter than flowers, tinged purple; corolla blue. **Habitat** Woodland clearings, coppice, scrub, hedge banks, unimproved grassland, on damp, fertile, neutral to mildly acid soils; to 760 m. **Dist**. Native. Common throughout BI. (Most of Europe except extreme N.) **Fls** May–Jul.

Ground-ivy
Glechoma hederacea

Trailing, stoloniferous perennial to 30 cm. **Stems** Rooting at nodes, flowering branches ascending. **Leaves** *Long-stalked, leaf blades kidney-shaped*, 10–30 mm across. **Flowers** Inflorescence whorls few-flowered; corolla 15–20 mm, blue. **Habitat** Woodland rides, scrub, hedgerows, permanent grassland, waste ground, shaded gardens, on calcareous or heavy soils; to 465 m. **Dist**. Native. Common throughout BI, but rare in N Scotland, W Ireland. (All Europe.) **Fls** Mar–May.

Selfheal
Prunella vulgaris

Ascending to erect, sparsely pubescent perennial to 30 cm. **Leaves** Stalked; leaf blades 20–50 mm, ± entire. **Flowers** In dense-flowered terminal head *with pair of leaves at base; bracts different from leaves, orbicular, with long white hairs*; calyx 2-lipped; *corolla 10–14 mm*, purple or, rarely, white. **Habitat** Permanent grasslands, meadows, pastures, lawns, waste ground, on neutral or calcareous soils; to 845 m. **Dist**. Native. Ubiquitous throughout BI. (All Europe.) **Fls** Jun–Sep.

Balm
Melissa officinalis

Erect, much-branched, *lemon-scented*, sparsely pubescent perennial to 60 cm. **Leaves** Stalked; leaf blades 30–70 mm, ovate. **Flowers** In axillary whorls; *calyx 2-lipped; corolla 2-lipped*, 8–15 mm, *pale yellow becoming pinkish*. **Habitat** Road verges, banks, tips, close to habitation. **Dist**. Introduced. Widely naturalised in S Britain as garden escape. (S Europe.) **Fls** Aug–Sep.

bracts leaf-like; *calyx 2-lipped, 2 teeth of lower lip longer than 3 teeth of upper lip*; upper lip of corolla flat; *stamens shorter than corolla*. **Similar spp**. Sometimes confused with *Origanum vulgare* (p.167), with which it often grows. **Habitat** Banks, hedgerows, scrub, rough grassland, on dry calcareous soils. **Dist**. Native. Widespread in S England, getting scarcer N to central Scotland; absent from Ireland. (Most of Europe except extreme N.) **Fls** Jul–Sep.

Basil Thyme
Clinopodium acinos VU. *(R)

Small, erect, pubescent annual to 20 cm. **Leaves** Stalked, 0.5–1.5 cm, ovate, obscurely toothed. **Flowers** Inflorescence whorls 3–8-flowered; calyx tube swollen near base; *corolla 7–10 mm, violet with white markings*. **Habitat** Dry calcareous grassland, arable land, stony waste ground. **Dist**. Native. Rather local in lowland England; introduced in Ireland. (Most of Europe except extreme N; rare in S.) **Fls** May–Sep.

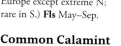
calyx

Skullcap
Scutellaria galericulata

Erect, sparsely pubescent, rhizomatous perennial to 50 cm. **Leaves** Ovate-lanceolate, 20–50 mm, *with 8–23 shallow teeth*. **Flowers** In axillary pairs; calyx 2-lipped; *corolla 2-lipped, 10–20 mm, deep blue*. **Habitat** Margins of ponds, lakes, rivers, streams, dykes and canals, fens, wet meadows, wet woods, dune slacks, avoiding acid soils; lowland to 365 m. **Dist**. Native. Throughout BI, but scarce in NW Scotland, Ireland. (All Europe.) **Fls** Jun–Sep.

Wild Basil to Calamint
▶ *Clinopodium*

calyx

Wild Basil
Clinopodium vulgare

Erect, pubescent, rhizomatous perennial to 80 cm. **Leaves** Stem leaves stalked, 1.5–5 cm. **Flowers** In *dense axillary whorls without a common stalk*, whorls >8-flowered;

Common Calamint
Clinopodium ascendens

Erect, little-branched, rhizomatous, pubescent perennial to 60 cm. **Leaves** Stalked; leaf blades 2–4 cm, *obscurely toothed*. **Flowers** *Stalks in upper inflorescence clusters usually unbranched, those of lower clusters branched once; lower 2 calyx teeth upward-curving and longer than upper 3 teeth; ring of hairs in calyx tube not*

protruding at fruiting;
corolla 10–15 mm,
lilac with darker spots
on lower lip. **Habitat**
Hedgerows, banks, scrub,
rough grassland, on dry
calcareous or sandy soils.
Dist. Native. Lowland
England, W Wales,
S Ireland. (W, S and
S-central Europe.)
Fls Jul–Sep.

COMMON CALAMINT

Wild Thyme
Thymus polytrichus

Mat-forming, aromatic
woody perennial to
*c.*7 cm. **Stems** Long, creeping, rooting
branches; *stems below inflorescence 4-angled,
with 2 opposite sides densely hairy and other
2 sides ± glabrous.* **Leaves** 4–8 mm, held
flat. **Flowers** *In rounded*, rarely somewhat
elongated, *inflorescence.* **Habitat** Close-
grazed permanent grassland, maritime and
mountain heaths, cliffs, limestone pavement,
mature sand-dunes, on dry calcareous or
acid soils. **Dist**. Native. Throughout BI, but
± confined to chalk areas in S England and
coastal in Ireland. (W Europe.)
Fls May–Aug.

calyx

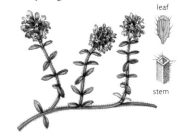

leaf

stem

Mint ▶ *Mentha*
The mints are not always easy to identify.
They are very variable and hybridise
freely, and many forms are cultivated and
frequently escape.

Corn Mint
Mentha arvensis

Erect, rhizomatous, pubescent
perennial to 60 cm. **Leaves**
Stalked, 2–6.5 cm. **Flowers**
*In well-separated axillary
whorls*; bracts leaf-like;
calyx hairy all over, 1.5–
2.5 mm, *teeth triangular,
≤0.5 mm*; corolla hairy on
outside; *stamens protruding.*
Habitat Woodland rides
and clearings, roadsides,
arable fields, damp pastures;
to 390 m. **Dist**. Native.
Frequent throughout BI.
(Most of Europe.)
Fls May–Oct.

Water Mint
Mentha aquatica

Erect, strongly aromatic,
sparsely pubescent or glab-rous
perennial to 90 cm. **Leaves**
Ovate, stalked, 2–6 cm.
Flowers *In terminal head,
c.*2 cm across, with 1–2 axillary
whorls below; pedicels and
calyx hairy; *stamens protruding.*
Habitat Wet meadows,
marshes, fens, damp
woodlands, margins of dykes,
ponds, streams and rivers;
to 455 m. **Dist**. Native.
Common throughout BI.
(All Europe except extreme
N.) **Fls** Jul–Oct.

Spear Mint
Mentha spicata

Strongly aromatic, erect,
usually glabrous, branched,
rhizomatous perennial to 90 cm. The
commonest cultivated pot-herb. **Leaves**

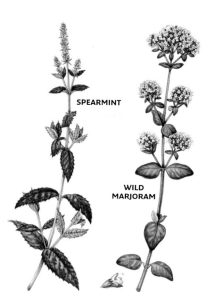

SPEARMINT

WILD MARJORAM

Gipsywort
Lycopus europaeus

Erect, sparsely pubescent, rhizomatous perennial to 100 cm. **Leaves** To 10 cm, deeply lobed. **Flowers** Small, *c.*3 mm, in separated axillary inflorescence; bracts leaf-like; corolla of 4 ± equal lobes, white with purple dots; 2 stamens, protruding. **Habitat** Marshes, fens, wet woodlands, margins of rivers, canals, dykes, ponds and lakes; to 485 m. **Dist**. Native. Common throughout BI, but rare in Scotland except W, and local in Ireland. (Most of Europe except extreme N.) **Fls** Jun–Sep.

Sessile, lanceolate, 4–9 cm, coarsely toothed, teeth pointing forward. **Flowers** *In terminal spike,* 3–6 cm. **Habitat** Damp roadsides, waste ground, as throw-out from cultivation. **Dist**. Archaeophyte (native origins unknown). Naturalised throughout BI, but scarce in N Scotland and rare in Ireland. (Naturalised throughout Europe.) **Fls** Aug–Sep.

Wild Marjoram
Origanum vulgare

Erect, sparsely pubescent, aromatic perennial to 80 cm. **Leaves** Ovate, 1.5–4.5 cm. **Flowers** In dense terminal inflorescence; calyx ± equally 5-toothed; corolla 6–8 mm, stamens protruding. **Habitat** Rough permanent grassland, hedge banks, scrub, roadsides, on dry calcareous soils; to 410 m. **Dist**. Native. Common throughout most of BI, but absent from N Scotland. (Most of Europe.) **Fls** Jul–Sep.

Wild Clary
Salvia verbenaca

Erect, pubescent perennial to 80 cm. **Leaves** Lower leaves 4–12 cm, distinctly lobed. **Flowers** In interrupted terminal spike; calyx 6–8 mm, glandular, with long white hairs; corolla eglandular, 6–10 mm, with 2 white spots at base of lower lip. **Habitat** Rough grassland, old pastures, roadsides, churchyards, dunes, on well-drained calcareous or sandy soils. **Dist**. Native. Local in England SE of line from Wash to Severn; rare and coastal in Ireland. (S and W Europe.) **Fls** May–Aug.

VERBENACEAE
Vervains
••

Vervain
Verbena officinalis

Erect, branched,
roughly hairy,
perennial to 75 cm.
Leaves Opposite;
lower leaves stalked,
deeply pinnately
lobed. **Flowers** In
elongated, slender
terminal spikes,
violet; 5 sepals; corolla
2-lipped with 5 lobes,
3.5–5 mm; 4 stamens.
Habitat Rough grassland,
scrub, roadsides, bare
ground, on well-drained
calcareous soils. **Dist**.
Archaeophyte. Declining.
Widespread in S England, S
Wales; rare further N and in Ireland. (Most
of Europe except N.) **Fls** Jul–Sep.

HIPPURIDACEAE
Mare's-tail
••

Mare's-tail
Hippuris vulgaris

Rhizomatous, submerged or
emergent aquatic perennial to
100 cm. **Stems** Emergent, stiff,
erect. **Leaves** *6–12 in a whorl;
linear, sessile, entire,* 1–7.5 cm;
leaves of submerged shoots
longer, more flaccid. **Flowers**
Greenish, solitary in axils of
shoots; *perianth absent; 1
stamen.* **Habitat** Shallow,
usually calcium-rich
lakes, ponds,
slow-moving
streams, dykes;

occasionally on mud, when smaller in all its
parts. Usually lowland but to 900 m. **Dist**.
Native. Throughout BI. (Most of Europe.)
Fls Jun–Jul.

CALLITRICHACEAE
Starworts
••

Aquatic or mud-growing annuals or
perennials. Leaves opposite, entire, linear-
ovate; flowers monoecious, axillary, usually
solitary, perianth absent, stamen 1. A very
difficult group to identify and in some cases
accurate identification is not possible without
microscopic examination of the pollen grains.
Seven British species of which *C. stagnalis* is
the most common and widespread.

Common Water-starwort
Callitriche stagnalis

Aquatic or mud-growing annual or
perennial. **Leaves** *Submerged leaves narrowly
ovate, never linear;* rosette and terrestrial
leaves broadly ovate to suborbicular.
Flowers Stamens 0.5–2 mm. **Fruits** *Ripe
fruits greyish with distinct wing (>12%
width of nutlet).* **Habitat** Shallow, still or
fast-moving clear, often calcium-rich water;
the common species of muddy woodland
rides. To 610 m. **Dist**. Native. Common
throughout BI. (Most of Europe except
extreme N.) **Fls** May–Sep.

PLANTAGINACEAE
Plantains

••••••••••••••••••••••••••••••••••

Annual or perennials with leaves in a basal
rosette. Flowers small, green or colourless,
solitary or in dense spikes on leafless stalks;
4 sepals and petals.

Greater Plantain
Plantago major

Robust, glabrous or pubescent perennial.
Leaves In a single rosette, 10–15 cm,
ovate, abruptly contracted into petiole,
petiole about as long as blade. **Flowers**
Inflorescence stalk 10–15 cm, not furrowed;
flowers *c*.3 mm, yellowish white. **Habitat**
Common plant of disturbed ground, paths,
tracks, gateways, gardens, cultivated ground
generally; tolerant of trampling. To 625 m.
Dist. Native. Ubiquitous throughout BI.
(All Europe.) **Fls** May–Aug.

Ribwort Plantain
Plantago lanceolata

Glabrous or pubescent perennial. **Leaves**
10–15 cm, narrowly ovate-lanceolate,
entire or weakly toothed, gradually tapered
into petiole. **Flowers** Inflorescence stalk
deeply furrowed, to 45 cm; spikes to
c.4 cm; flowers brownish, *c*.4 mm; corolla
lobes with prominent brown midrib.
Habitat Common on meadows, pastures,
grass heaths, verges, maritime and dune
grassland, cliffs; to 790 m. **Dist.** Ubiquitous
throughout BI. (All Europe except extreme
N.) **Fls** Apr–Aug.

Hoary Plantain
Plantago media

Pubescent perennial. **Leaves** 4–6 cm, ovate
to elliptic, 5–9-ribbed, almost sessile or
short-stalked. **Flowers** Inflorescence stalk
much longer than leaves, to 30 cm, not
furrowed; spike 2–6 cm; flowers whitish;
filaments purple. **Habitat** Permanent
meadows, pastures, rough grassland, on
well-drained, usually calcareous soils;
to 520 m. **Dist.** Native. Widespread in
England; rare in the SW, Wales, Scotland;
absent from Ireland as a native. (Most of
Europe.) **Fls** May–Aug.

waste ground, on dry sandy or gravelly soils; tolerant of trampling. **Dist**. Native. All round coasts of BI; also inland S and E England. (Coasts of Europe; also inland W Europe and Mediterranean.) **Fls** May–Jul.

Sea Plantain
Plantago maritima

Glabrous perennial. **Leaves** Narrow, entire or sparsely toothed; inflorescence stalk to 30 cm; spikes to 7 cm; in rosettes, one to many rosettes, forming tight clump. **Flowers** Brownish, *c*.3 mm; corolla lobes with broad brown midrib. **Habitat** Salt marshes, brackish grassland, sea cliffs, upland stream banks, rock ledges, scree. To 790 m. **Dist**. Native. All round coasts of BI; also inland NW Scotland, W Ireland. (Most of Europe, but rare in S.) **Fls** Jun–Aug.

HOARY PLANTAIN

Buck's-horn Plantain
Plantago coronopus

Pubescent annual to perennial. **Leaves** Very variable, linear, entire to toothed or deeply divided; in one to many rosettes. **Flowers** Inflorescence stalk to 20 cm; spikes to 4 cm; flowers brown, *c*.3 mm; stamens yellow. **Habitat** Heaths, cliffs, cliff tops, sand-dunes,

Shoreweed
Littorella uniflora

Aquatic, turf-forming, stoloniferous perennial. **Stems** Stolons far-creeping, producing rosettes at nodes. **Leaves** 2–10 cm, linear, sheathing at base, cylindrical and solid in section (cf. *Lobelia*

WILD PRIVET

dortmanna, p.186, of similar habitats).
Flowers Unisexual; 2–4 sepals and petals;
male flowers solitary, stalks as long as leaves;
female flowers one to a few, sessile at base of
male stalk; stamens long, 1–2 cm. **Habitat**
Shallow margins or exposed shores of acid
or nutrient-deficient lakes, ponds, reservoirs,
to depth of *c.*4 m; to 825 m. **Dist**. Native.
Widespread in upland Britain; rare and
declining in lowlands. (W and central
Europe.) **Fls** Jun–Aug.

OLEACEAE
Ash, privet and olive
• •

Trees or shrubs with opposite leaves that lack
stipules. Inflorescence often dense; flowers
regular; 0 or 4 small, fused sepals; 0 or 4
petals, united into tube at base; 2 stamens;
ovary superior.

Wild Privet
Ligustrum vulgare

Semi-evergreen shrub to 5 m. **Bark** Smooth.
Branches Young twigs minutely pubescent
(use a lens). **Leaves** Lanceolate, 3–6 cm.
Flowers 4–5 mm across, in thinly pubescent
inflorescence, 3–6 cm; corolla tube about as
long as lobes. **Fruits** Black berry. **Habitat**
Old hedgerows, scrub, wood borders, on
well-drained calcareous, base-rich soils;
to 490 m. **Dist**. Native. Widespread in
England, Wales to S Scotland; introduced
further N, Ireland. (S, W and central
Europe.) **Fls** Jun–Jul.

SCROPHULARIACEAE
Figworts and mulleins
• •

The Scrophulariaceae as traditionally defined
comprised a rather variable family of usually
annuals or perennials. Leaves are without
stipules, opposite or alternate, or rarely all
basal. Flowers are irregular, sometimes
weakly so, with basically 5 sepals, petals and
stamens, but there are numerous variations
on this theme; base of corolla is united into
a tube; ovary superior and 2-celled. Fruit is
a capsule. Plants with square stems and
opposite leaves, such as *Rhinanthus*, look like
members of the Lamiaceae, but the ovary is
quite different and lacks the distinct 4-celled
structure of members of that family. DNA
analysis has now confirmed that the old
Scrophulariaceae should be subdivided into
at least five separate families.

Figworts ▶ *Scrophularia*

Common Figwort
Scrophularia nodosa

Erect, glabrous perennial to 80 cm. **Stems**
Sharply 4-angled but not winged. **Leaves**
6–13 cm, ovate, acute, coarsely toothed;
petiole not winged. **Flowers** Calyx lobes
with very narrow, pale border; staminode

obovate, emarginate at tip. **Habitat** Woodland clearings, hedgerows, stream sides, shaded places, on damp, fertile soils. **Dist**. Native. Frequent throughout BI. (Most of Europe.) **Fls** Jun–Sep.

COMMON FIGWORT

Water Figwort
Scrophularia auriculata

Erect, glabrous perennial to 100 cm. **Stems** Distinctly winged. **Leaves** 6–12 cm, ovate, obtuse, bluntly toothed, sometimes with 1–2 small lobes at base; petiole winged. **Flowers** Calyx with broad, pale border; staminode ± orbicular, entire. **Habitat** Margins of rivers, dykes, canals, lakes and ponds, marshes, fens, wet woods, on fertile, neutral soils. **Dist**. Native. Frequent and widespread N to S Scotland. (W Europe, N to Netherlands.) **Fls** Jun–Sep.

Mulleins ▶ *Verbascum*
Hybrids between mulleins are frequent where the parents occur together. They are usually sterile and can be detected by rubbing the seed capsules between the fingers, which will break up into dust.

Great Mullein
Verbascum thapsus

Tall, erect biennial to 200 cm, densely clothed with soft whitish woolly hairs. **Leaves** Ovate-lanceolate, basal leaves to 45 cm, stem leaves decurrent. **Flowers** Large, 1.5–3 cm across, in dense, spike-like inflorescence; hairs on 3 upper filaments yellowish white, 2 lower filaments ± glabrous; anthers attached obliquely. **Habitat** Rough grassland, hedge banks, roadsides, waste ground, on dry sandy or calcareous soils. **Dist**. Native. Throughout almost all BI; absent from N Scotland. (All Europe except extreme N and SE.) **Fls** Jun–Aug.

Dark Mullein
Verbascum nigrum

Tall, erect, pubescent biennial to 120 cm. **Stems** Angled. **Leaves** Dark green above, pale beneath; basal leaves long-stalked. **Flowers** 12–22 mm across, 5–10 in each bract; all filaments with purple hairs; anthers transversely attached. **Habitat** Rough permanent grassland, road verges, banks, on dry calcareous soils. **Dist**. Native. Scattered throughout lowland England. (Most of Europe except N and extreme S.) **Fls** Jun–Oct.

PHRYMACEAE
Monkeyflowers
∙∙∙

Monkeyflower
Mimulus guttatus

Decumbent to erect perennial, to 75 cm.
Stems Glabrous below, glandular-pubescent
above. **Leaves** 1–7 cm, irregularly toothed.
Flowers Pedicels 1.5–3 cm; calyx becoming
inflated in fruit, upper tooth much longer
than rest; corolla 2.5–4.5 cm, yellow with
small red spots, base of lower lip with 2
swellings that almost close entrance to
throat. **Habitat** Wet marshy ground, edges
of rivers, streams and lakes, open woods.
Dist. Introduced (native of W North
America). Naturalised throughout BI, but
scarce in Ireland. (Naturalised throughout
much of Europe.) **Fls** Jul–Sep.

VERONICACEAE
Foxgloves and speedwells
∙∙∙

Foxglove
Digitalis purpurea

Tall, handsome, erect biennial to 150 cm,
with softly hairy stems, leaves and flower
stalks. Whole plant is
poisonous. **Leaves** To 30 cm.
Flowers Pinkish purple,
tubular, to 50 mm, in
a raceme. **Dist**. Native.
Common throughout BI.
Habitat Woodland clearings,
hedge banks, open heathland,
rocky hillsides, on acid, well-
drained soils. (W Europe,
N to central Norway.)
Fls Jun–Sep.

Round-leaved Fluellen
Kickxia spuria

Prostrate, trailing, summer-germinating
annual. Whole plant pubescent, with both
glandular and non-glandular hairs. **Stems**
To 50 cm. **Leaves** With short stalks, ovate
with rounded base. **Flowers** To 11 mm,
yellow, upper lip purple; *stalks with long
hairs*. **Habitat** Almost exclusively on
late-summer stubble fields on light soils.
Dist. Archaeophyte. Decreasing. Widely
distributed in S Britain. (Most of Europe
and Mediterranean.) **Fls** Jul–Oct.

Sharp-leaved Fluellen
Kickxia elatine *(R)

Prostrate, trailing, summer-germinating annual. Similar to *K. spuria*, but more slender, less hairy and hardly glandular. **Leaves** *Hastate.* **Flowers** To 11 mm, yellow, upper lip purple; *stalks glabrous.* **Habitat** Similar to *K. spuria.* **Dist**. Archaeophyte. Decreasing. Similar distribution to *K. spuria.* (Most of Europe and Mediterranean.) **Fls** Jul–Oct.

Toadflaxes ▶ *Linaria*

Common Toadflax
Linaria vulgaris

Erect, branched, glabrous grey-green perennial to 80 cm. **Leaves** Linear-lanceolate, to 8 cm. **Flowers** To 25 mm, in a raceme; yellow, base of lower petal orange; spur almost as long as corolla. **Habitat** Frequent plant of rough grassland, roadsides, hedge banks, waste ground, on well-drained calcareous or sandy soils. **Dist**. Native. Widely distributed in England, Wales; rare in Scotland, Ireland. (Most of Europe except extreme N and parts of Mediterranean.) **Fls** Jun–Oct.

Speedwells ▶ *Veronica*
Large genus of annuals and perennials that can present identification problems. Characterised by opposite leaves, and by blue flowers (rarely pink or white) with 4 sepals, 4 petals, 2 stamens; the upper petal is the largest, the lower the smallest.

Germander Speedwell
Veronica chamaedrys

Pubescent, stoloniferous perennial to 40 cm. **Stems** Prostrate, rooting at nodes, with 2 lines of long white hairs on opposite sides. **Leaves** 1–2.5 cm, ± sessile. **Flowers** In axillary, long-stalked, 10–20-flowered racemes; corolla *c.*10 mm across, sky-blue with white eye. **Fruits** Capsule, shorter than calyx. **Habitat** Familiar plant of hedge banks, verges, wood borders, rough grassland, upland scree, on well-drained or calcareous soils; to 750 m. **Dist**. Native. Throughout BI. (All Europe except extreme N.) **Fls** Mar–Jul.

Wood Speedwell
Veronica montana

Similar to *V. chamaedrys*, but stems hairy all round; leaves distinctly stalked, 5–15 mm;

racemes 2–5-flowered; bracts much shorter than pedicels; corolla *c.*7 mm across, lilac-blue. **Habitat** Well established in damp woodlands, coppice, hedge banks, on loamy, sandy soils; to 435 m. **Dist.** Native. Throughout BI, but rare in N Scotland. (W, central and S Europe.) **Fls** Apr–Jul.

Heath Speedwell
Veronica officinalis

Pubescent, mat-forming, creeping perennial to 40 cm. **Stems** Rooting at nodes, hairy all round. **Leaves** 2–3 cm, at least the lowest shortly stalked. **Flowers** In long-stalked, many-flowered racemes, usually emerging from both of a pair of leaves; bracts *c.*2× as long as pedicels; corolla *c.*6 mm across, lilac. **Fruits** Capsule, longer than calyx.

Habitat Grass heaths, woodland clearings, commons, pastures, often on ant-hills; acid, well-drained soils. To 880 m. **Dist.** Native. Common throughout BI. (All Europe.) **Fls** May–Aug.

Thyme-leaved Speedwell
Veronica serpyllifolia

Creeping perennial, rooting at nodes, to 30 cm. **Stems** Flowering stems ascending. **Leaves** 1–2 cm, ± entire, glabrous. **Flowers** In terminal, many-flowered racemes; bracts longer than pedicels; corolla 5–10 mm across, white or pale blue; style about as long as calyx. **Fruits** Capsule, about as long as calyx. **Dist.** Native. Widespread and common throughout BI to 825 m. **Habitat** Short grassland, commons, woodland rides, rock ledges, weed of gardens, on damp acid soils. (All Europe.) **Fls** Mar–Oct. **Note** The common plant is ssp. *serpyllifolia.* Ssp. *humifusa*, with more orbicular leaves, glandular-pubescent racemes and larger, bright blue flowers, 7–10 mm across, is a local plant of montane rock ledges and flushes to 1160 m in the Scottish Highlands and, rarely, N England and N Wales.

Brooklime
Veronica beccabunga

Creeping, ascending, glabrous perennial to 60 cm. **Leaves** Rather fleshy, ovate, short-stalked. **Flowers** In opposite, 10–20-flowered racemes; bracts as long as or shorter than pedicels; corolla 10 cm across, a deep, bright blue. **Habitat** Shallow margins of ponds, rivers, streams and dykes, wet meadows, marshes, woodland rides; to 845 m. **Dist.** Native. Frequent throughout BI. (Most of Europe except extreme N.) **Fls** May–Sep.

BROOKLIME

marshy meadows; lowland to 380 m. **Dist**. Native. Throughout BI; frequent in S, local further N. (Most of Europe except extreme N.) **Fls** Jun–Aug.

Pink Water-speedwell
Veronica catenata

Similar to *V. anagallis-aquatica*, but stems tinged purplish, leaves narrower, racemes more spreading, bracts longer than pedicels, corolla pink, pedicels spreading after flowering. **Habitat** Similar to *V. anagallis-aquatica*, with which it often grows and hybridises. **Dist**. Native. Throughout BI.

Blue Water-speedwell
Veronica anagallis-aquatica

Creeping, ascending, glabrous annual to 30 cm. **Leaves** Sessile, 5–12 cm, ovate-lanceolate. **Flowers** In opposite, 10–50-flowered racemes; bracts as long as or shorter than pedicels; corolla 5–6 mm across, pale blue; pedicels ascending after flowering. **Habitat** Shallow margins of pools, drainage ditches, rivers and streams,

Frequent in S Britain but rare and coastal in N and W; widespread in Ireland. (Most of Europe except N.) **Fls** Jun–Aug.

Marsh Speedwell
Veronica scutellata

Creeping, ascending, glabrous, sparsely branched perennial to 50 cm. **Leaves** Sessile, yellowish green, 2–4 cm, linear-lanceolate. **Flowers** In alternate, few-flowered racemes; corolla 5–8 mm across, whitish or lilac with dark lines. **Habitat** Shallow margins of ponds, pools, ditches and dykes, wet meadows, hillside flushes, on acid, calcium-poor soils; to 780 m. **Dist.** Native. Throughout BI; commoner in N and W. (Most of Europe, but rare in S.) **Fls** Jun–Aug.

Wall Speedwell
Veronica arvensis

Small, erect, pubescent annual to 25 cm. **Leaves** To 15 mm, coarsely and bluntly toothed. **Flowers** ± sessile, small, 2–3 mm across, in long racemes; bracts entire, longer than flowers; corolla shorter than calyx, deep blue. **Fruits** Capsule, about as long as broad. **Habitat** Dry, open areas, including arable fields, open grassland (ant-hills), sand-dunes, walls, banks, paths; to 820 m. **Dist.** Native. Common throughout BI. (All Europe.) **Fls** Mar–Oct.

Green Field-speedwell
Veronica agrestis

Prostrate to ascending, pubescent annual to 30 cm. **Leaves** Ovate. **Flowers** Solitary, in leaf axils; *corolla 4–8 mm across, pale blue with lower petal white.* **Fruits** Capsule, *with spreading glandular hairs only, lobes diverging*

at narrow angle. **Habitat** Arable fields, cultivated land, on well-drained sandy soils; to 410 m. **Dist.** Archaeophyte. Declining significantly. Throughout BI, but scarce in Scotland, Ireland. (Most of Europe except extreme N and SE.) **Fls** Year-round.

Grey Field-speedwell
Veronica polita

Branched, procumbent, pubescent annual to 40 cm. Similar to *V. agrestis*, but lower leaves broader than long; *calyx lobes ovate, overlapping near base; flowers bright blue; capsule with short, crisped, glandless hairs and few spreading, glandular hairs.* **Habitat** Arable fields, cultivated ground, gardens, on light sandy or calcareous soils. **Dist.**

Introduced. Throughout BI; frequent in central and S England, but scarce and declining elsewhere. (Most of Europe except extreme N.) **Fls** Year-round.

Common Field-speedwell
Veronica persica

Branched, decumbent, pubescent annual to 40 cm. **Leaves** 1–3 cm, ovate, strongly toothed. **Flowers** Solitary, axillary, *8–12 mm across, bright blue, lower petal almost white*; pedicels longer than leaves. **Fruits** *Lobes of capsule divergent, c.2× as broad as long.* **Habitat** Arable fields, gardens, waste ground, on fertile soils.

Dist. Introduced. Common throughout BI, becoming scarce in N Scotland. (Native of Caucasus and Iran; naturalised throughout Europe.) **Fls** Year-round.

Slender Speedwell
Veronica filiformis

Mat-forming, pubescent perennial with numerous creeping stems, to 50 cm. **Leaves** c.*5 mm, orbicular to kidney-shaped*, bluntly toothed, stalks short. **Flowers** *Pedicels slender, much longer than leaves; corolla*

8–15 mm across, purplish blue. **Fruits** Rare. **Habitat** Lawns, churchyards, parks, stream sides; lowland to 450 m. **Dist**. Introduced. Common, increasing. Throughout BI, but scarce in N Scotland, S Ireland. (Native of N Turkey and Caucasus; naturalised in N, W and central Europe.) **Fls** Apr–Jun.

Ivy-leaved Speedwell
Veronica hederifolia

Prostrate, pubescent annual to 60 cm. **Leaves** *Kidney-shaped, with 1–3 large teeth or lobes*, light green, rather thick. **Flowers** Pedicels shorter than leaves; sepals ovate, cordate at base; corolla shorter than calyx. **Fruits** *Glabrous capsule.* **Habitat** Weed of cultivation, arable fields, gardens, waste

ground; to 380 m. **Dist**. Archaeophyte. Throughout BI, but rare in N Scotland, W Ireland. (Most of Europe except extreme N.) **Fls** Apr–May. **Note** Has 2 subspecies that are not always possible to separate. Ssp. *hederifolia* has apical leaf lobe that is wider than long; pedicel 3–4× as long as calyx; corolla mostly ≥6 mm across, whitish blue; and blue anthers. Ssp. *lucorum* has apical leaf lobe that is longer than wide; pedicel 3.5–7× as long as calyx; corolla ≤6 mm across, whitish to pale lilac; and white to pale blue anthers. It also occurs in more shaded habitats than ssp. *hederifolia*, including woodland rides and hedgerows.

OROBANCHACEAE

Yellow-rattle
Rhinanthus minor

Erect, pubescent, simple or branched annual to 50 cm. **Flowers** In terminal leafy spike; calyx mid-green, strongly inflated in fruit; corolla 12–15 mm, dorsal edge of tube straight, lower lip turned down, teeth of upper lip violet, broader than long. **Habitat** Partial parasite of nutrient-poor calcareous grassland, hay meadows, fens, montane grassland; to 1065 m. **Dist**. Native. Frequent throughout BI. (Most of Europe except Mediterranean.) **Fls** May–Sep. **Note** Extremely variable and variously divided into a number of subspecies based on branching, leaf arrangement and hairiness, and distinguished by habitat and flowering time.

Eyebrights ▶ *Euphrasia*

Eyebrights are all annual partial parasites on the roots of various grassland perennials. All species show great variability and most hybridise freely. However, they do have distinct geographical distributions and habitat preferences, such as between acid and calcareous soils. Eyebrights are extremely difficult to identify. There are about 18 British species of which *E. nemorosa* is the most common and widespread.

Eyebright
Euphrasia nemorosa

A rather variable species, 10–20 cm. **Leaves** Lower ones longer than internodes, upper ones shorter than internodes. **Flowers** 5–7.5 mm. **Fruit** Capsule 5–6 mm, about as long as calyx teeth. **Habitat** Grassy heaths, commons, chalk downs, dunes, woodland rides. **Dist.** Widespread throughout most of BI, but less frequent in N Scotland. (N, central and W Europe.) **Fls** Jul–Sep.

Common Cow-wheat
Melampyrum pratense

Erect, usually glabrous, branched annual to 60 cm. **Leaves** 1.5–10 cm, ± sessile, lanceolate. **Flowers** Axillary, in pairs, held horizontal; bracts leaf-like; corolla 11–17 mm, *lower lip straight, corolla tube longer than calyx*. **Habitat** Heathy woodlands, moorlands, on acid soils; scrub, hedgerows, woodlands, on calcareous soils. **Dist**. Native. Widespread throughout most of BI, especially N and W. (Most of Europe.) **Fls** May–Oct.

COMMON COW-WHEAT

Red Bartsia
Odontites vernus

Erect, pubescent, usually branched, purple-tinted annual to 50 cm. Very variable, with a number of named subspecies. **Flowers** In terminal inflorescence; bracts leaf-like; calyx 4-toothed; corolla 8–10 mm, 2-lipped. **Habitat** Rough grassland, tracksides, arable fields, waste ground, sandy shores, salt marshes. **Dist**. Native. Common throughout BI. (Most of Europe.) **Fls** Jun–Aug.

Alpine Bartsia
Bartsia alpina

Erect, pubescent, rhizomatous, unbranched perennial to 20 cm. **Leaves** 1–2 cm. **Flowers** *In short, glandular inflorescence; bracts purplish; corolla 20 mm*, upper lip much longer than lower. **Habitat**

Damp upland pastures, seepage lines, rock ledges, on base-rich soils; calcareous mires. To 950 m. **Dist**. Native. Very rare. Central Scotland, N England. (N Europe, mts of S Europe.) **Fls** Jun–Aug.

Yellow Bartsia
Parentucellia viscosa

Erect, unbranched annual to 50 cm, *covered by sticky glandular hairs*. **Flowers** Axillary; bracts leaf-like; corolla 16–24 mm, lower lip much longer than upper. **Habitat** Damp sandy grassland, dune slacks, heath pasture; casual elsewhere. **Dist**. Native. S and SW England, S Wales, N and S Ireland. (S and W Europe.) **Fls** Jun–Oct.

Lousewort
Pedicularis sylvatica

Decumbent to erect, ± glabrous, much-branched perennial to 25 cm. **Flowers** In terminal, 3–10-flowered inflorescence; bracts leaf-like; *calyx glabrous*; corolla 2–2.4 cm, *upper lip with 2 teeth,* one on each side near tip. **Habitat** Damp acid grassland, heath, moors, drier parts of bogs; to 915 m. **Dist**. Native. Throughout BI, but rare in East Anglia. (W and central Europe.) **Fls** Apr–Sep.

Marsh Lousewort/Red-rattle
Pedicularis palustris

Erect, single-stemmed,
branching, ± glabrous
annual to 60 cm.
Similar to *P. sylvatica*,
but taller, *calyx
pubescent, upper lip
of corolla with 4
teeth*. **Habitat**
Fens, marshes,
wet meadows,
valley bogs,
hillside flushes;
to 550 m.
Dist. Native.
Widespread
in W and N
Britain, Ireland;
rare elsewhere. (Most of
Europe.) **Fls** May–Sep.

Broomrapes ▶ *Orobanche*
Root parasites lacking chlorophyll.
Erect perennials; leaves scale-
like, alternate. Flowers
zygomorphic, in racemes
or spikes; calyx 4-lobed or
2-lipped; corolla 2-lipped;
4 stamens.

Knapweed Broomrape/Tall Broomrape
Orobanche elatior

Parasitic on Greater
Knapweed *Centaurea
scabiosa* (p.201).
Stems Flowering stems
to 70 cm. **Flowers**
Numerous, in dense spikes;
bracts as long as flowers;
*calyx lobes fused beneath
corolla*; corolla 18–25 mm,
pale yellow, tinged purple,

glandular-pubescent, *upper lip finely toothed;
stamens attached well above base of corolla
tube, lower part of filaments hairy; stigmas
yellow*. **Habitat** Chalk and limestone
grassland, road verges. **Dist**. Native. Local,
declining. S and E England. (All Europe
except N and extreme S.) **Fls** Jun–Jul.

Ivy Broomrape
Orobanche hederae *(NI)

Parasitic on Ivy *Hedera helix*.
Stems Flowering stems
reddish or purple, to 60 cm.
Flowers Rather few; bracts as
long as or longer than flowers;
*corolla constricted towards tip,
12–20 mm, cream, veined
purple, lower lip with acute
lobes*; stamens attached above
base of corolla tube, *lower part
of filaments almost glabrous;
stigmas yellow*. **Habitat** Coastal
cliffs, rocky woodland, hedge
banks. **Dist**. Native. Local.
Coastal areas of S and SW England,
Wales; scattered in Ireland. (W,
S and SW Europe.)
Fls Jun–Jul.

Common Broomrape
Orobanche minor

Very variable on a wide
variety of hosts, especially
Fabaceae and Asteraceae;
ssp. *maritima* parasitic on
Sea Carrot *Daucus carota*
ssp. *gummifer* (p.149).
Stems Flowering stems
yellowish tinged with red, to
60 cm. **Flowers** Bracts about
as long as flowers; corolla
10–16 mm, *upper edge of
corolla tube slightly and ±
regularly curved; stamens*

attached 2–3 mm above base of corolla tube, *filaments ± glabrous throughout*; stigmas purple. **Habitat** Rough grassland, cultivated land, usually on dry soils; var. *maritima* on sand-dunes, cliffs, of S coast. **Dist.** Native. Frequent in England, Wales; casual elsewhere. (W, S and S-central Europe.) **Fls** Jun–Sep.

LENTIBULARIACEAE
Bladderworts and butterworts
••

Small family of insectivorous aquatic or bog plants related to Scrophulariaceae. Flowers solitary or in a raceme; calyx 5-lobed or 2-lipped; corolla 2-lipped and spurred; 2 stamens. Fruits are a capsule.

Bladderworts ► *Utricularia*
Rootless aquatics, free-floating or with lower part of stems in bottom mud. Difficult to name; accurate identification often relies on microscopic examination of bladders, especially as some species rarely flower. The following notes rely on examination of fresh plants; the leaf characters need a strong lens.

Greater Bladderwort, Bladderwort
Utricularia vulgaris, Utricularia australis

Free-floating, to 100 cm. **Stems and Leaves** All of one sort. **Flowers** Yellow, *lower lip*

**GREATER
BLADDERWORT**

with strongly reflexed margins; flower stalks 8–15 mm, *not elongating after flowering.* **Habitat** Ponds, ditches, lakes, grazing marshes, in rather infertile base-rich waters. **Dist.** Native. Very local, declining. Throughout BI, especially East Anglia, Somerset Levels, N Ireland. (Most of Europe, but rare in S.) **Fls** Jul–Aug. **Note** *U. australis* similar but stems to 60 cm; *lower lip of flowers flat or with upturned margins*; flower stalks 8–15 mm at flowering, *elongating to 10–30 mm after*. In still, usually acid but also calcareous waters; lowland to 335 m. Dist. and Fls as *U. vulgaris* but scattered throughout BI. (Most of Europe except extreme N.)

BLADDERWORT

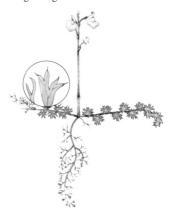

Lesser Bladderwort
Utricularia minor

Stems Slender, to 40 cm, of 2 kinds: free-floating with green leaves and few bladders;

colourless, free-floating or ± buried in substratum, with bladders on reduced leaves. **Leaves** Segments entire, without bristles. **Flowers** Flowering stems 4–15 cm, 2–6-flowered; corolla 6–8 mm, pale yellow; spur very short, 1–2 mm, blunt. **Habitat** Acid bog pools, peat cuttings, ditches; to 650 m. **Dist.** Native. Throughout BI: widespread in N and W; rare and declining elsewhere. (Most of Europe, but rare in Mediterranean.) **Fls** Jun–Sep.

Butterworts ▶ *Pinguicula*
Perennial insectivorous plants. Whole plant covered by sticky glands. Leaves in basal rosette, entire, margins inrolled. Flowering stems leafless; flowers solitary; corolla 2-lipped, spurred.

Common Butterwort
Pinguicula vulgaris

Leaves 2–8 cm, yellow-green. **Flowers** Flowering stems 5–15 cm; corolla 14–22 mm including spur, spur 4–7 mm, *lobes of lower lip longer than broad, divergent.* **Habitat** Bare, wet acid peat, wet rocks, on wet heaths, moorland, acid bogs, flushes, moss-rich fens. **Dist.** Native. Widespread in N and W BI; rare and declining elsewhere. (N, W and central Europe.) **Fls** May–Jul.

Pale Butterwort
Pinguicula lusitanica

Leaves 1–2 cm, yellowish purple. **Flowers** Flowering stems 3–15 cm; *flowers pale lilac*; corolla 7–11 mm including spur, spur 2–4 mm, lower lip notched. **Habitat** Short, grazed turf,

damp, bare peat, wet heaths, wet moorland flushes, drainage ditches. **Dist.** Native. Widespread in S and SW England, W Scotland, Ireland; rare in SW Wales. (W Europe.) **Fls** Jun–Oct.

CAMPANULACEAE
Bellflowers
••

Annual or perennial plants, often showy and frequently with blue or purple flowers. Leaves are alternate, simple and without stipules. Flowers are solitary, or arranged in open inflorescences, or in spherical heads or spikes; 5 sepals and petals, fused into a tube at the base; 5 stamens attached to the receptacle, and with their anthers often fused into a ring surrounding the style; ovary inferior. Fruit is usually a capsule.

Bellflowers ▶ *Campanula*

Spreading Bellflower
Campanula patula EN.

Erect, coarsely pubescent biennial to 60 cm. **Leaves** Lower *leaf blades ovate, decurrent down petiole*; stem leaves narrow, sessile. **Flowers** Erect, *in much-branched inflorescence*, stalks slender; *bracteoles attached at middle of flower stalks*; corolla 15–20 mm, *broadly funnel-shaped,* lobed to halfway to base, *lobes spreading.* **Habitat** Open woodland, rock outcrops, hedge banks, on well-drained sandy soils. **Dist.** Native. Local, declining. Welsh border counties. (Most of Europe except S.) **Fls** Jul–Sep.

Clustered Bellflower
Campanula glomerata

Erect, pubescent perennial to 20(–50) cm. **Leaves** *Basal leaves long-stalked, blade 2–4 cm, ovate, rounded at base; stem leaves sessile, ± clasping stem.* **Flowers** *Erect, sessile, in a terminal head; corolla 15–20 mm,* bright purplish blue, lobes almost as long as tube. **Habitat** Grazed or rough chalk grassland, open scrub, limestone cliffs, dunes; to 355 m. **Dist**. Native. Throughout England, local but widespread in S; rare in Wales, Scotland; absent from Ireland. (Most of Europe except extreme S and N.) **Fls** May–Sep.

Harebell
Campanula rotundifolia

Slender, glabrous, stoloniferous perennial to 40 cm. **Leaves** *Basal leaves orbicular, long-stalked, cordate; stem leaves linear, sessile.* **Flowers** *Nodding,* in usually branched inflorescence, buds erect; calyx lobes linear, spreading; corolla *c.*12–20 mm, lobes *c.* ½ as long as tube; 3 stigmas. **Habitat** Grassy hillsides, heaths, downs, dunes, cliffs, hedge banks, on dry acid or calcareous soils; to 1160 m. **Dist**. Native. Common throughout BI, but rare in SW England and in Ireland except for W. (Most of Europe, but rare in S.) **Fls** Jul–Sep.

Nettle-leaved Bellflower
Campanula trachelium *(R)

Tall, erect, unbranched, hispid perennial to 100 cm. **Stems** *Sharply angled.* **Leaves** *Basal leaves cordate; lower and middle stem leaves stalked*, blade *c.*10 cm, cordate, coarsely toothed. **Flowers** In leafy inflorescence with short branches; *corolla* blue-purple, *25–35 mm,* lobes shorter than tube. **Habitat** Wood margins, scrub, hedgerows, shaded banks, on dry calcareous soils; to 320 m. **Dist**. Native. England N to Humber; rare in SW England, Wales, Ireland. (Most of Europe except N.) **Fls** Jul–Sep.

Giant Bellflower
Campanula latifolia

Tall, handsome, softly pubescent perennial to 120 cm. **Stems** *Bluntly angled.* **Leaves** *Basal leaves narrowing to petiole; lower and middle stem leaves sessile.* **Flowers** *Corolla blue-purple, 40–55 cm,* lobes shorter than tube. **Habitat** Woods, shaded hedge banks, on moist calcareous or mildly acid soils; to 390 m. **Dist**. Native. Central England N to central Scotland; naturalised elsewhere. (Most of Europe except extreme N; rare in SW and Mediterranean.) **Fls** Jul–Aug.

Venus's-looking-glass
Legousia hybrida

Erect, hispid annual to 30 cm. **Leaves** 10–30 mm, sessile, *oblong, margins undulate*. **Flowers** Erect, in terminal few-flowered inflorescence; *calyx teeth elliptic-lanceolate*, c.2× *as long as corolla*; c.½ *as long as ovary; corolla 8–15 mm across*. **Fruits** *Capsule, 15–30 mm*. **Habitat** Arable fields on light sandy or calcareous soils. **Dist.** Archaeophyte. Local, declining. England, SE of line from Humber to Severn. (W and S Europe.) **Fls** May–Aug.

IVY-LEAVED BELLFLOWER

Ivy-leaved Bellflower
Wahlenbergia hederacea

Slender, glabrous, creeping perennial to 30 cm. **Leaves** *All stalked*, blades 5–10 mm, ± *orbicular, angled, cordate*. **Flowers** Solitary, nodding; peduncles longer than petioles; corolla pale blue, 6–10 mm, bell-shaped. **Habitat** Wet grassy flushes, margins of springs and streams, wet woodland rides, on acid soils; to 485 m. **Dist.** Native. SW England, Wales; rare elsewhere. (W Europe.) **Fls** Jul–Aug.

Round-headed Rampion
Phyteuma orbiculare

Erect, glabrous or sparsely pubescent perennial to 50 cm. **Leaves** Basal leaves long-stalked, blade lanceolate to ovate; stem leaves few, sessile, narrow. **Flowers** In globose inflorescence, 1–2 cm across; corolla blue-violet, 5–8 mm, *curved in bud*. **Habitat** Species-rich chalk grassland on warm, dry slopes. **Dist.** Native. Very local. S England. (W, central and E Europe.) **Fls** Jul–Aug.

Sheep's-bit
Jasione montana

Decumbent, *pubescent*, simple or branched biennial to 50 cm. **Leaves** Linear-oblong, undulate, basal leaves stalked, stem leaves sessile. **Flowers** In terminal globose head, 5–35 mm across; corolla blue, *c*.5 mm, *straight in bud, split nearly to base when open*; anthers fused; 2 stigmas, short.

SHEEP'S-BIT

Habitat Heaths, rough grassland, rocky hillsides, sea cliffs, dunes, walls, hedge banks, maritime heaths, on acid soils. **Dist.** Native. Widespread in W Britain except NW Scotland, scattered elsewhere; mostly coastal in Ireland. (Most of Europe except extreme N.) **Fls** May–Aug.

Water Lobelia
Lobelia dortmanna

Glabrous, erect, aquatic perennial to 60 cm. **Stems** Smooth, leafless. **Leaves** In submerged basal rosette, 2–4 cm, linear, entire. **Flowers** 12–20 mm, 3–10 in lax, elongated inflorescence, nodding, pale lilac. **Habitat** Shallow water of acid, nutrient-deficient mountain tarns, lakes; to 745 m. **Dist.** Native. Widespread and frequent in upland areas of Scotland, Lake District, Wales, W Ireland. (N and N-central Europe.) **Fls** Jul–Aug. **Note** Non-flowering plants can be distinguished from other smooth-leaved submerged aquatics of upland lakes by the compressed leaves, which have 2 hollow tubes in section. The familiar annual garden lobelia is *Lobelia erinus*.

RUBIACEAE
Bedstraws
••••••••••••••••••••••••••••••••••••••

Distinctive family, easily recognised by whorls of 4 or more 'leaves' arranged regularly along stem. In fact, only 2 are leaves, the rest leaf-like stipules. Annual, perennial or evergreen climbers, with small flowers in branched terminal or axillary inflorescences. Sepals minute or absent; 4–5 petals, united into tube at base; 4–5 stamens; ovary inferior. Fruits various, usually comprising 2 fused nutlets or a berry.

Field Madder
Sherardia arvensis

Prostrate, glabrous annual to 40 cm. **Stems** Spreading. **Leaves** 4–6 (including stipules) per whorl, margins with forward-pointing prickles. **Flowers** 3 mm across, in dense clusters with ring of 8–10 leaf-like bracts below; corolla 4–5 mm, mauve-lilac, funnel-shaped, tube *c.*2× as long as lobes. **Habitat** Arable fields, pathsides, sand-dunes, waste ground, on well-drained acid or calcareous soils; to 365 m. **Dist.** Native. Throughout BI, becoming scarce in N Scotland. (All Europe.) **Fls** May–Oct.

Squinancywort
Asperula cynanchica

Slender, prostrate to ascending, much-branched, glabrous perennial to 40 cm. **Leaves** Basal leaves soon withering; 4 upper leaves per whorl, linear, glabrous, unequal. **Flowers** 3–4 mm across, in few-flowered inflorescence; corolla pale pink, funnel-shaped, lobes shorter than tube. **Habitat** Short, grazed turf, dry calcareous grassland, dunes; to 305 m. **Dist**. Native. Frequent on calcareous soils of lowland England N to Lake District, S Wales, W Ireland. (Most of Europe except N.) **Fls** Jun–Jul.

Bedstraws ▶ *Galium*

Woodruff
Galium odoratum

Rhizomatous perennial to 45 cm, smelling of hay when dried. **Stems** Erect, unbranched, ± glabrous. **Leaves** Elliptical, 6–9 per whorl, upper leaves 2.5–4 cm. **Flowers** *c*.6 mm across, in umbel-like inflorescence; corolla pure white, funnel-shaped, tube about as long as lobes. **Fruits** With hooked bristles. **Habitat** Deciduous

woodlands, coppice, hedge banks, on damp calcareous or base-rich soils; to 640 m. **Dist**. Native. Throughout BI. (Most of Europe, but rare in Mediterranean.) **Fls** May–Jun.

Northern Bedstraw
Galium boreale

Erect, rhizomatous perennial to 45 cm. **Stems** Ascending. **Leaves** Lanceolate-elliptic, 1–4 cm, 3-veined, 4 per whorl. **Flowers** 3 mm across, in pyramidal inflorescence. **Fruits** With hooked bristles. **Habitat** Rough montane grassland, rocky slopes, scree, cliffs, stream sides, on calcareous or base-rich soils; to 1065 m. Also river shingle, dunes. **Dist**. Native. N Britain, Wales, Ireland. (Most of Europe, but rare in Mediterranean.) **Fls** Jul–Aug.

Fen Bedstraw
Galium uliginosum

Scrambling perennial to 60 cm. **Stems** 4-angled, angles rough, with downward-directed prickles. **Leaves** 5–10 mm, 6–8 per whorl, linear-lanceolate, mucronate, margins with backward-directed prickles. **Flowers** 2.5–3 mm across, in narrow inflorescence. **Habitat** Calcareous or base-rich marshes, fens; to 750 m. **Dist**. Native. Throughout BI except NW Scotland, S Ireland. (Most of Europe except extreme N.) **Fls** Jul–Aug.

Common Marsh-bedstraw
Galium palustre

Ascending or scrambling perennial to 100 cm. Very variable (*see* 'Note'). **Stems** 4-angled. **Leaves** 4–6 per whorl, linear-oblong to elliptic; tip blunt, not mucronate. **Flowers** 3–4.5 mm across, in spreading inflorescence; pedicels spreading after flowering. **Fruits** Smooth. **Habitat** Marshes, fens, wet woodlands, edges of ponds, lakes, streams and ditches; to 825 m. **Dist**. Native. Common throughout BI. (Almost all Europe.) **Fls** Jun–Jul. **Note** The 2 most widespread forms are ssp. *palustre*, with most leaves 4–10 mm, flowers 2–3.5 mm across, fruits 1.2–1.5 mm long; and ssp. *elongatum*, with leaves 12–30 mm, flowers 3.5–5.5 mm across, fruits 2.5–3.5 mm long.

Hedge Bedstraw
Galium album

Decumbent to erect, glabrous or pubescent, stoloniferous perennial to 120 cm. Very variable, with several named subspecies. **Stems** 4-angled. **Leaves** 8–25 mm, 5–8 per whorl, linear-obovate with apical point, margins with forward-directed prickles. **Flowers** 2–5 mm across. **Fruits** Smooth to wrinkled. **Habitat** Hedgerows, scrub, wood margins, rough grassland, road verges, waste ground; to 845 m. **Dist**. Native. Common throughout BI, but scarce in N Scotland; introduced in Ireland. (All Europe.) **Fls** Jun–Jul.

Lady's Bedstraw
Galium verum

Decumbent to erect, sparsely pubescent, stoloniferous perennial to 100 cm. **Leaves** 6–25 mm, linear, dark green, with revolute margins, 8–12 per whorl. **Flowers** 2–4 mm across, bright yellow. **Fruits** Smooth. **Habitat** Dry calcareous grassland, hay meadows, hedge banks, dunes, machair, cliff tops, verges; to 780 m. **Dist**. Native. Common throughout BI. (Most of Europe.) **Fls** Jul–Aug. **Note** Dwarf prostrate plants with leaves that are longer than internodes, frequent on dunes and cliff tops, are var. *maritimum*. The hybrid with *G. mollugo*, *G. × pomeranicum*, intermediate with pale yellow flowers, is frequent where the parents grow together.

Heath Bedstraw
Galium saxatile

Prostrate, mat-forming perennial to 20 cm. **Stems** Numerous non-flowering branches and much-branched ascending flowering shoots. **Leaves** 7–10 mm, 6–8 per whorl, *obovate,* mucronate, *margins with forward-*

Habitat Short, grazed limestone grassland, scree, limestone pavement; to 975 m. **Dist**. Native. Restricted to areas of hard limestone upland or basic igneous rocks. S Wales to Orkney, W Ireland. (NW Europe.) **Fls** Jun–Jul. **Note** Grows together with *G. saxatile* in some upland grasslands, when it can be distinguished by the marginal leaf prickles.

Wall Bedstraw
Galium parisiense VU.

Slender, almost prostrate annual to 30 cm. **Stems** Rough, with small, downward-directed prickles. **Leaves** 3–12 mm, 5–7 per whorl, linear-oblong, *eventually reflexed, with forward-directed marginal prickles.*

Flowers *Tiny, 0.5 mm across; corolla reddish* outside. **Fruits** Glabrous, blackish. **Habitat** Old walls, bare patches on dry, open calcareous grassland. **Dist**. Native. Rare, declining. Mostly East Anglia. (S, W and central Europe.) **Fls** Jun–Jul.

Cleavers/Goosegrass
Galium aparine

Prostrate, 'sticky', scrambling to erect annual, to 120 cm. **Stems** *Very rough, with numerous backward-directed prickles.* **Leaves** 12–50 mm, 6–8 per whorl, linear-oblanceolate, margins with

pointing prickles. **Flowers** 3 mm across. **Fruits** Glabrous, with pointed tubercles. **Habitat** Heath, moorland, grassland, open rocky woodlands, on acid soils; to 1215 m. **Dist**. Native. Common throughout BI. (W and W-central Europe.) **Fls** Jun–Aug.

Limestone Bedstraw
Galium sterneri

Prostrate, mat-forming perennial. Similar to *G. saxatile*, but more non-flowering shoots; *leaves* narrower, *oblanceolate* and *prickles on the margins pointing backwards; fruits with high-domed acute tubercles.*

backward-directed prickles. **Flowers** In 2–5-flowered axillary inflorescences. **Fruits** *4–6 mm, covered with hooked white bristles.* **Habitat** Hedgerows, cultivated ground, scrub, banks of streams and rivers, scree, shingle beaches, waste ground, on fertile soils. **Dist**. Native. Cosmopolitan weed. Abundant throughout BI. (All Europe.) **Fls** Jun–Aug.

CLEAVERS

Crosswort
Cruciata laevipes

Erect, *densely pubescent perennial* to 70 cm. **Leaves** *Pubescent, yellow-green,* 10–20 mm, 4 per whorl, 3-veined. **Flowers** *In dense axillary clusters; corolla yellow,* 4-lobed. **Habitat** Rough grassland, scrub, hedge banks, verges, wood borders, on well-drained neutral or calcareous soils; to 550 m. **Dist**. Native. Throughout Britain, N to central Scotland; absent from Ireland. (W, central and S Europe.) **Fls** May–Jun.

Wild Madder
Rubia peregrina

Robust, *scrambling evergreen* perennial to 120 cm. **Stems** Glabrous, 4-angled, rough, with backward-directed prickles. **Leaves** *Thick, shining, 4–6 per whorl*, 1.5–6 cm, 1-veined, margins with curved prickles. **Flowers** 5 mm across, *corolla* yellowish green, *5-lobed*. **Fruits** Berry-like, black. **Habitat** Coastal scrub, walls, cliffs, hedge banks. **Dist**. Native. SW England, Wales, S Ireland. (S and W Europe.) **Fls** Jun–Aug.

ADOXACEAE
Moschatel family

Moschatel/Townhall Clock
Adoxa moschatellina *(NI)

Rhizomatous perennial to 15 cm. **Stems** Flowering stems erect, with 2 opposite leaves. **Leaves** Ternate, long-stalked. **Flowers** Light green, in 5-flowered cube-shaped head, consisting of 1 terminal and 4 lateral flowers (the townhall clock); terminal flower with 4 corolla lobes, lateral flowers with 5; anthers yellow. **Habitat** Woodlands, coppice, lanesides, hedge banks, shaded stream sides, on damp, fertile soils; to 1065 m. **Dist**. Native. Throughout Britain except NW Scotland; very rare in Ireland. (Most of Europe; restricted to mts in S.) **Fls** Apr–May.

MOSCHATEL

CAPRIFOLIACEAE
Elders, viburnums and
honeysuckles

Deciduous or evergreen shrubs or woody
climbers. Leaves opposite, stipules usually
absent. Flowers bisexual; 5 sepals, fused at
base; 5 petals, fused at base, sometimes
2-lipped; 4–5 stamens; ovary inferior. Fruits
berry-like, rarely an achene or capsule.

Elder
Sambucus nigra

Deciduous shrub or small tree to 10 m.
Bark Deeply fissured,
corky. **Branches** With
prominent lenticels.

Leaves With 5 leaflets, these 3–9 cm, ovate
(deeply dissected in var. *laciniata*); *stipules
absent*. **Flowers** In flat-topped inflorescence;
corolla 5 mm across. **Fruits** *Black*. **Habitat**
Woods, scrub, hedgerows, waste ground,
roadsides, railway banks, sand-dunes,
on fertile soils; to 470 m. **Dist**. Native.
Common throughout BI except extreme N
Scotland. (Most of Europe except extreme
N.) **Fls** Aug–Sep.

Guelder Rose
Viburnum opulus

Deciduous shrub to 4 m. **Stems** Twigs
glabrous, buds with scales. **Leaves** Blades
5–8 cm, irregularly 3-lobed, glabrous
above, deep red in autumn. **Flowers** In
inflorescence with *large outer sterile flowers
surrounding smaller fertile ones*. **Fruits** Red.
Habitat Woods, hedgerows, scrub, fen
carr, on neutral and calcareous soils. **Dist**.
Native. Throughout BI, becoming scarcer
to N. (All Europe except N and parts of
Mediterranean.) **Fls** Jun–Jul.

Wayfaring-tree
Viburnum lantana

Deciduous shrub to 6 m. **Branches** Twigs
and *buds pubescent; buds naked*. **Leaves**
Blades 5–10 cm, regularly toothed, densely
hairy beneath. **Flowers** All fertile. **Fruits**
Compressed, red becoming black. **Habitat**

WAYFARING-
TREE

Scrub, wood margins, hedgerows, on dry,
base-rich or calcareous soils. **Dist**. Native
SE of line from Wash to Severn; naturalised
further N. (Central and S Europe.) **Fls**
May–Jun.

Honeysuckle
Lonicera periclymenum

Scrambling or twining, climbing deciduous
shrub to 6 m. **Leaves** Ovate, 30–70 mm,
sessile or shortly stalked; leaves below
inflorescence not fused at base. **Flowers** In
terminal heads; corolla 40–50 mm, cream,
yellowish purple, deeply 2-lipped, upper lip
with 4 lobes, lower lip entire. **Fruits** Red

berry. **Habitat** Woodland, scrub, hedgerows;
to 610 m. **Dist**. Native. Common
throughout BI. (W, central and S Europe.)
Fls Jun–Sep.

VALERIANACEAE
Valerians
••

Annuals or perennials with opposite leaves
that lack stipules. Flowers small with inferior
ovary; corolla tubular, funnel-shaped,
5-lobed, often spurred or pouched at base;
calyx minute or absent, sometimes forming a
feathery pappus at fruiting; 1 or 3 stamens.

Common Valerian
Valeriana officinalis

Tall, erect, ± glabrous perennial to 150 cm.
Very variable. **Leaves** To *c.*20 cm, pinnate
with terminal leaflet, leaflets entire or
irregularly toothed. **Flowers** In dense
terminal inflorescence; corolla *c.*5 mm
across, pale pink. **Habitat** Marshes, fens,
alpine meadows, wet woods; also rough
grassland on dry calcareous soils. **Dist**.
Native. Frequent throughout BI. (Most of
Europe except extreme S.) **Fls** Jun–Aug.

Marsh Valerian
Valeriana dioica

Erect, ± glabrous,
stoloniferous
perennial to 30 cm.
Leaves Basal leaves
entire, long-stalked,
2–3 cm; stem leaves
sessile, pinnate.
Flowers Pinkish,
dioecious, male
*c.*5 mm across,
female 2 mm.
Habitat Marshes,
fens, wet
meadows, wet
woodlands. **Dist**.
Native. Throughout Britain, N
to S Scotland; absent from Ireland. (W and
central Europe.) **Fls** May–Jun.

Red Valerian
Centranthus ruber

Erect, glabrous, glaucous perennial to
80 cm. **Leaves** Ovate, entire, lower leaves
stalked, upper leaves sessile. **Flowers** Red
or white, in dense terminal inflorescences;
corolla tube
8–10 mm,
spur long,
5–12 mm.
Habitat Sea
cliffs, waste
ground, old
walls, buildings.
Dist. Introduced.
Popular garden
plant, naturalised
throughout
most of
BI except
N Scotland.
(Mediterranean.)
Fls Jun–Aug.

Cornsalads ► *Valerianella*
Small annuals with characteristic repeatedly
forked, branching stems. Leaves simple,
entire or sparsely toothed or lobed. Flowers
in terminal open inflorescence; corolla
neither pouched nor spurred; 3 stamens.
Ripe fruits are essential to identify the 5
British species.

Common Cornsalad
Valerianella locusta

Habitat Disturbed ground, arable land,
hedge banks, rocks, cliffs, walls, dunes,
shingle. **Dist**. Native. Frequent throughout
BI, but mostly coastal in N. (Most of
Europe except N.) **Fls** Apr–Jun.

seed

Keeled Cornsalad
Valerianella carinata

Habitat Walls, paths, railways, gardens.
Dist. Archaeophyte. Throughout much of
S Britain, Ireland, especially SW England.
Increasing, more common in SW than
V. locusta. (S, W and central
Europe.) **Fls** Apr–Jun.

seed

DIPSACACEAE
Teasels

••

Herbs with erect stems and opposite leaves.
Flowers in dense heads, surrounded by calyx-
like whorl of bracts (involucral bracts); with or
without bracts mixed with flowers (receptacle
bracts); each flower surrounded by tubular
epicalyx; calyx small, cup-shaped or divided
into 4–5 segments or with numerous fine
bristles; corolla with 4–5 lobes or 2-lipped; 2
or 4 stamens, long-protruding; ovary inferior.

Wild Teasel
Dipsacus fullonum

Tall, erect biennial to 200 cm. **Stems**
Branched, glabrous, spiny. **Leaves** Basal
leaves in rosette, withering in 2nd spring,
with swollen-based prickles; stem leaves
lanceolate, fused across stem to form water-
collecting cup. **Flowering heads** In ovoid
heads; *involucral bracts curving upwards,
often as long as heads; receptacle bracts
longer than flowers, spine on tip straight.*
Habitat Rough grassland, roadsides, banks
of streams and rivers, waste ground. **Dist**.
Native. Throughout BI, but rare in N

Scotland, Ireland. (S, W and central
Europe.) **Fls** Jul–Aug.

Small Teasel
Dipsacus pilosus

Erect, branched biennial to 150 cm. **Stems**
Angled, with weak prickles. **Leaves** Basal
leaves in a rosette, ovate, long-stalked; stem
leaves short-stalked, upper with pair of
basal leaflets. **Flowers** *In spherical heads,
2–2.5 cm*; involucral bracts and bracts
among florets spine-tipped with long silky
hairs; *corolla 6–9 mm, white.* **Habitat** Damp
woods, ditches, stream sides, hedge banks,
especially on calcareous soils. **Dist**. Native.
Rather local, scattered throughout England.
(W and central Europe.) **Fls** Aug.

Field Scabious
Knautia arvensis

Erect, branched perennial to 100 cm.
Stems Roughly hairy. **Leaves** Basal leaves
in overwintering rosette; stem leaves deeply
pinnate, with large terminal lobe. **Flowers**
In heads, 3–4 cm across; *involucral bracts
ovate-lanceolate*, hairy, in 2 rows, shorter
than flowers; *outer flowers larger than inner*;
calyx cup-shaped, with 8 narrow teeth;

corolla 4-lobed. **Habitat** Rough grassland, hedge banks, roadsides, wood margins, on dry calcareous soils; to 365 m. **Dist**. Native. Throughout BI except N Scotland, W Ireland. (Most of Europe except Mediterranean.) **Fls** Jul–Sep.

Devil's-bit Scabious
Succisa pratensis

Erect, branched, sparsely hairy perennial to 100 cm. **Leaves** *Basal leaves ovate-lanceolate*, short-stalked; stem leaves few, entire or sparsely toothed. **Flowers** *Bluish purple, ± equal in size*, in heads, 1.5–2.5 mm across; involucral bracts broadly lanceolate, in 2–3 rows; calyx cup-shaped, with 5 teeth; *corolla 4-lobed*, 4–7 mm. **Habitat** Wet meadows, marshes, fens, wet heathland, woodland rides, on mildly acid soils; also chalk and limestone grassland. To 970 m. **Dist**. Native. Common throughout BI. (Most of Europe except extreme N and Mediterranean.) **Fls** Jun–Oct.

Small Scabious
Scabiosa columbaria

Slender, erect perennial to 70 cm. **Stems** Branching, sparsely hairy. **Leaves** Basal leaves stalked, obovate, variously lobed; stem leaves deeply pinnate, with narrow lobes. **Flowers** Bluish lilac, outer much larger than inner, in heads, 1.5–3.5 cm across; *c.10 involucral bracts, almost linear*, in 1 row; calyx cup-shaped, with 5 narrow, spreading teeth; *corolla 5-lobed*. **Habitat** Common, well-drained calcareous grassland to 610 m. **Dist**. Native. Widespread N to S Scotland, absent Ireland (All Europe except N.) **Fls** Jul–Aug.

ASTERACEAE (COMPOSITAE)
Composites
••

The familiar daisy, dandelion or thistle-like 'flowers' of the composites in fact consist of heads of a number of small individual flowers (*florets*). Each individual floret consists of an inferior ovary with a single style that has a 2-lobed stigma. There are 5 stamens, their anthers joined to form a tube through which the style projects. There are 3 kinds of corolla: *discoid*, in which the corolla is regular and funnel-shaped, with 5 short, triangular corolla lobes; *tubular*, with a long slender corolla tube that has 5 long, narrow lobes and with the style usually long and protruding; and *ray florets*, where the corolla is fused into a petal-like *ligule*, usually with 3 or 5 teeth at the tip. The calyx is absent or represented by a plume of silky hairs, the *pappus* – the familiar 'dandelion clock'.

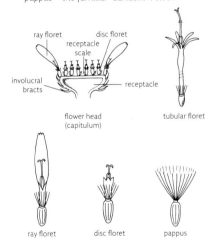

ray floret — disc floret
receptacle scale
involucral bracts — receptacle
flower head (capitulum) — tubular floret
ray floret — disc floret — pappus

Carline Thistle
Carlina vulgaris

Erect, thistle-like biennial or monocarpic perennial to 60 cm. **Leaves** Pinnately lobed, spiny; basal leaves cottony beneath.

Flowering heads 2–4 cm across, 1–3 per inflorescence; *involucral bracts spiny, inner longer than outer, straw-coloured and stiffly spreading,* looking like ray florets. **Habitat** Dry calcareous grassland, coastal cliffs, dunes; to 455 m. **Dist.** Native. Throughout BI, but mostly coastal in SW, Wales, Scotland. (Most of Europe except extreme N.) **Fls** Jul–Oct.

Burdocks ▶ *Arctium*
Robust biennials with erect, much-branched stems. Lower leaves are large, stalked, ovate, cordate, simple and untoothed. Flowering heads are globose, covered with numerous stiff, hooked involucral bracts (the burs); corolla is purple. Fruiting heads are dispersed by animals. Rather a difficult group, about which the experts differ!

Greater Burdock
Arctium lappa

Robust, much-branched, to 130 cm. **Leaves** *Petioles solid.* **Flowering heads** 3–4 cm across, long-stalked, in corymb-like inflorescence. **Habitat** Stream sides, roadsides, field borders, waste ground. **Dist.** Archaeophyte. Widespread in England N to

Humber; rare Wales, SW England; absent from Scotland, Ireland. (Most of Europe except extreme N.) **Fls** Jul–Sep.

Lesser Burdock
Arctium minus

Leaves *Petioles hollow.* **Flowering heads** 15–32 × 11–24 mm, those at ends of inflorescence sessile or short-stalked; middle involucral bracts ≤1.6 mm wide; involucre shorter or longer than corolla; corolla glandular-hairy or glabrous. **Habitat** Wood margins, roadside verges, hedgerows, scrub, dunes, waste ground; to 390 m. **Dist**. Native. Throughout BI. (Most of Europe except extreme N.) **Fls** Jul–Sep.

Slender Thistle
Carduus tenuiflorus

Erect annual or biennial to 100 cm. **Stems** *With continuous broad, spiny wings right up to heads.* **Leaves** Cottony beneath. **Flowering heads** *Cylindrical, sessile, 3–10 forming tight clusters*; inner involucral bracts as long as or longer than florets. **Habitat** Roadsides, waste ground close to sea, coastal grassland, sea walls, seabird colonies. **Dist**. Native. Coastal areas of BI except W Scotland, W Ireland; casual inland. (W Europe.) **Fls** Jun–Aug.

Welted Thistle
Carduus crispus

Tall, branched biennial thistle to 150 cm. **Stems** Spiny, winged margin ceasing just below flowering heads. **Flowering heads** *15–25 mm across, erect, almost spherical, in dense clusters of 3–5; involucral bracts not narrowed just above base*, tips of outer bracts recurved; corolla 12–15 mm. **Habitat** Roadsides, hedgerows, stream sides, rough grassland, waste ground, on fertile soils; lowland to 365 m. **Dist**. Native. Widely distributed as far N as central Scotland; local in E Ireland. (Most of Europe except parts of S.) **Fls** Jun–Aug.

Musk Thistle
Carduus nutans

Erect, usually branched biennial thistle
to 100 cm. **Stems** With white cottony
hairs; spiny, winged margin ceasing some
way below flowering heads. **Flowering
heads** *Large, 30–60 mm across, spherical,
drooping, usually solitary; outer involucral
bracts strongly reflexed, lanceolate, contracted
abruptly just above base*; corolla 15–25 mm.
Habitat Rough pastures, waste ground,
roadsides, on calcareous soils. **Dist.** Native.
Widely distributed as far N as central
Scotland; casual in N Scotland, Ireland. (W
and central Europe.) **Fls** May–Aug.

Thistles ▶ *Cirsium*

Spear Thistle
Cirsium vulgare

Tall, robust, branched biennial thistle to
150 cm. **Stems** With discontinuous spiny
wings. **Leaves** *Upper surface bristly, dull,
slightly glaucous; stem leaves decurrent, with*
narrow, elongated terminal lobe. **Flowering
heads** 2.5–5 cm, 2–3 per cluster, short-
stalked. **Habitat** Common weed of pastures,

rough grassland, roadsides, waste ground,
on fertile, base-rich soils; to 685 m. **Dist.**
Ubiquitous throughout BI. (All Europe.)
Fls Jul–Oct.

Woolly Thistle
Cirsium eriophorum

Tall, robust, branched biennial thistle to
150 cm. **Stems** *Unwinged, not prickly,
with cottony hairs.* **Leaves** *Deeply pinnately*

lobed; *upper surface bristly, dull*; tips of segments usually 2-lobed, one pointing up, the other down. **Flowering heads** *3–5 cm, solitary, erect; involucre with long white hairs (cottony).* **Habitat** Rough grasslands, scrub, railway banks, roadsides, quarries, on dry calcareous soils; to 310 m. **Dist.** Native. Rather local. Central England N to Yorkshire. (W and central Europe.) **Fls** Jul–Sep.

Melancholy Thistle
Cirsium heterophyllum *(NI)

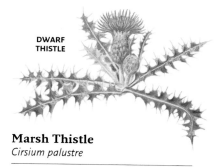

DWARF THISTLE

Tall, handsome perennial thistle to 120 cm. **Leaves** Basal leaves elliptic-lanceolate, long-stalked; *middle stem leaves with broad auricled base clasping stem, green above, white-felted beneath, margins with soft teeth*; upper stem leaves few, small. **Flowering heads** *Large, 3.5–5 cm, usually solitary*; involucral bracts ± glabrous. **Habitat** Hay meadows, roadsides, open woodland; to 760 m. **Dist**. Native. Widespread in N England, Scotland; very rare in Wales, Ireland. (N Europe.) **Fls** Jul–Aug.

Dwarf Thistle
Cirsium acaule

Perennial. **Leaves** Very spiny, forming basal rosette. **Flowering heads** one to a few, 3–4 cm, *sessile,* rarely with short stems. **Habitat** Species-rich, short calcareous grassland; to 425 m. **Dist**. Native. Widespread in S Britain, SE of line from Humber to Severn. (Most of Europe except N and Mediterranean.) **Fls** Jul–Sep.

Marsh Thistle
Cirsium palustre

Tall biennial thistle to 200 cm. **Stems** *Spiny-winged throughout, leafy to top.* **Leaves** *Stem leaves sessile, decurrent, hairy above,* hairs blackish. **Flowering heads** 1.5–2 cm, short-stalked, in clusters at ends of often arching branches; flowers purple, sometimes white. **Habitat** Marshes, fens, wet pastures, wet woodlands, upland flushes, communities of tall herbs; to 760 m. **Dist**. Native. Widespread throughout BI. (Most of Europe, but rare in Mediterranean.) **Fls** Jul–Sep.

COTTON THISTLE

Creeping Thistle
Cirsium arvense

Erect, branched, *rhizomatous* perennial to 120 cm. **Stems** Unwinged, leafy to top. **Leaves** Not forming basal rosette, very spiny, upper surface glabrous. **Flowering heads** 1.5–2.5 cm, short-stalked, solitary or in clusters of 2–4; florets dull purple, *upper part of corolla shorter than basal tube and divided almost to base into 5 segments.* **Habitat** Pastures, meadows, rough grassland, roadsides, waste ground, on fertile soils; to 845 m. **Dist**. Native. Ubiquitous throughout BI. (All Europe.) **Fls** Jul–Sep.

Cotton Thistle
Onopordum acanthium

Tall, erect greyish-white biennial thistle to 250 cm. **Stems** With continuous broad, spiny wings. **Leaves** *With cottony hairs on both surfaces.* **Flowering heads** 3–5 cm, solitary; involucral bracts spreading or reflexed; florets pale purple; receptacle without hairs or bristles. **Habitat** Field margins, hedgerows, waste ground, rubbish tips. **Dist**. Archaeophyte. Naturalised throughout lowland England; scarce elsewhere. (W, central and E Europe.) **Fls** Jul–Sep.

Saw-wort
Serratula tinctoria

Erect, slender, sparsely branched, glabrous, partially dioecious perennial to 90 cm. **Leaves** *12–25 cm, lobed to pinnate, with bristle-tipped teeth.* **Flowering heads** 1.5–2 cm, in open inflorescence; receptacle with thin scales; *involucral bracts ovate, not spiny, appressed.* **Habitat** Heathy and calcareous grassland, hay and fen meadows,

commons, wood margins, cliff tops; to 560 m. **Dist**. Native. Throughout England (especially SW), Wales; absent from Ireland, most of Scotland. (Most of Europe except much of Scandinavia and Mediterranean.) **Fls** Jul–Sep.

Knapweeds ▶ *Centaurea*

Greater Knapweed
Centaurea scabiosa

Erect, branched, ± pubescent perennial to 90 cm. **Leaves** *10–25 cm, usually deeply pinnately lobed*. **Flowering heads** 3–5 cm, solitary, long-stalked, partially radiate; *involucral bracts with blackish-brown toothed, crescent-shaped apical portion decurrent down sides of basal section*. **Habitat** Rough grassland, scrub, roadsides, hedge banks, cliffs, usually on calcareous soils; to 320 m. **Dist**. Native. Widespread in England; local and mostly coastal elsewhere. (Most of Europe except S.) **Fls** Jul–Sep.

Cornflower
Centaurea cyanus

Erect, branched annual to 90 cm. **Stems** Slender, grooved, branching. **Leaves** *Lower leaves stalked, pinnately branched*; upper leaves linear, simple, sessile; all leaves *greyish, pubescent*. **Flowering heads** 1.5–3 cm across, solitary, partially radiate; involucral bracts with decurrent apical portion, teeth of upper bracts silvery; *outer florets bright blue*. **Habitat** Rubbish tips, waste places, roadsides. **Dist**. Archaeophyte. Formerly common arable weed, now casual garden escape. Throughout BI, but rare in Scotland, Ireland. (SE Europe.) **Fls** Jun–Aug.

Common Knapweed
Centaurea nigra

Erect, branching, hairy perennial to 100 cm. **Leaves** Entire to lobed. **Flowering heads** 2–4 cm across; capitula (excluding flowers) 15–20 mm across, short-stalked, stalks swollen beneath heads, solitary, usually discoid but sometimes partially radiate; *apical portion of involucral bracts separated from basal portion by distinct constriction, apical portion dark brown-black, regularly toothed, teeth long*; florets reddish purple. **Habitat** Rough grassland, meadows, pastures, roadsides, sea cliffs, waste ground; to 580 m. **Dist**. Native. Common throughout BI. (W and central Europe.) **Fls** Jun–Sep.

Chicory
Cichorium intybus

Erect to spreading, much-branched perennial, to 120 cm. **Stems** Stiff, glabrous or pubescent. **Leaves** Lower stem leaves lobed or toothed; upper stem leaves lanceolate, sessile, clasping stem with pointed auricles. **Flowering heads** Ligulate, 2.5–4 cm across; florets blue. **Fruits** Pappus consisting of short scales. **Habitat** Rough grassland, roadside verges, field margins, on dry soils; to 275 m. **Dist**. Archaeophyte. Declining. Throughout most of BI, but rare in Scotland, Ireland. (Most of Europe, but widely naturalised.) **Fls** Jul–Oct.

Nipplewort
Lapsana communis

Erect, branched annual to 90 cm. **Stems** Hairy below, glabrous above. **Leaves** *Lower leaves lobed, terminal lobe much larger than laterals.* **Flowering heads** 1.5–2 cm across, 15–20 in open panicles; 8–10 involucral bracts, erect; *8–15 florets.* **Fruits** *Pappus absent.* **Habitat** Disturbed and shaded habitats, hedgerows, roadsides, walls, wood borders, gardens, waste ground. **Dist**. Native. Common throughout BI. (All Europe.) **Fls** Jul–Sep.

Cat's-ear
Hypochaeris radicata

Perennial to 60 cm. **Stems** Flowering stems swollen below heads, *usually with few branches and several small, scale-like bracts.* **Leaves** 7–25 cm, in basal rosette, roughly hairy, *hairs unbranched.* **Flowering heads** 2.5–4 cm across, ligules *c*.4× as long as wide, *receptacle scales present.* **Fruits** Central achenes 8–17 mm. **Habitat** Pastures,

meadows, lawns, grass
heaths, roadsides,
dunes, on mildly
acid soils. **Dist**.
Native. Ubiquitous
and common
throughout BI
except Shetland.
(Most of Europe
except NE.)
Fls Jun–Sep.

Rough Hawkbit
Leontodon hispidus

Perennial to 60 cm. **Stems**
Flowering stems unbranched,
usually densely hairy above.
Leaves With forked 'Y'-shaped hairs, in
basal rosette. **Flowering heads** Solitary,
25–40 mm across; *involucral bracts
conspicuously hairy*; outer ligules usually
reddish beneath. **Fruits** *All achenes with
pappus of hairs*. **Habitat** Hay meadows,
pastures, rough grazing, roadside verges,
on well-drained calcareous soils; to 575 m.

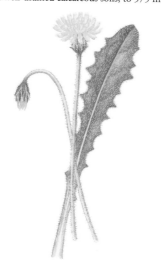

Dist. Native. Throughout most of BI, N
to S Scotland; local in Ireland, rare in SW.
(Most of Europe.) **Fls** Jun–Sep.

Lesser Hawkbit
Leontodon saxatilis

Perennial to 30 cm. **Stems** *Flowering stems*
unbranched, *glabrous or sparsely hairy.*
Leaves With forked 'Y'-shaped hairs along
margins, in basal rosette. **Flowering heads**
Solitary, 12–20 mm across; *involucral bracts
sparsely hairy*; outer ligules usually greyish
beneath. **Fruits** *Outer achenes with no
pappus of hairs.* **Habitat** Heaths, commons,
grazed grassland, roadsides, dunes, on well-
drained calcareous or sandy soils; to 500 m.

Dist. Native. Throughout BI, N to central
Scotland. (S, W and central Europe.) **Fls**
Jun–Sep.

Autumn Hawkbit
Scorzoneroides autumnalis

Perennial to 60 cm. **Stems** Flowering stems
glabrous, *usually with few branches, scale-like
bracts beneath heads.* **Leaves** Usually deeply
lobed, with narrow segments; in basal
rosette; glabrous or with sparse simple hairs.
Flowering heads 12–35 mm across; outer
ligules streaked reddish beneath. **Fruits**

Pappus consisting of 1 row of feathery (branched) hairs. **Habitat** Meadows, pastures, grass heaths, commons, roadsides, scree, salt marshes, dunes; to 975 m. **Dist**. Native. Ubiquitous throughout BI. (Most of Europe, but local in S.) **Fls** Jun–Oct.

Bristly Oxtongue
Helminthotheca echioides

Erect, branched, bristly annual or biennial 90 cm. **Leaves** Stem leaves sessile, ± cordate, clasping, coarsely toothed, covered by rough bristles. **Flowering heads** 2–2.5 cm across, *3–5 outer involucral bracts, broad, leaf-like; beak as long as body.* **Fruits** Pappus white. **Habitat** Roadsides, rough ground, field margins, riverbanks, sea walls, on heavy calcareous soils. **Dist**. Archaeophyte.

AUTUMN HAWKBIT

Widespread SE of line from Humber to Severn; scattered elsewhere. (S Europe.) **Fls** Jun–Oct.

Hawkweed Oxtongue
Picris hieracioides

Erect, branched, bristly biennial or perennial to 90 cm. **Leaves** Stem leaves lanceolate, slightly clasping, margins undulate. **Flowering heads** 2–3.5 cm across; *inner and outer involucral bracts narrow, similar, outer ± spreading, recurved.* **Fruits** Short-beaked achenes. **Habitat** Chalk and limestone grassland, roadsides, railway banks, quarries, on calcareous soils. **Dist**. Native. Widespread SE of line from Humber to Severn, S Wales. (Most of Europe.) **Fls** Jul–Sep.

Goat's-beard
Tragopogon pratensis

Erect annual to perennial, to 70 cm. Has 2 widespread subspecies, ssp. *pratensis* and ssp. *minor*, which should be identified only when flowers are open on sunny mornings. **Leaves** *Glabrous, linear-lanceolate, long-pointed, entire, sheathing at base,* with conspicuous white midrib. **Flowering heads** Large; involucral bracts in 1 row; ligules as long as involucral bracts in ssp. *pratensis*, *c.* ½ as long in ssp. *minor*. **Fruits** Pappus and fruiting heads very large. **Habitat** Ssp. *pratensis* on dry grassland, roadsides, waste ground. Ssp. *minor* similar, but also rough grassland, sand-dunes; to 365 m. **Dist**.

Ssp. *pratensis* introduced; casual in lowland England. Ssp. *minor* native; widespread N to central Scotland, scattered in Ireland. (Ssp. *pratensis* in most of Europe; ssp. *minor* in W and central Europe.) **Fls** Jun–Jul.

Sow-thistles ▶ *Sonchus*

Perennial Sow-thistle
Sonchus arvensis

Tall, erect, rhizomatous perennial to 150 cm. **Leaves** Basal leaves ± pinnately lobed, lobes

with spiny teeth; *stem leaves sessile with rounded auricles.* **Flowering heads** 4–5 cm across, deep yellow; *inflorescence branches and involucres densely covered by yellow glandular hairs.* **Fruits** Dark brown achenes, 3–3.5 mm. **Habitat** Banks of streams and rivers, arable land, road verges, sea walls, drift lines. **Dist**. Native. Widely distributed throughout BI, but scarce in N Scotland. (Most of Europe.) **Fls** Jul–Oct.

Smooth Sow-thistle
Sonchus oleraceus

Erect, glabrous annual to 150 cm. **Leaves** Variable, somewhat glaucous, not spinous, *with acute, spreading auricles.* **Flowering heads** 1.5–3.5 cm across, ligules yellow. **Fruits** *Achenes, transversely wrinkled between ribs.* **Habitat** Common weed of gardens, arable land, roadsides, disturbed ground,

on fertile soils. **Dist**. Native. Widespread throughout lowland BI, but scarce in N Scotland. (Most of Europe.) **Fls** Jun–Aug.

Prickly Sow-thistle
Sonchus asper

Erect, glabrous annual to 120 cm. Very variable. Similar to *S. oleraceus*, but upper surface of leaves shining green, not glaucous; *stem leaves with rounded spinous auricles appressed to stem*; flowering heads 1.5–2.5 cm across; ligules deeper yellow; *achenes smooth between ribs*. In doubtful cases, the only certain way to distinguish it from *S. oleraceus* is on the sculpturing of the achenes. **Habitat** Rough grassland, roadside verges, gardens, arable fields, coastal habitats, waste places. **Dist**. Native. Common throughout BI. (All Europe except extreme N.) **Fls** Jun–Aug.

PRICKLY SOW-THISTLE

Prickly Lettuce
Lactuca serriola

Tall, erect annual or biennial to 200 cm. **Leaves** Pinnately lobed to unlobed, *midribs whitish*, margins and underside of midrib sharply toothed, sessile with pointed auricles; *stem leaves held vertically in N–S plane*. **Flowering heads** 8–10 mm across, in elongated inflorescence; involucre cylindrical, glabrous. **Fruits** Olive-grey *achenes, 3–4 mm (excluding beak)*.

Habitat Disturbed ground, roadsides, sea walls, coastal habitats; lowland. **Dist**. Archaeophyte. England N to Humber; rare in SW, Wales. (Most of Europe.) **Fls** Jul–Sep.

Hawk's-beards ► *Crepis*

Marsh Hawk's-beard
Crepis paludosa

Erect, glabrous perennial to 90 cm. **Leaves** *Stem leaves sharply toothed*, base sessile, clasping *with pointed auricles*. **Flowering heads** 15–25 mm across, few; involucre with numerous black glandular and non-glandular hairs. **Fruits** Straw-coloured achenes 4–5 mm, not beaked; *pappus of stiff, brittle yellow-brown hairs*. **Habitat** Wet meadows, pastures, stream sides, fens, marshes, wet woodland; to 915 m. **Dist**. Native. Widespread in N Britain, N Ireland. (N and central Europe.) **Fls** Jul–Sep.

MARSH HAWK'S-BEARD

Smooth Hawk's-beard
Crepis capillaris

Erect, branched, ± *glabrous annual* to 75 cm. Very variable. **Leaves** Lower leaves with toothed lobes; *stem leaves clasping, with long, arrow-shaped lobes.* **Flowering heads** 10–13 mm across, erect in bud; inner surface of inner bracts glabrous, outer bracts appressed. **Fruits** Achenes, not beaked, 1.5–2.5 mm, with 10 ribs. **Habitat** Grassland, roadsides, heaths, waste ground, old walls; to 445 m. **Dist**. Native. Common throughout BI. (W, central and S Europe.) **Fls** Jun–Sep.

Beaked Hawk's-beard
Crepis vesicaria

Erect, branched, *hispid biennial* to 80 cm. **Leaves** Thinly pubescent; basal leaves stalked, variously lobed; stem leaves clasping. **Flowering heads** 15– 25 mm across; *florets yellow, orange-striped beneath; outer bracts spreading.* **Fruits** *Achenes, 4–5 mm, with slender beak as long as achene when ripe.* **Habitat** Roadsides, rough grassland, waste ground. **Dist**. Introduced. Abundant and widespread as far N as Humber; absent from Scotland, N Ireland. (S, central and W Europe.) **Fls** May–Jul.

Hawkweeds
Hieracium spp.

Erect perennials, exceedingly difficult to identify to species level as all are *apomictic*, i.e. producing seed without fertilisation. Seedlings are thus genetically identical

HAWKWEED

Mouse-ear-hawkweeds ▶ *Pilosella*
Stoloniferous perennials. *Flowering stem ±
leafless (scapigerous). Leaves in a basal rosette,
elliptical, without marginal teeth, the lower
surface densely white-felted,* the upper surface
with scattered long, stiff hairs. Involucre
hairy; ligules red-streaked beneath.

Mouse-ear-hawkweed
Pilosella officinarum

Very variable, with 7 subspecies. **Stems**
Stolons long, with small, well-spaced leaves,
not usually ending in rosettes; flowering
stem 5–30 cm. **Flowering heads** Solitary,
15–25 mm across. **Habitat** Short turf, grass
heaths, dunes, banks, walls, cliffs, on dry
sandy or calcareous soils; to 915 m. **Dist.**
Native. Widely distributed throughout BI.
(All Europe.) **Fls** May–Aug.

to the seed parent; in effect, 'cloning' by
seed. This can give rise to a large number
of genetically invariable populations, each
of which can be recognised as separate
species (sometimes referred to as '*micro-
species*'). There are currently 412 species of
Hieracium recognised in the BI, many of
which are rare endemics and a number of
which are probably introduced. No attempt
has been made to deal with these here.
Leaves Varying arrangement of basal and
stem leaves. **Flowering heads** *Involucral
bracts in several overlapping rows, absence
of receptacle scales.* **Fruits** *Pappus of 1 row
of pale brown or dirty white simple hairs.*
Similar spp. Often confused with species of
hawk's-beards, but these have the involucral
bracts in 2 rows. **Habitat** Found in a wide
range of habitats, but prefer dry, open or
rocky places, including cliffs, limestone
pavement, hillside grassland, rock ledges,
rocky stream sides, roadsides, walls and
quarries; to 1220 m.

Fox-and-cubs
Pilosella aurantiaca

Erect, stoloniferous or rhizomatous
perennial. **Stems** Flowering stems to 40 cm,
branched, with 2–12 heads. **Leaves** Rosette
leaves large, 6–20 cm. **Flowering heads**
10–20 mm across; *ligules orange-brown to
red.* **Habitat** Hedge banks, grassy roadsides,

walls, churchyards; to 445 m. **Dist**. Introduced. Naturalised. Garden escape. (N and central Europe.) **Fls** May–Jul.

Wall Lettuce
Mycelis muralis

Erect, branched, *glabrous perennial* to 100 cm. **Leaves** Lower leaves pinnately lobed, with large, triangular terminal lobe;

stem leaves sessile, clasping. **Flowering heads** 12–15 mm across, in large, open inflorescence; *5 florets per head*. **Habitat** Shaded hedge banks, calcareous woods, rocks, walls, grikes in limestone pavement; to 500 m. **Dist**. Native. Throughout most of Britain, but rare in Scotland; introduced in Ireland. (All Europe except N.) **Fls** Jul–Sep.

Dandelions
Taraxacum spp.

Usually glabrous perennials. Like hawkweeds (*see* above), they are apomicts and pose the same problems of identification. There are currently 232 species recognised in the BI; as with the hawkweeds, no attempt is made to deal with these here. **Stems** Leafless flowering stem arises from basal leaf rosette. **Leaves** All in basal rosette. **Flowering heads** Solitary; involucral bracts in 2 different rows; receptacle bracts absent. **Fruits** Pappus in several rows of simple white hairs (the dandelion 'clock'). **Habitat** Native species occur in chalk grassland, fens, flushes, stream sides, sand-dunes, cliffs. Most introduced species are abundant plants of disturbed ground such as roadsides, pastures, gardens, waste ground. **Dist**. More than 40 species are endemic, 100-plus are probably introduced, and the remainder are native. Throughout BI. **Fls** Mar–Oct.

Mountain Everlasting
Antennaria dioica

Erect, stoloniferous, dioecious perennial to 20 cm. **Stems** *Covered by whitish woolly hairs.* **Leaves** *Mostly basal, 1–4 cm, white-woolly beneath.* **Flowering heads** *In tight clusters*; florets tubular, female 12 mm across; male *c*.6 mm; involucral bracts of male plants ovate, white; of female plants linear-lanceolate, pink. **Habitat** Upland grassland, dwarf shrub heaths, stream sides, rock ledges; to 885 m. Also sand-dunes, machair, cliff tops, limestone grassland. **Dist**. Native. Declining. Widespread in upland Britain; rare and local in lowlands. (N and central Europe.) **Fls** Jun–Jul.

Cudweeds ▶ *Filago* and *Gnaphalium*
Filago and *Gnaphalium* look very similar; both are densely hairy or woolly annuals or perennials with heads of small yellowish or brownish florets, the heads in tight sessile clusters in the axils of leaves. The technical difference between them is that *Filago* has receptacle bracts mixed with the outer florets whilst there are no receptacle bracts in *Gnaphalium*. However, this character is often not easy to see. In practice, the two genera can usually be distinguished in the field. The stem and branches of *Filago* all end in axillary clusters, but the main stem is successively overtopped by the lower lateral branches, giving the whole plant a distinct 'jizz'. In addition, the leaves of most *Filago* are usually ± erect, whereas those of *Gnaphalium* are more spreading.

Common Cudweed
Filago vulgaris

Erect annual to 40 cm. **Stems** Densely white-woolly, usually branched. **Leaves** *Widest below middle*, erect, 1–2 cm, undulate, *upper leaves not overtopping clusters.* **Flowering heads** *20–40* in ± sessile clusters; involucral bracts in 5 rows, inner with pointed yellow tips. **Habitat** Dry, open grassland, grass heaths, arable land, tracks on sandy soils, dunes. **Dist**. Native. Declining. Lowland Britain, especially East Anglia; rare in Scotland, Ireland. (Central and S Europe.) **Fls** Jul–Aug.

Small Cudweed
Filago minima *(R)

Slender, ± erect, branched annual to 25 cm. Plant covered by silky silvery hairs. **Stems** Erect. **Leaves** *Erect, closely appressed to*

stem, 4–10 mm, linear-lanceolate, *apical leaves not overtopping clusters*. **Flowering heads** 3–6 forming clusters. **Habitat** Grass heaths, commons, arable fields, pathsides, waste ground, pits, on dry, open sandy or gravelly soils; to 365 m. **Dist**. Native. Local, declining. Scattered throughout BI. (Much of Europe except N.) **Fls** Jun–Sep.

Heath Cudweed
Gnaphalium sylvaticum
EN. *(R)

Erect perennial to 60 cm. **Stems** Whitish woolly; short, leafy non-flowering shoots. **Leaves** *Linear-lanceolate, 1-veined*, glabrous above, woolly beneath, *diminishing in size up stem*. **Flowering heads** 2–8 or solitary, in *elongated, spike-like inflorescence > ½ length of stem*; involucral bracts with central green stripe and broad papery margins. **Habitat** Open heathy woodlands, heaths, dunes; to 850 m. **Dist**. Native.

Throughout BI but now local and seriously declining. (Most of Europe except extreme N.) **Fls** Jul–Sep.

Marsh Cudweed
Gnaphalium uliginosum

Much-branched decumbent to erect annual, to 20 cm, densely covered by woolly hairs. **Leaves** Linear-lanceolate, 1–5 cm. **Flowering heads** *In dense, sessile, terminal clusters*, 3–10 heads per cluster, *overtopped by apical leaves*; involucral bracts brown. **Habitat** Open trampled areas, pond margins, woodland rides, arable fields, heaths, gardens, on seasonally flooded clay or acid sandy soils. **Dist**. Native. Widely distributed throughout BI. (Most of Europe except extreme N.) **Fls** Jul–Aug.

Ploughman's-spikenard
Inula conyzae

Erect, softly pubescent biennial or perennial to 130 cm. **Stems** Simple or branched, often reddish. **Leaves** *Basal leaves ovate*; stem leaves lanceolate, ± sessile,

PLOUGHMAN'S-SPIKENARD

GOLDEN-SAMPHIRE

all toothed. **Flowering heads** *7–12 mm across, numerous, in terminal clusters; florets yellow, marginal ray florets absent*; involucral bracts in many rows, green with pale bases. **Similar spp**. The basal leaves closely resemble those of Foxglove *Digitalis purpurea* (p.173), but that invariably grows on acid soils. **Habitat** Rough grassland, scrub, dunes, broken ground, quarries, roadsides, on dry calcareous soils. **Dist**. Native. Widespread in England, Wales, N to S Scotland. (Central and SE Europe, N to Denmark.) **Fls** Jul–Sep.

Golden-samphire
Inula crithmoides

Erect, glabrous maritime perennial to 90 cm. **Stems** *Fleshy*, branched. **Leaves** 2.5–6 cm, *linear, fleshy, glabrous, simple or with 3 teeth at apex*. **Flowering heads** 23–28 mm across, few in corymb-like inflorescence; ray florets golden yellow. **Habitat** Calcareous maritime cliffs, salt marshes. **Dist.** Native. Local. Coasts of S Britain from Suffolk to N Wales; SW and E Ireland. (Coasts of W and S Europe.) **Fls** Jul–Aug.

Common Fleabane
Pulicaria dysenterica

Erect, stoloniferous, sparsely hairy, clump-forming perennial to 60 cm. **Leaves** 3–8 cm, densely, softly hairy; *stem leaves* oblong-lanceolate, *cordate, clasping*.

Flowering heads 15–30 mm across, in loose inflorescence; *ray florets much longer than involucral bracts.* **Habitat** Damp roadsides, ditches, banks of streams and rivers, marshes, fens, wet meadows, dune slacks. **Dist**. Native. Widespread and common in England, Wales; ± absent from Scotland; scattered in Ireland. (All Europe except N.) **Fls** Aug–Sep.

Blue Fleabane
Erigeron acris *(NI)

Slender, erect, branched annual or biennial to 60 cm. **Stems** *Roughly hairy*, reddish. **Leaves** Stem leaves numerous, lanceolate, *entire*. **Flowering heads** 12–18 mm across, one to several per inflorescence; *ray florets purplish mauve, erect, not much longer than disc florets.* **Habitat** Dry, open permanent grassland, mature sand-dunes, banks, old walls, on well-drained calcareous soils. **Dist**. Native. Widespread in England SE of line from Humber to Severn; local and coastal in SW England, Wales; scarce in Ireland. (Most of Europe.) **Fls** Jul–Aug.

Mexican Fleabane
Erigeron karvinskianus

Much-branched, slender perennial to 25 cm. **Stems** Leafy. **Leaves** Lower leaves obovate, *coarsely toothed*; upper leaves linear, entire. **Flowering heads** 17–20 mm across, very 'daisy-like', in open, leafy inflorescence; *ligules white above*, pink beneath. **Habitat** Old walls, rock outcrops, cliffs. **Dist.** Introduced (native of Mexico). Widely naturalised as garden escape. Common in S and SW England, Channel Is; scattered elsewhere. (S and W Europe) **Fls** Jul–Aug.

Canadian Fleabane
Conyza canadensis

Tall, erect, much-branched yellowish-green annual to 100 cm. **Leaves** Stem leaves numerous, 3–12 cm, linear-lanceolate. **Flowering heads** 3–5 mm across, in elongated inflorescence; *involucral bracts glabrous.* **Habitat** Increasingly common urban weed of waste ground, pavements, walls, railway ballast, cultivated ground.

CANADIAN FLEABANE

Dist. Introduced (native of North America). Spreading. Widespread in lowland England, but scarce in SW, Wales; rare in Ireland. (Throughout Europe.) **Fls** Aug–Sep. **Note** *C. canadensis* is the commonest and most widespread of several species of North and South American *Conyza* that are well established in BI and appear to be spreading.

Michaelmas-daisies ▶ *Aster*

A number of North American Michaelmas-daisies have long been cultivated in British gardens, and several are commonly established on rough ground, waste places, roadsides and railway banks. The numerous cultivars and hybrids makes identification difficult; details of the involucral bracts are especially useful in this.

Common Michaelmas-daisy

Aster × salignus (*A. lanceolatus* × *A. novi-belgii*)

Commonest naturalised Michaelmas-daisy. Very similar to *A. lanceolatus*, but stems to 130 cm; leaves narrowed to semi-clasping base with short auricles; flowering heads 15–25 mm across; inflorescence wider than *A. lanceolatus*; *involucral bracts 5–7 mm, widest below middle, tips reddish; ligules whitish to pale blue*. **Habitat** *See* above. **Fls** Sep–Nov.

Sea Aster

Aster tripolium

Erect, *glabrous*, short-lived *maritime* perennial to 100 cm. **Leaves** Lanceolate, 7–12 cm, *fleshy, glabrous*. **Flowering heads** 8–30 mm across; involucral bracts few, blunt; ligules blue-purple or absent (var. *flosculosus*). **Habitat** Salt marshes, creek sides, brackish ditches, tidal rivers, sea cliffs. **Dist**. Native. All round coasts of BI. (Most European coasts.) **Fls** Jul–Oct.

Daisy
Bellis perennis

Perennial. **Stems** Flowering stems to 12 cm, leafless, hairy. **Leaves** 2–4 cm, all in basal rosette. **Flowering heads** 16–25 mm across, ray florets white, disc yellow. **Habitat** Familiar plant of lawns, pastures, roadside verges; also characteristic of grazed, mown, trampled grasslands, dune slacks, stream sides, upland flushes. To 915 m. **Dist.** Native. Common throughout BI. (All Europe.) **Fls** Mar–Oct.

FEVERFEW

Feverfew
Tanacetum parthenium

Erect, branched, somewhat downy, strongly aromatic perennial to 70 cm. **Leaves** *Yellowish green, deeply pinnately lobed.* **Flowering heads** Numerous, radiate, 15–25 mm across, in open corymb-like inflorescence; ray florets white, disc yellow. **Habitat** Naturalised on old walls, gardens, tips, waste ground. **Dist.** Archaeophyte. Frequent throughout BI, but scarce in N Scotland, W Ireland. (SE Europe.) **Fls** Jul–Aug.

Tansy
Tanacetum vulgare

Tall, robust, rhizomatous, *aromatic* perennial to 120 cm. **Leaves** 15–25 cm, oblong in outline, *pinnate.* **Flowering heads** *Discoid, yellow,* 7–12 mm across, in dense corymb-like inflorescence. **Dist.** Native throughout Britain, but scarce in N Scotland; introduced in Ireland. **Habitat** Rough grassland, roadsides, riverbanks, waste ground; to 380 m. (Most of Europe.) **Fls** Jul–Sep.

Yarrow
Achillea millefolium

Stoloniferous, pubescent, aromatic perennial
to 80 cm. **Leaves** *Lanceolate, 5–15 cm, deeply
dissected, 2–3-pinnate.* **Flowering heads**
Radiate, 4–6 mm across, *in dense, terminal,
corymb-like inflorescence;* ray florets white, disc
cream. **Habitat** All grassland habitats from
sea-level to 1210 m, lawns, dunes, shingle,
waste ground. **Dist**. Native. Common
throughout BI. (All Europe.) **Fls** Jun–Sep.

SNEEZEWORT

Sneezewort
Achillea ptarmica

Erect perennial to 60 cm. **Stems** Simple
or branched, glabrous below, pubescent
above. **Leaves** *1.5–8 cm, linear-lanceolate,
sharply toothed.* **Flowering heads** *Radiate,
12–18 mm across,* few in open inflorescence;
ray florets white, disc cream. **Habitat** Damp
grasslands, meadows, grazed commons,
marshes, wet heaths, stream sides, hillside
flushes; to 770 m. **Dist**. Native. Throughout
BI, but scarce in S Ireland and decreasing
E and SE England. (All Europe except
Mediterranean.) **Fls** Jul–Aug.

Corn Marigold
Glebionis segetum VU.

*Glabrous, glaucous
annual* to 50 cm.
Stems Simple or
branched. **Leaves**
2–8 cm, coarsely
toothed or pinnately
lobed. **Flowering
heads** *Solitary,*
long-stalked,
35–65 mm
across, radiate;
*ray florets golden
yellow,* disc yellow.
Habitat Disturbed and
waste ground, arable
weed of light sandy
soils; to 410 m. **Dist**.
Archaeophyte. Declining. Throughout BI.
(E Mediterranean.) **Fls** Jun–Aug.

Oxeye Daisy
Leucanthemum vulgare

Erect, branched, slender perennial with non-
flowering rosettes and simple or branched
flowering stems to 70 cm. **Leaves** Basal

Flowering heads Numerous, 1–2 mm across; florets all tubular. **Habitat** Drier parts of salt marshes; also sea walls, shingle, cliffs, brackish dykes, rough ground near sea. **Dist.** Native. All round coast of Britain except W and N Scotland; rare in Ireland. (Atlantic and Mediterranean coasts of Europe; inland saline areas of E Europe.) **Fls** Aug–Sep.

Mugwort
Artemisia vulgaris

Tall, robust, tufted, aromatic perennial to 150 cm. **Stems** *Becoming glabrous, central pith >¾ width of stem.* **Leaves** 5–8 cm, deeply divided, dark green, glabrous above, whitish pubescent beneath, ultimate segments lanceolate, 3–6 mm wide. **Flowering heads** 3–4 mm across, numerous; in inflorescence, hardly leafy, *branches straight, erect.* **Habitat** Roadsides, hedge banks, riverbanks, waste ground, on fertile soils; to 350 m. **Dist.** Archaeophyte. Common throughout most of BI, but sparse in N Scotland and most of Ireland. (All Europe except extreme N.) **Fls** Jul–Sep.

Wormwood
Artemisia absinthium

Tufted, aromatic perennial to 90 cm, with *non-flowering rosettes.* **Stems** *Erect, silky-hairy.* **Leaves** Deeply pinnately divided, *greyish pubescent, lobes 2–4 mm wide.* **Flowering heads** Numerous, 3–5 mm,

leaves 1–8 cm, spathulate, long-stalked, bluntly toothed; upper stem leaves sessile. **Flowering heads** *Radiate, 25–60 mm across, solitary*; involucral bracts 6–8 mm. **Habitat** Dry grasslands, coastal cliffs, dunes, waste ground, roadside verges, railway banks, on neutral or calcareous soils; to 845 m. **Dist.** Native. Common throughout most of BI. (All Europe.) **Fls** Jul–Sep.

Mugworts ▶ *Artemisia*

Sea Wormwood
Artemisia maritimum

Strongly aromatic, white-downy, rhizomatous perennial with non-flowering rosettes. **Stems** Decumbent to erect flowering shoots, to 50 cm. **Leaves** *White-woolly,* 2–5 cm, deeply pinnately divided, *ultimate segments linear, ≤1 mm wide.*

wider than long,
drooping; *receptacle
hairy*. **Habitat**
Roadsides, waste
ground, railway sidings;
to 370 m. **Dist**.
Archaeophyte.
Widely distributed in
England, Wales;
mostly coastal in
E Scotland; rare
in Ireland. (Most
of Europe except
extreme N and S.)
Fls Jul–Aug.

**WORM-
WOOD**

Chamomile and Mayweeds ▶ *Chamaemelum, Matricaria* and *Tripleurospermum*

A distinctive, similar-looking group of
composites, with radiate flower heads
(occasionally discoid) comprising usually
white ray florets (sometimes yellow)
and yellow disc florets. The leaves are
1–3-pinnate and deeply dissected into
narrow linear segments. Identification
depends primarily on the presence of
receptacle bracts and details of the achenes,
as well as on whether the plants are hairy.

Chamomile
Chamaemelum nobile VU.

Pleasantly aromatic, prostrate to erect,
branched, pubescent *perennial* to 30 cm.
Leaves 1.5–5 cm. **Flowering heads**
18–25 mm across, solitary, on long stalks;
*receptacle scales oblong, blunt; base of corolla
tube of disc florets enlarged and enclosing
tip of achene*. **Habitat** Seasonally wet,
grazed, acid sandy grassland, village greens,
commons, maritime grassland, cliffs; to
465 m. **Dist**. Native. Local, declining.
S and SW Britain, SW Ireland. (W Europe.)
Fls Jun–Jul. **Note** Non-flowering form
cultivated as chamomile lawns is cultivar
'Treneague'.

CHAMOMILE

Pineapple-weed
Matricaria discoidea

Much-branched, erect, glabrous annual
to 30 cm. **Flowering heads** 5–8 mm
across, solitary, on short stalks, *discoid;
ray florets absent*. **Habitat** Disturbed or
trampled fertile ground, tracks, arable
fields, gateways, roadsides; to 845 m. **Dist**.
Introduced (native of NE Asia). Naturalised
and common throughout BI. (Naturalised
throughout Europe.) **Fls** Jun–Aug.

Scented Mayweed
Matricaria chamomilla

Pleasantly aromatic, erect, much-branched,
glabrous annual to 60 cm. **Flowering heads**
12–22 mm across; *receptacle markedly
conical, hollow*, receptacle scales absent;
ligules becoming reflexed soon after flowers

open. **Habitat** Arable fields, waste ground, on light, fertile, mildly acid soils; to 365 m. **Dist**. Archaeophyte. Common throughout most of England, Wales; scarce in Scotland, Ireland. (Most of Europe.) **Fls** Jun–Aug.

Scentless Mayweed
Tripleurospermum inodorum

achene

flower

Non-aromatic, prostrate to erect, much-branched, glabrous annual to 60 cm. **Leaves** Leaflets not succulent. **Flowering heads** 15–40 mm across, solitary, on long stalks; *receptacle slightly convex, solid.* **Fruits** *Achenes, with 2 dark brown, ± circular oil glands towards top of outer face*; ribs separated. **Habitat** Common weed of arable fields, tracks, roadsides, waste ground, on disturbed, fertile soils; to 530 m. **Dist**. Archaeophyte. Throughout BI, but scarce in NW Scotland, W Ireland. (N and central Europe.) **Fls** Jul–Sep.

Sea Mayweed
Tripleurospermum maritimum

Perennial, similar to *T. inodorum,* but ± prostrate, mat-forming; *leaflets shorter, rather succulent; oil glands on achenes elongated, ribs almost touching.* **Habitat** Shingle beaches, cliffs, sea walls, sand, waste ground close to sea. **Dist**. Native. Common all round coasts of BI. (N Europe.) **Fls** Jul–Sep.

achene

flower

Ragworts and groundsels ▶ *Senecio*
Annuals or perennials with discoid or radiate flower heads; the involucral bracts are mostly in one row or with a few short outer ones; disc florets and ray florets are both yellow.

Common Ragwort
Senecio jacobaea

Erect, branched, non-stoloniferous biennial or perennial to 100 cm. **Leaves** Stem *leaves* irregularly lobed, glabrous above, *sparsely hairy on veins beneath*, several pairs of lateral lobes, terminal lobe not much broader than laterals. **Flowering heads** 15–25 mm across, *in dense inflorescence*, so that neighbouring heads in contact or overlapping; outer involucral bracts *c*.¼ as long as inner. **Habitat** Rough grassland, rabbit-grazed pasture, scrub, woodland rides, waste ground, roadsides, sand-dunes; to 670 m. **Dist**. Native. Common throughout BI. (Most of Europe, but rare in extreme N and S.) **Fls** Jun–Oct.

COMMON RAGWORT

Hoary Ragwort
Senecio erucifolius

Tall, stiffly erect, stoloniferous perennial to 120 cm. **Leaves** Stem *leaves deeply pinnately lobed, terminal lobe small, narrow, acute, margins revolute, whole surface grey-pubescent beneath*. **Flowering heads** 15–20 mm across; outer involucral bracts *c*. ½ as long as inner. **Habitat** Rough grassland, roadsides, field borders, railway banks, on calcareous or clay soils; also waste ground, shingle, dunes. **Dist**.

Native. Lowland England, Wales; absent from Scotland; rare in Ireland. (Most of Europe except N.) **Fls** Jul–Aug.

Marsh Ragwort
Senecio aquaticus

Erect, non-stoloniferous, glabrous or sparsely pubescent biennial to 80 cm. **Leaves** Stem leaves with large, ovate terminal lobe and a few smaller lateral lobes. **Flowering heads** 25–30 mm across; *inflorescence spreading so that neighbouring heads not in contact*. **Habitat** Wet meadows, marshes, by streams, ponds and ditches; to 460 m. **Dist**. Native. Throughout lowland BI, but declining in SE. (S, W and central Europe.) **Fls** Jul–Aug.

Oxford Ragwort
Senecio squalidus

Decumbent to erect, ± glabrous annual or short-lived perennial, to 30 cm. Very variable. **Leaves** Deeply lobed. **Flowering heads** *16–20 mm across*, in open inflorescence; *involucral bracts all black-tipped; 12–15 ray florets*. **Habitat**

Habitat Ubiquitous weed of waste ground, gardens, arable fields; to 550 m. Also on dunes, shingle, cliffs. **Dist**. Native. Throughout BI. (All Europe except extreme N.) **Fls** Jan–Dec.

Heath Groundsel
Senecio sylvaticus

Erect, pubescent annual to 70 cm. **Stems** *Glandular but not sticky.* **Leaves** *Yellow-green*, deeply pinnately lobed; pubescent, becoming glabrous. **Flowering heads** Numerous, 5–6 mm across; peduncles and involucral bracts with short glandular hairs; *8–14 ray florets, short, revolute.*

Naturalised on waste ground, walls, railways, roadsides. **Dist**. Introduced. Widespread throughout England, Wales; spreading in Scotland, Ireland. (Native of Sicily.) **Fls** May–Dec.

Groundsel
Senecio vulgaris

Erect, irregularly branched annual to 30 cm. **Leaves** Pinnately lobed, glabrous or with cottony hairs. **Flowering heads** 4–5 mm across, *discoid; ray florets usually absent,* or *≤5 mm if present; outer involucral bracts black-tipped.* **Fruits** Achenes, ≤2.5 mm.

Habitat Heaths, commons, open woodland, cliffs, on sandy soils; to 365 m. **Dist**. Native. Rather local, throughout BI. (Central Europe.) **Fls** Jul–Sep.

Sticky Groundsel
Senecio viscosus

Erect, branched, *sticky annual, with dense glandular hairs,* to 60 cm. **Leaves** Dark green, deeply pinnately lobed, very sticky.

STICKY GROUNDSEL

stalks; florets bright yellow. **Habitat** Damp woods, stream sides, roadsides. **Dist**. Introduced. Naturalised throughout most of BI as escape from cultivation, but rare in Ireland. (W Europe.) **Fls** May–Jul.

Colt's-foot
Tussilago farfara

Rosette-forming, rhizomatous perennial. **Stems** *Flowering stems erect, to 15 cm, appearing long before leaves*. **Leaves** All basal, 20–30 cm across, densely white-felted beneath, cordate, shallowly lobed, *lobes with small blackish teeth*. **Flowering heads** Radiate, solitary, 15–35 mm across, yellow. **Habitat** Disturbed ground, shingle, dunes, eroding cliffs, scree, riverbanks, waste ground, verges; to 1065 m. **Dist**. Native. Throughout BI. (All Europe except extreme N.) **Fls** Mar–Apr.

Flowering heads 10–15 mm across, long-stalked; 13 *ray florets, revolute*. **Habitat** Free-draining sands, gravels, on roadsides, railways, banks, walls, waste ground, dunes, shingle; to 430 m. **Dist**. Introduced. Naturalised throughout most of BI, but rare in N Scotland, Ireland; spreading. (All Europe except extreme N.) **Fls** Jul–Sep.

Leopard's-bane
Doronicum pardalianches

Rosette-forming, rhizomatous perennial to 90 cm. **Stems** Flowering stems leafy. **Leaves** *Rosette leaves long-stalked, ovate, cordate, pubescent*. **Flowering heads** *Radiate, 40–60 mm across*, several on long

Butterburs ▶ *Petasites*
Dioecious, rhizomatous perennials with large, cordate basal leaves. Flowering stems are leafless but with few to several scale leaves. Flowering heads are in dense, spike-like terminal inflorescences. Stems and leaves are downy with white-cottony hairs.

Butterbur
Petasites hybridus

Flowering stems Erect, to 40 cm, with many narrow *scale leaves, <10 mm wide*. **Leaves** 10–90 cm across, long-stalked, shallowly lobed, marginal teeth uneven, *sides of basal sinus convergent*. **Flowering heads** *Pale purplish, in ± cylindrical inflorescence,* appearing before leaves. **Habitat** Damp woodlands, banks of rivers and streams, wet meadows; to 380 m. **Dist**. Native. Throughout BI, but scarce in N Scotland; female plants mostly in N and central England. (Most of Europe.) **Fls** Mar–May.

Winter Heliotrope
Petasites fragrans

Flowering stems To 25 cm; scale leaves 2–7 cm, sometimes with fully developed blade. **Leaves** *Persisting through winter,* 10–20 cm across, roundish, green on both surfaces, slightly pubescent beneath, marginal teeth all ± same size. **Flowering heads** *c.6–20, lilac, marginal flowers ligulate,* vanilla-scented; in rather loose inflorescence. **Habitat** Hedge banks, roadsides verges, stream sides, waste ground, forming large, persistent colonies. **Dist**. Introduced (native of N Africa). Naturalised throughout BI; common in S, but rare in N Scotland.

(Naturalised in central and S Europe.) **Fls** Dec–Mar, with leaves.

Nodding Bur-marigold
Bidens cernua

Erect, branched annual to 75 cm. **Leaves** *Unlobed*, strongly toothed, sessile, with long, drawn-out, acute apex. **Flowering heads** *Solitary*, discoid, 15–25 mm across, *drooping*; receptacle scales 6–8 mm, oblanceolate. **Fruits** Achene, with 4 terminal barbed spines. **Habitat** Wet meadows, sides of ditches, dykes, streams and ponds, especially where drying out in summer. **Dist**. Native. Throughout BI, but commoner in S and scarce in Scotland. (Most of Europe.) **Fls** Jul–Sep.

Trifid Bur-marigold
Bidens tripartita

Erect, branched annual to 75 cm. **Leaves** Most *3-lobed*, coarsely toothed; petioles winged. **Flowering heads** 15–25 mm across, solitary, ± *erect*; receptacle scales 8–10 mm, broadly linear, acute. **Fruits** Achene, with 2–4 terminal, upwardly barbed spines. **Habitat** Wet meadows, margins of streams, rivers, ditches, ponds and lakes. **Dist**. Native. Throughout most of BI, but scarce or absent in much of Scotland. (All Europe except extreme N.) **Fls** Jul–Sep.

Hemp-agrimony
Eupatorium cannabinum

Tall, robust, clump-forming perennial to 150 cm. **Leaves** *Basal leaves deeply 3(–5)-lobed*, lobes toothed. **Flowering heads** *Discoid, 2–5 mm across, numerous, in dense terminal inflorescence; flowers pinkish purple.*

Habitat Tall herbaceous vegetation of fens, marshes, damp woods, sides of rivers and ponds, wet ditches; also calcareous scrub. **Dist**. Native. Throughout BI, but scarce and mostly coastal in Scotland. (Most of Europe.) **Fls** Jul–Sep.

BUTOMACEAE
Flowering rushes

Flowering Rush
Butomus umbellatus

Tall, handsome, glabrous, erect perennial to 150 cm. **Stems** Smooth. **Leaves** Triangular in section. **Flowers** Forming an umbel, individual flower stalks up to 10 cm; 3 sepals and petals, pink; 9 stamens. **Habitat** Shallow water of margins of ponds, slow-moving rivers, dykes and canals, on fertile soils. **Dist**. Native. Local throughout England; rare in Wales, Ireland; introduced in Scotland. (Most of Europe.) **Fls** Jul–Sep.

ALISMATACEAE
Water-plantains
•••

Glabrous aquatic or emergent annuals or perennials. Leaves basal, entire, stalked. Flowers in simple umbels or whorls, regular; 3 sepals, green; 3 petals, white or mauve; ≥6 stamens; ovary superior. Fruits are usually a head of achenes.

Arrowhead
Sagittaria sagittifolia

Erect, glabrous, submerged or emergent aquatic perennial to *c*.90 cm. **Leaves** Submerged leaves linear, grass-like; floating leaves narrowly ovate; erect leaves long-stalked, blade *sagittate*, to 20 cm. **Flowers** Monoecious, 3–5 in a whorl, 20–30 mm across; inflorescence stalk longer than leaves. **Habitat** Characteristic of shallow, unpolluted waters of ponds, dykes, canals, slow-flowing rivers, on fertile soils. **Dist**. Native. Widespread in England; rare in Wales, Ireland. (Most of Europe.) **Fls** Jul–Aug.

Water-plantain
Alisma plantago-aquatica

Tall, robust, glabrous perennial to 1 m. **Leaves** Emergent leaves long-stalked, blade to 20 cm, rounded to cordate at base; submerged leaves linear, 30–80 cm. **Flowers** 7–12 mm across, opening in the afternoon, in much-branched inflorescence,

20–100 cm; *inner petals blunt. Style arising from below middle of fruit.* **Habitat** Shallow water or wet fertile mud of marginal vegetation of drainage dykes, slow-flowing rivers, canals, ponds, lakes. **Dist**. Native. Frequent throughout BI. (Most of Europe.) **Fls** Jun–Aug.

HYDROCHARITACEAE
Frogbits and waterweeds
•••

Frogbit
Hydrocharis morsus-ranae VU.

Free-floating, stoloniferous aquatic with roots hanging in water. Overwinters by means of perennating buds that sink to mud in autumn. **Leaves** *In basal rosette, stalks long; blades orbicular, cordate, 1.5–5 cm across.* **Flowers** *Conspicuous,* unisexual, 20–30 mm across; 3 sepals, green; 3 petals, larger than sepals, white; 9–12 stamens. **Fruits** Berry-like capsule (rarely formed). **Habitat** Slow-flowing ditches, dykes, canals, pools, ponds, in calcareous or base-rich water. **Dist**.

FROGBIT

Native. Very local, declining. Throughout BI except Scotland. (Most of Europe.) **Fls** Jul–Aug.

Waterweeds ▶ *Elodea*

Canadian Waterweed
Elodea canadensis

Dioecious, submerged perennial, rooted in mud. All British plants are female. **Stems** Long, to 3 m, branched. **Leaves** *Upper leaves mostly in whorls of 3, not strongly recurved, 0.8–2.3 mm wide below tip, leaf tip blunt.* **Flowers** Inconspicuous, solitary, in axils of leaves; 3 sepals; 3 petals, 1.5–3 mm, narrower than sepals, white; female flowers reach surface by long, slender, stalk-like

elongation of perianth tube; male flowers break off and float. **Habitat** Most kinds of ponds, canals, dykes, slow-moving rivers, on fertile soils; to 440 m. **Dist**. Introduced (native of North America). Established throughout BI. Common, but now being replaced by *E. nuttallii* (*see* below). (Naturalised throughout much of Europe.) **Fls** May–Oct.

Nuttall's Waterweed
Elodea nuttallii

Submerged perennial. All British plants are female. Similar to *E. canadensis*, but upper leaves mostly in *whorls of 4, strongly recurved and twisted, narrower, 0.2–0.7 mm wide below tip*, margins minutely toothed in upper half, *leaf tip acute.* **Habitat** Similar to *E. canadensis*. **Dist**. Introduced (native North America). First recorded in 1966 and spreading rapidly, in places replacing *E. canadensis*. Now common and widespread in England. (Spreading in Europe.)

JUNCAGINACEAE
Arrowgrasses

Glabrous, rhizomatous, 'plantain-like' perennials. Leaves all in a basal rosette, sessile, with sheathing base, linear, cylindrical, with ligule. Flowers inconspicuous, in a terminal spike; 6 tepals; 6 stamens. Fruits consisting of 3–6 separating carpels.

Sea Arrowgrass
Triglochin maritimum

Robust, rhizomatous
perennial to 50 cm.
Leaves Half-cylindrical,
not furrowed. **Flowers**
Inflorescence not
elongating after
flowering. **Fruits**
3–4 mm, not
appressed to
inflorescence axis.
Habitat Common
plant of salt marshes,
brackish grazing
marshes. **Dist**. Native.
All round coasts of
BI. (All Europe except
Mediterranean.)
Fls Jul–Sep.

Marsh Arrowgrass
Triglochin palustris

Similar to
T. maritimum, but
more slender; leaves
half-cylindrical,
deeply furrowed on
upper surface towards
base; inflorescence
elongating after
flowering; fruits
7–10 mm, appressed
to inflorescence
axis. **Habitat** Wet
meadows, fens,
marshes, spring
flushes, on
calcareous or
mildly acid soils;
to 970 m. **Dist**. Native.
Throughout BI, but scarce in
SE and SW. (All Europe
except Mediterranean.)
Fls Jun–Aug.

PONDWEEDS
....

There are three families of submerged or
floating aquatic plants that look superficially
similar. All have leafy submerged flowering
stems with opposite or alternate and
submerged leaves, and/or floating linear or
narrowly ovate leaves.

POTAMOGETONACEAE
Pondweeds
....

Pondweeds ▶ *Potamogeton*
Pondweeds can sometimes be difficult to
identify. It is important to look carefully
at the leaf shape, the number of leaf veins,
and details of the stipules and fruits (these
are described under the individual species
descriptions). Lengths of fruits include
the beak. Numerous hybrids have been
recorded, but these are not common and
are usually sterile.

Broad-leaved Pondweed
Potamogeton natans

Leaves Floating leaves stalked, blade 2.5–
12.5 cm, thick and opaque, ovate-elliptic,
*decurrent for short distance down stalk and
therefore appearing jointed just below blade;*

fruit

submerged leaves linear, without expanded *blade*; stipules 40–170 mm. **Flowers** In dense cyclindrical inflorescence. **Fruits** 4–5 mm. **Habitat** Ponds, lakes, slow-moving streams, rivers, dykes and canals, in clear, mildly acid to calcareous water. **Dist**. Native. Common throughout BI. (All Europe.) **Fls** May–Sep.

Bog Pondweed
Potamogeton polygonifolius

Leaves Floating leaves thick and opaque, secondary veins inconspicuous, similar in shape to *P. natans*, but *without 'joint' on petiole below blade; submerged leaves stalked, blade narrowly elliptic*, to 16 cm; stipules 10–15 mm. **Fruits** 1.9–2.6 mm.

fruit

Habitat Small ponds, bog pools, wet *Sphagnum* lawns, spring heads, streams, in shallow acid, often peaty water; to 780 m. **Dist**. Native. Common in N and W Britain and parts of S. (W and central Europe.) **Fls** May–Oct.

Shining Pondweed
Potamogeton lucens

Leaves *Floating leaves absent*; submerged leaves large, 75–200 mm, *yellowish green*, translucent, elliptic, apex with short point, *margin finely toothed; petioles short*, to 10 mm, or leaves appearing ± sessile; *stipules 35–80 mm, winged*. **Fruits** 3.2–4.5 mm.

fruit

Habitat Lakes, canals, rivers, fenland drains, in clear, calcium-rich water to depths of 4 m. **Dist.** Native. Widespread in England SE of line from Humber to Wash, central Ireland; scarce elsewhere. (Most of Europe.) **Fls** Jun–Sep.

Various-leaved Pondweed
Potamogeton gramineus

Leaves Floating leaves elliptic, opaque, blade 19– 70 mm; *submerged leaves translucent, narrowly elliptic, sessile, margins finely toothed, tip usually with short tooth, 40–90 mm, 4.5–12× as long as wide*; stipules 10–25 mm.

fruit

Fruits 2.4–3.1 mm. **Habitat** Rivers, streams, canals, lakes, ditches, in acid to base-rich shallow water. **Dist**. Native. Widespread in N England, Scotland, Ireland; rare elsewhere. (Much of Europe, but rare in Mediterranean.) **Fls** Jun–Sep.

Red Pondweed
Potamogeton alpinus

fruit

Leaves Floating leaves ovate-elliptic, 45–90 mm, narrowing to short stalk, blunt, entire; submerged *leaves often reddish, especially when dry*, 70–180 × 10–25 mm, narrowly oblong-elliptic, *sessile, blunt, entire*, with 7–11 longitudinal veins, *midrib bordered by broad band of lacunae at base*; stipules 20–60 mm, shorter than internodes. **Fruits** 2.6–3.7 mm. **Habitat** Lakes, canals, dykes, ponds, streams, in neutral to mildly acid water; to 945 m. **Dist**. Native. Widespread in N Britain, N Ireland; rare elsewhere. (Much of Europe, but rare in S.) **Fls** Jun–Sep.

Perfoliate Pondweed
Potamogeton perfoliatus

Robust aquatic plant. **Leaves** Floating leaves absent; *submerged leaves 20–115 mm, 1.3–10× as long as wide, lanceolate to ovate, thin, translucent, sessile, cordate, ± completely*

fruit

clasping stem; stipules 2.5–22 mm, soon disappearing. **Fruits** 2.6–3.5 mm. **Habitat** Mildly acid to neutral lakes, ponds, canals, slow-flowing streams; to 780 m. **Dist**. Native. Widespread throughout most of BI. (All Europe.) **Fls** Jun–Sep.

Lesser Pondweed
Potamogeton pusillus

Stems Slender, to 70 cm, compressed, richly branched in shallow water. **Leaves**

cross-section of stipule

fruit

Submerged leaves 0.8–1.4 mm wide, linear, tapering or abruptly narrowing to acute tip; *3 longitudinal veins, midrib prominent, not bordered by lacunae; stipules 5–17 mm, tubular for most of their length when young,* splitting later. **Fruits** 1.8–2.3 mm. **Habitat** Lakes, pools, canals, ditches, dykes, streams, in calcareous or brackish water. **Dist**. Native. Widely distributed throughout BI, but rather local. (Most of Europe.) **Fls** Jun–Sep.

Small Pondweed
Potamogeton berchtoldii

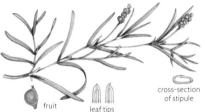

cross-section of stipule

fruit   leaf tips

Stems To 60 cm, slender, only slightly compressed. **Leaves** *Submerged leaves 0.8–1.8 mm wide, linear; 3 longitudinal veins,* without faint intermediate veins, midrib bordered by band of lacunae at least at base; *stipules 5–15 mm, open.* **Fruits** 1.8–2.7 mm. **Similar spp**. Very similar to *P. pusillus* (p.229), but differing in the open stipules, which need to be examined carefully. **Habitat** Occurring in almost the full range of aquatic habitats, but avoiding peaty water and, unlike *P. pusillus*, not tolerant of brackish conditions; to 500 m. **Dist**. Native. Throughout BI. (Most of Europe.) **Fls** Jun–Sep.

Curled Pondweed
Potamogeton crispus

Stems Robust, compressed, to 150 cm. **Leaves** *Submerged leaves 5–12 mm wide,* sessile, linear-oblong, tips usually blunt, *margins toothed, upper leaves strongly*

fruit

undulate; 3–5 longitudinal veins, midrib bordered by band of lacunae; stipules 4–17 mm, open. **Fruits** 4–6.2 mm. **Habitat** Shallow lakes, ponds, streams, canals, drainage dykes; lowland to 350 m. **Dist**. Native. Frequent throughout BI, but rare in N Scotland. (Most of Europe.) **Fls** May–Oct.

Fennel Pondweed
Potamogeton pectinatus

Stems *To 225 cm, richly branched.* **Leaves** Submerged leaves 0.2–4 mm wide, midrib bordered on each side by longitudinal air channel; *leaf sheath open, ligule 5–15 mm.*

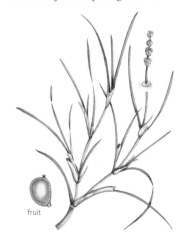

fruit

Fruits *3.3–4.7 mm.* **Habitat** Eutrophic or brackish water of ponds, lakes, canals, rivers, streams, drainage dykes. **Dist**. Native. Throughout lowland BI, but scarce in N Scotland. (Most of Europe.) **Fls** May–Sep.

Horned Pondweed
Zannichellia palustris

Submerged fresh- and brackish-water aquatic perennial. **Stems** Slender, much branched, leafy, to 40 cm. **Leaves** Linear, mostly opposite, 0.2–1.3 mm wide. **Flowers** Monoecious, in sessile axillary groups consisting of 1 male and 2–5 female flowers; perianth absent. **Fruits** 2.6–5 mm,

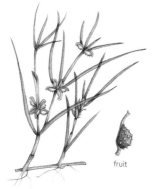

fruit

with distinct beak, 0.4–2.6 mm. **Similar spp**. Superficially similar to some grass-leaved pondweeds, especially *Potamogeton pectinatus* (opposite), but distinguished by opposite leaves and clusters of axillary flowers. **Habitat** Shallow lakes, ponds, ditches, streams, brackish dykes and lagoons; lowland to 380 m. **Dist**. Native. Throughout BI; frequent in S, scarce in N and W. (All Europe.) **Fls** May–Aug.

RUPPIACEAE
Tasselweeds

Small family of submerged, brackish-water aquatic perennials. Leaves linear with sheathing bases, mostly alternate, but upper opposite. Inflorescence few-flowered, terminal, short and umbel-like; perianth absent; 2 stamens, but appearing as 4 as anthers widely bilobed.

Beaked Tasselweed
Ruppia maritima

Slender aquatic perennial. **Stems** Much branched, to 30 cm. **Leaves** 0.4–0.9 mm wide. **Flowers** Peduncles ≤2.5 mm, straight or curved. **Fruits** 2–2.8 mm. **Habitat** Shallow water of brackish lagoons, creeks, drainage dykes. **Dist**. Native. All round coasts of BI, but declining in S. (Most of Europe.) **Fls** Jul–Sep.

fruit

ZOSTERACEAE
Eelgrasses

Submerged, rhizomatous marine perennials, with alternate grass-like leaves in opposite ranks; leaves sheathing at base with ligule. Flowers monoecious, small, inconspicuous, enclosed within leaf sheath, perianth absent.

Eelgrass
Zostera marina

Stems Flowering stems much branched. **Leaves** 5–10 mm wide, rounded, mucronate at tip, with 5–11 veins, sheaths tubular. **Flowers** Stigma 2× as long as style. **Fruits** 3–3.5 mm. **Habitat** In sub-tidal zone, from low-water springs to 4 m, on gravel, sand, sandy mud. **Dist**. Native. Declining owing to disease. All round coasts of BI, but rare in E. (All Europe except extreme N.) **Fls** Jun–Sep.

EELGRASS

fruit

Dwarf Eelgrass
Zostera noltei VU.

Slender, creeping, inter-tidal perennial. **Stems** Flowering stems unbranched. **Leaves**

fruit

Very narrow, 0.5–1.5 mm wide, notched at tip, with 3 veins, sheaths open. **Fruits** 1.5–2 mm. **Habitat** Estuaries, mudflats, creeks, runnels, between mid-tide level and low-water springs. **Dist**. Native. Scattered all round coasts of BI. (All Europe except N.) **Fls** Jun–Oct.

ARACEAE
Arums
••

Large, essentially tropical family of mostly glabrous, rhizomatous or tuberous herbs, but also shrubs, climbers and epiphytes. Flowers commonly monoecious, small and packed together on a club-shaped spadix, this usually enclosed within a large leaf-like bract – the spathe. There are 2 native British species.

Lords-and-ladies/Cuckoo-pint
Arum maculatum

Erect, glabrous perennial to 50 cm. **Leaves** Appearing in spring; petioles long; blade

7–20 cm, often black-spotted, triangular-hastate, midrib dark green. **Flowers** Spathe 10–25 cm, erect, base completely enclosing flowers at base of spadix; *spadix 7–12 cm, c. ½ as long as spathe, upper sterile portion dull purple (rarely yellow)*; flowers unisexual, in compact whorls, males above, females below. **Fruits** Red, berry-like. **Habitat** Hedgerows, woodlands, coppice, on moist, fertile soils; lowland to 425 m. **Dist**. Native. Common. England, Wales, Ireland; introduced in Scotland. (W, central and S Europe.) **Fls** Apr–May.

Sweet-flag
Acorus calamus

Tall, rhizomatous perennial to 100 cm. **Leaves** *Linear, rather sedge-like, 50–125 × 0.7–2.5 cm, transversely wrinkled; midrib prominent, with strong smell of tangerines* when crushed. **Flowers** *Spadix appearing lateral, without spathe, 5–9 cm, yellowish green.* **Habitat** Shallow, nutrient-rich water at water's edge. **Dist**. Introduced (native of Asia and North America). Naturalised throughout BI, but rare in N and W. **Fls** May–Jul.

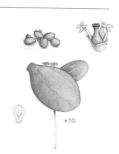

LEMNACEAE
Duckweeds
● ●

Small, floating aquatic plants that form a green carpet on the surface of stagnant water. Each plant consists of a small, simple frond, with or without roots; the minute single-sex flowers are borne in hollows on the frond surface. Duckweeds include the smallest flowering plants known.

Common Duckweed
Lemna minor

Fronds 2–5 mm, with 3 veins, dark shining green, obovate, each with 1 root. **Habitat** Stagnant or slow-moving nutrient-rich waters, damp exposed mud; lowland to 500 m. **Dist**. Native. Common throughout BI, but rare in NW Scotland. (All Europe.) **Fls** Jun–Jul.

Ivy-leaved Duckweed
Lemna trisulca

Fronds 3–15 mm, with 3 veins, thin, tapering to short stalk, each with 1 root, cohering in branched groups, floating beneath surface. **Habitat** Stagnant or slow-moving moderate to eutrophic water, ponds, ditches; lowland to 340 m. **Dist**. Native. Frequent throughout BI, N to central Scotland. (All Europe except extreme N.)

Fat Duckweed
Lemna gibba

Fronds 1–8 mm, with 4–5 veins, often turning very reddish purple, underside strongly swollen, each with

1 root. **Habitat** Stagnant or slow-moving water in ditches, ponds, canals; tolerant of brackish water. **Dist**. Native. Rather local. Lowland England; scarce elsewhere. (Europe except N.) **Fls** Jun–Jul, rarely.

Greater Duckweed
Spirodela polyrhiza

Fronds 3–10 mm, with 5–15 veins, underside reddish, each with 5–15 roots. **Habitat** Still or slow-moving base-rich ponds, drainage dykes, canals. **Dist**. Native. Local. Lowland England, Ireland. (All Europe except N and SW.) **Fls** Rarely.

×10

JUNCACEAE
Rushes and wood-rushes

Perennial or, less often, annual, wind-pollinated herbs with cylindrical, channelled or grass-like leaves. Leaves are either alternate or, more usually, all basal. They are distinguished from other grass-like plants by the small, regular (lily-like) bisexual flowers, with 6 tepals (3+3), 6 stamens, 3 stigmas and the 1–3-celled superior ovary. Flowers are arranged in terminal inflorescences that often appear lateral, and the tepals are usually greenish or brownish. Many rushes are characteristic plants of wet habitats.

Heath Rush
Juncus squarrosus

Densely tufted, wiry perennial to 50 cm. **Leaves** *All basal*, 8–15 cm, *linear, stiff, reflexed, upper surface deeply channelled.*

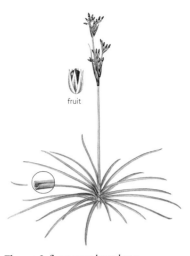

fruit

Flowers Inflorescence branches ± erect; lowest bract much shorter than inflorescence; tepals dark brown. **Habitat** Moorland, damp heaths, acid grassland, bogs, upland flushes; to 1040 m. **Dist**. Native. Common throughout BI, but scarce and declining in lowland England. (NW, W and central Europe.) **Fls** Jun–Jul.

Slender Rush
Juncus tenuis

fruit

Tufted perennial. **Stems** Flowering stems 15–35 cm, erect. **Leaves** Most basal, 10–25 cm, linear, yellowish green. **Flowers** *Lowest bracts much longer than inflorescence; inflorescence diffuse; tepals yellowish, lanceolate, acute.* **Habitat** Frequent on damp, open ground, paths, tracksides, heathland and woodland rides, lake margins. **Dist**. Introduced (native of North and South

America). Widespread in S and W BI; scattered elsewhere. (N, W and central Europe.) **Fls** Jun–Sep.

Saltmarsh Rush
Juncus gerardii

Very similar to *J. compressus*, but *lowest bract usually shorter than inflorescence; anthers 2–3× as long as filaments; styles as long as or slightly longer than ovary; capsule about as long as perianth*, ovoid. **Habitat** Upper levels of salt marshes, wet brackish grassland, cliff-top turf. **Dist**. Native. Common all round coasts of BI. (All European coasts, saline habitats inland.) **Fls** Jun–Jul.

Three-leaved Rush
Juncus trifidus

Slender, densely tufted, patch-forming alpine perennial. **Stems** Flowering stems to 30 cm, *with 1–2 leaves and leaf-like lower bract, all longer than inflorescence*. **Flowers** Sessile, 1–3 in tight cluster; tepals brown. **Fruits** Capsule, longer than perianth. **Habitat** Abundant on bare, exposed mountain plateaux, rock crevices, on acid or calcareous rock; to 1310 m. **Dist**. Native. Central and NW Scotland. (Arctic Europe, mts of central and S Europe.) **Fls** Jun–Aug.

fruit

fruit

Toad Rush
Juncus bufonius

Erect to procumbent tufted annual to 35 cm. **Stems** Simple or much branched. **Leaves** *0.5–2 cm × <1 mm, bristle-like*, dark green. **Flowers** Inflorescence leafy, much branched; *tepals without dark lines, all acute*. **Fruits** Capsule, shorter than inner perianth segments. **Habitat** All kinds of seasonally wet, open habitats, dune slacks, estuarine mud. **Dist**. Native. Common throughout BI. (All Europe.) **Fls** Aug–Sep.

Jointed Rush
Juncus articulatus

Prostrate to ascending, tufted, rhizomatous perennial to 80 cm. **Leaves** *Curved, laterally compressed*, with inconspicuous transverse septa. **Flowers** Inflorescence repeatedly branched, branches diverging at acute angle; perianth dark brown to black; *inner and outer tepals same length, acute*. **Fruits** *Shining black ovoid, mucronate capsule*. **Habitat** Marshes, fens, dune slacks, damp woodland rides, margins of ponds, lakes and streams, on base-rich or calcareous soils; to 810 m. **Dist**. Native. Common throughout BI. (All Europe.) **Fls** Jun–Sep.

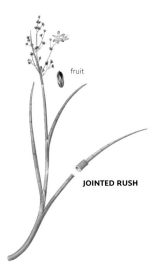

fruit

JOINTED RUSH

fruit

Sharp-flowered Rush
Juncus acutiflorus

Tall, stiffly erect, rhizomatous perennial to 100 cm. **Leaves** *Straight, ± cylindrical in section*, with conspicuous transverse septa. **Flowers** Inflorescence repeatedly branched, branches diverging at acute angle; perianth brown; *tepals acute, tapering to fine points, the outer recurved at tip.* **Fruits** *Brown capsule, evenly tapered to fine point.* **Habitat** Wet pastures, marshes, wet heaths, bogs, pond sides, on acid soils; to 685 m. **Dist**. Native. Common throughout BI. (W, central and S Europe.) **Fls** Jul–Sep.

Bulbous Rush
Juncus bulbosus

Small, slender perennial, greatly varying in habit and stature. **Stems**

fruit

inside leaf

Tufted, procumbent, rooting at nodes or free-floating, often with *swollen base*. **Leaves** Filiform, with numerous indistinct septa. **Flowers** *Inflorescence diffuse, sparse, often proliferating into small, leafy non-flowering shoots*; outer tepals acute, inner blunt. **Fruits** Blunt capsule. **Habitat** Frequent on bare mud or peat, woodland rides, wet heaths, mires, on acid soils; or free-floating. **Dist.** Native. Throughout BI, but scarce in English lowlands. (Most of Europe except SE.) **Fls** Jun–Sep.

Three-flowered Rush
Juncus triglumis

fruit

Stiffly erect, small, tufted perennial to 20 cm. **Leaves** All basal, curved. **Flowers** *(2–)3 all at ± same level forming terminal cluster*; lowest bract shorter than inflorescence. **Fruits** Blunt, mucronate capsule, 4–5.5 mm, slightly exceeding perianth. **Habitat**

Wet, gravelly base-rich flushes, rock ledges; to 1065 m. **Dist**. Native. Mts of N Wales and N England, Scottish Highlands. (N Europe, mts of S and E Europe.) **Fls** Jun–Jul.

Sea Rush
Juncus maritimus

Erect, densely tufted, robust perennial to 100 cm. **Leaves** *Sharply pointed*. **Flowers** In much-branched inflorescence, appearing lateral, shorter than sharply pointed bract; *tepals 3–4.5 mm, straw-coloured*, inner blunt, outer acute. **Fruits** Ovoid, mucronate *capsule, about as long as perianth*. **Habitat** Upper parts of salt marshes, dune slacks. **Dist**. Native. All round coasts of BI except NW Scotland. (All European coasts except extreme N; also inland E-central Europe.) **Fls** Jul–Aug.

Hard Rush
Juncus inflexus

Densely tufted grey-green rhizomatous perennial to 120 cm. **Stems** *Stiffly erect, dull, glaucous, prominently ridged, pith interrupted*. **Flowers** Inflorescence apparently lateral, diffuse; tepals narrow, unequal. **Fruits** Dark brown, glossy capsule, as long as perianth. **Habitat** Wet meadows, banks of ponds, lakes, dykes and rivers on base-rich soils, dune slacks. **Dist**. Native. Common throughout BI as far N as central Scotland. (All Europe except N.) **Fls** Jun–Aug.

Soft Rush
Juncus effusus

Densely tufted, stiffly erect perennial to 150 cm. **Stems** *Bright green, smooth, glossy, pith continuous*. **Flowers** Inflorescence apparently lateral, diffuse or compacted into tight head (var. *subglomeratus*); tepals narrow, sharp-pointed. **Fruits** Yellowish-brown ovoid, blunt capsule, shorter than perianth. **Habitat** Marshes, bogs, wet grassland, margins of streams, ponds, rivers and dykes, wet woods, usually on neutral or acid soils; to 845 m. **Dist**. Native. Common throughout BI. (All Europe except Arctic.) **Fls** Jun–Aug.

fruit

tight-headed form

smooth stem

Compact Rush
Juncus conglomeratus

Densely tufted, erect perennial to 100 cm. Similar to *J. effusus*, but less robust, *stems rather greyish green, not glossy, with numerous fine ribs below inflorescence; inflorescence a tight head*. **Habitat** Marshes, bogs, wet heaths, wet grassland, ditches, lakes, rivers, damp woods; more restricted to acid soils than *J. effusus*. To 840 m. **Dist**. Native. Throughout BI. (Most of Europe.) **Fls** May–Jul.

flower

fruit

fine-ridged stem

Wood-rushes ▶ *Luzula*

Hairy Wood-rush
Luzula pilosa

Erect, tufted, grass-like perennial to 30 cm. **Leaves** *Basal leaves 3–4 mm* broad, sparsely hairy. **Flowers** Single, dark brown, in lax inflorescence with *slender, spreading*

fruit

inside leaf

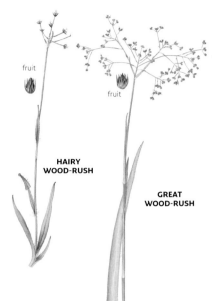

HAIRY WOOD-RUSH

GREAT WOOD-RUSH

Field Wood-rush
Luzula campestris

Erect, loosely tufted, *rhizomatous* perennial to 15 cm. **Leaves** Grass-like, 2–4 mm broad, with long, colourless hairs. **Flowers** Inflorescence of 1 sessile and 3–6 stalked clusters of 3–12 flowers; tepals dark brown; *anthers 3–4× as long as filaments.* **Habitat**

branches. **Fruits** Inflorescence branches reflexed; tepals shorter than or as long as capsule; seeds with hooked appendage, > ½ as long as rest of seed. **Habitat** Deciduous woodland, coppice, hedge banks, usually on acid soils; to 670 m. **Dist**. Native. Common throughout most of BI, but scarce in parts of Ireland. (Most of Europe except extreme S.) **Fls** Apr–Jun.

Great Wood-rush
Luzula sylvatica

Tall, erect, mat- or tussock-forming, robust, rhizomatous perennial to 80 cm. **Leaves** *Basal leaves 8–12 mm wide*, glossy, sparsely hairy. **Flowers** Brown, in groups of 3–5 in lax terminal inflorescence. **Fruits** Inflorescence branches spreading; tepals about as long as capsule. **Habitat** Woodlands, shaded stream sides, heaths, moors, upland stream sides, on acid soils; to 1040 m. **Dist**. Native. Throughout BI, but scarce in E England. (S, W and central Europe.) **Fls** May–Jun.

Short, infertile, usually acid grassland; to 1005 m. **Dist**. Native. Common throughout BI. (Most of Europe except extreme N.) **Fls** Mar–Jun.

Heath Wood-rush
Luzula multiflora

Erect, densely tufted perennial *without rhizomes*, to 40 cm. Very variable, with a number of named subspecies based on characters of the seed, of which the 2 most widespread and equally common are ssp. *congesta* and ssp. *multiflora*. **Leaves** Grass-like, 3–4 mm broad, sparsely hairy. **Flowers** In sessile clusters in

ssp. *multiflora*

ssp. *congesta*

compact head (ssp. *congesta*), or in stalked clusters (ssp. *multiflora*); peduncles smooth; outer and inner tepals equal, outer tepals 2.6–3.3 mm; *anthers 0.8–2.2× as long as filaments*; style 0.4–0.9 mm. **Fruits** Seeds 1.2–1.5 mm in ssp. *congesta*, 0.8–1.2 mm in ssp. *multiflora*. **Habitat** Acid grassland, open woods, heaths, moors, bogs; to 1020 m. **Dist**. Native. Common throughout BI. (Most of Europe.) **Fls** Apr–Jun.

Spiked Wood-rush
Luzula spicata

Small, tufted, stoloniferous alpine perennial to 30 cm. **Stems** *Erect*. **Leaves** Basal leaves 1–2 mm wide, recurved, slightly channelled. **Flowers** In *dense, drooping, spike-like inflorescence* of many several-flowered sessile clusters. **Fruits** Blackish capsule, 2.1–2.5 mm. **Habitat** Open stony ground, ledges, scree, cliffs, on acid rocks; to 1220 m. **Dist**. Native. Widespread in Scottish mts. (Arctic and N Europe, mts of S Europe.) **Fls** Jun–Jul.

fruit

TYPHACEAE
Bur-reeds and bulrushes
. . . .

Bur-reeds ▶ *Sparganium*
Rhizomatous aquatic perennials, with branched or unbranched stems. Leaves long and narrow with sheathing bases. Flowers unisexual, in tight, spherical heads, female heads at base of inflorescence, male heads above; individual flowers minute, with

3–6 scale-like tepals; male flowers with ≥3 stamens, females with a single ovary.

Branched Bur-reed
Sparganium erectum

Robust, erect perennial to 150 cm. **Leaves** 10–15 mm wide, erect, keeled. **Inflorescences** *Branched; 6–9 male heads*, mostly on branches above the 1–3 female heads. **Habitat** Shallow margins of rivers, dykes, lakes, ponds and canals, in nutrient-rich water; to 425 m. **Dist**. Native. Common throughout BI, but scarce in NW Scotland. (All Europe.) **Fls** Jun–Aug. **Note** Separated into 4 subspecies based on the shape of the fruits; there is no apparent habitat difference between these and they often grow together.

Bulrushes ▶ *Typha*
Tall, robust, rhizomatous perennials growing in shallow water. Stems erect, unbranched. Leaves flat, grey-green, arranged on two opposite sides of stem, with sheathing bases. Inflorescence a cylindrical spike of closely packed tiny flowers, the lower part brown and with female flowers, the upper narrower and yellow, and consisting of male flowers; perianth consisting of numerous bristles and/or scales.

Bulrush/ Reedmace
Typha latifolia

Tall, robust aquatic or semi-aquatic rhizomatous perennial to 3 m. **Leaves** *8–25 mm wide*, bluish green. **Inflorescences** *18–30 mm wide, with male and female parts ± contiguous*, male part 6–14 cm, female part 8–15 cm. **Habitat** Shallow, nutrient-rich water or bare mud at margins of lakes, pools, canals, ditches and slow-moving rivers; to 500 m. **Dist**. Native. Throughout BI, but scarce or absent in NW Scotland. (All Europe.) **Fls** Jun–Jul.

Lesser Bulrush
Typha angustifolia

Similar to *T. latifolia*, but *leaves* narrower, *3–6 mm wide*; *inflorescence* narrower, *13–25 mm wide, with male and female parts separated by 3–8 cm of bare stem*. **Habitat** Similar to *T. latifolia*, but preferring deeper water and tolerant of less nutrient-rich conditions. **Dist**. Native. Widespread but local throughout lowland England; rare and scattered in rest of BI. (All Europe.) **Fls** Jun–Jul.

LILIACEAE
Lily family

The Liliaceae traditionally comprised a large variable family, with often colourful and conspicuous, usually regular flowers, with 6 petal-like tepals, 6 stamens and a 3-celled

inferior or superior ovary. DNA analysis has now confirmed that the old Liliaceae should be subdivided into at least nine separate families and these have been incorporated in the text where appropriate. The similar-looking Iridaceae has only 3 stamens.

Martagon Lily
Lilium martagon

Tall, attractive, bulbous perennial to 200 cm. **Leaves** *In whorls*, 7–20 cm. **Flowers** 3–10, *pink-purple*, *c.*40 mm across. **Habitat** Wood margins, coppice, orchards, derelict gardens. **Dist**. Introduced. Naturalised as a garden escape in scattered localities throughout Britain. (Most of Europe.) **Fls** Aug–Sep.

Yellow Star-of-Bethlehem
Gagea lutea

Bulbous perennial to 25 cm. **Leaves** *Single linear-lanceolate basal leaf* with hooded tip, to 45 cm × 15 mm, often curled; 2 stem leaves. **Flowers** *1–7, in umbel-like inflorescence*; tepals yellow with green band on outside, free, spreading. **Habitat** Damp woodland on deep, rich calcareous loams. **Dist**. Native. Widely scattered throughout Britain; absent from Ireland. (Most of Europe.) **Fls** Mar–May.

YELLOW STAR-OF-BETHLEHEM

LILY-OF-THE-VALLEY

ASPARAGACEAE
Hyacinth family

Lily-of-the-valley
Convallaria majalis

Perennial to 35 cm with long, creeping, much-branched rhizomes. **Leaves** *In pairs on long stalks*, 5–20 × 3–7 cm. **Flowers** *Nodding, sweet-scented*, 6–12 in a 1-sided raceme. **Fruits** Red berry. **Habitat** Dry, open woodlands on nutrient-poor, usually base-rich soils, especially ash woods on limestone; also a frequent garden escape. **Dist**. Native. Scattered throughout Britain. (Most of Europe except extreme N and S.) **Fls** May–Jun.

Solomon's-seal
Polygonatum multiflorum

Glabrous, rhizomatous perennial to 80 cm. **Stems** *Smooth*, arching. **Leaves**

SOLOMON'S-SEAL

5–12 cm, all cauline, alternate. **Flowers** *Tubular*, 9–15 mm, *contracted in middle*, in 2–5-flowered axillary clusters; *filaments of stamens hairy*. **Fruits** Bluish-black berry.

Similar spp. Garden Solomon's-seal *P. ×
hybridum* (*P. odoratum* × *P. multiflorum*)
is the commonest Solomon's-seal grown in
gardens, and frequently occurs as an escape
of cultivation throughout BI. It is often
confused with *P. multiflorum*, but the stems
are ridged or slightly angled and the flowers
are 15–22 mm. **Habitat** Dry woodlands,
usually on chalk or limestone. **Dist**. Native.
Local and scattered N to Lake District,
centred on central-S England; introduced
elsewhere in BI. (Most of Europe except
SW.) **Fls** May–Jun.

Star-of-Bethlehem
Ornithogalum umbellatum

Similar to
O. pyrenaicum,
but *leaves
with white
stripe running
down midrib*;
flowers
30–40 mm
across, shorter
than or as long
as pedicels,
4–12 in *corymbose
inflorescence, lower
pedicels up to 10 cm,
much longer than
upper*. **Habitat** Rough
grassland, open woods,
roadside verges. **Dist**.
Introduced; possibly
native in Breckland (East
Anglia). Throughout BI, but
very rare in Ireland. (S and
S-central Europe.) **Fls** Apr–Jun.

Bluebell
Hyacinthoides non-scripta *(B)

(Protected by law against sale.)
Glabrous, bulbous perennial to 50 cm.
Leaves All basal, 7–15(–20) mm wide.

Flowers
Drooping,
10–28 mm
across, 4–16 in
1-sided, drooping
inflorescence; bracts
in pairs, blue; tepals
united at base,
parallel-sided so
*flowers cylindrical,
tips revolute; stamens
unequal in length,
anthers cream or yellow.*
Habitat Abundant and
often forming extensive
carpets in deciduous
woodland, hedge banks,
coastal cliffs, upland acid
grassland; to 685 m. **Dist**.
Native. Throughout BI
except Orkney, Shetland.
(W Europe.) **Fls** Apr–Jun.

Spanish Bluebell
*Hyacinthoides
hispanica*

Similar to
H. non-scripta,
but leaves
broader, to
35 mm wide;
inflorescence
not 1-sided,
flowers erect
or spreading,
15–22 mm
long, 15–25 mm
across, becoming
saucer-shaped,
*tips of petals
not revolute,
stamens equal in
length*, anthers blue.
Dist. Introduced.
Cultivated in
gardens and

occasionally naturalised in suitable habitats. (Spain, Portugal.) **Fls** Apr–May. **Note** Most bluebells commonly cultivated in gardens are the hybrid between *H. non-scripta* and *H. hispanica*, *H.* × *variabilis*, which is fully fertile and will back-cross with *H. non-scripta*. It is a frequent escape, occurring in woods, hedgerows, churchyards, roadsides and rough ground throughout the BI. It is intermediate in character between the parents, but usually more difficult to separate from *H. hispanica*; the flowers are 12–17 mm long and 10–20 mm across, and mauve, pink or white.

Spring Squill
Scilla verna

Glabrous bulbous perennial to 30 cm. **Stems** Smooth. **Leaves** All basal, 2–7, long-linear. **Flowers** 10–16 mm across, 2–12, forming dense inflorescence; *1 bract per flower, longer than pedicels*; tepals free. **Dist.** Native. Rather local. SW and W coasts of BI from Devon to Shetland; E coast of Ireland. **Habitat** Short, dry grassland close to sea, cliff tops, maritime heath. (W Europe.)

Fls Apr–May. **Note Autumn Squill** *S. autumnalis* is similar to *S. verna* but leaves appear after flowers, inflorescence becoming lax, 4–20 flowered, no bracts. Native, in similar habitats but very local in SW England, Channel Is. **Fls** *Jul–Sep*.

Garden Asparagus
Asparagus officinalis

Rhizomatous perennial. **Stems** Much-branched; erect to 1.5 m. **Leaves** Reduced to small scales with clusters of 4–15 green needle-like 'cladodes' in their axils that perform the function of leaves, cladodes 10–20 mm, flexible; pedicels 6–10 mm. **Flowers** Unisexual, 1–2 in axils of scale leaves on main stem; tepals fused at base, 4.5–6.5 mm, greenish to pale yellow. **Fruit** A red berry. **Habitat** Naturalised as escape from cultivation, sandy heaths, dunes. **Dist.** Archaeophyte. central, S and E England. **Fls** Jul–Sep.

SPRING SQUILL AUTUMN SQUILL

BUTCHER'S-BROOM

Wild Asparagus
Asparagus prostratus EN

Differs from *A. officinalis* in stems to 30 cm, procumbent; cladodes 4–10 mm, rigid, glaucous; pedicels 2–6 mm. **Habitat** Rocky sea cliffs, sand dunes. **Dist**. Native, very local in SW England, S Wales, SE Ireland, Channel Is. (Coasts of W Europe.) **Fls** Jul–Sep.

Butcher's-broom
Ruscus aculeatus

Erect, rhizomatous, much-branched evergreen shrub to 80 cm. **Leaves** Reduced to minute scales with broad, leaf-like cladodes in their axils; cladodes dark green, 10–30 mm, ovate, thick, spine-tipped. **Flowers** 1, on upper surface of cladode, unisexual, *c.*3 mm across; tepals free, greenish. **Fruits** Red berry. **Habitat** Dry woods, hedgerows, coastal cliffs. **Dist**. Native. Rather local. S England, S Wales, Channel Is; sparsely naturalised in similar habitats in rest of BI. (W, S and S-central Europe.) **Fls** Jan–Mar.

ALLIACEAE

Onions ▶ *Allium*
Onions, chives and leeks are bulbous perennials that mostly have a characteristic smell of onion or garlic. Leaves usually all basal, linear or cylindrical. Flowers arranged in a terminal umbel, and sometimes replaced by bulbils; whole inflorescence is at first enclosed within a thin, papery spathe, which splits on flowering into 1 or 2 bracts; tepals free; 6 stamens. Fruits a capsule.

Ramsons
Allium ursinum

Stems To 50 cm, 2-angled. **Leaves** 2–3, basal, *narrowly ovate, rounded at base*, 10–25 cm long, 4–7 cm broad; petiole to 20 cm, twisted. **Flowers** In 6–20-flowered umbel, without bulbils; 2 bracts, shorter than pedicels; *tepals spreading*, 7–12 mm, white. **Habitat** Damp woodlands on rich, loamy, mildly acid to calcareous soils, hedge banks, coastal cliffs, limestone pavement; to 430 m. **Dist**. Native. Widespread and common throughout BI, but becoming scarce in N Scotland. (Most of Europe except extreme N and S.) **Fls** Apr–Jun.

RAMSONS

Field Garlic
Allium oleraceum VU.

Stems To 100 cm, smooth. **Leaves** 2–4, to 30 cm long, *cylindrical, lower part hollow*, ribbed beneath. **Flowers** In 5–40-flowered umbel, with few to many bulbils, or sometimes with bulbils only; *2 bracts, long-pointed, much longer than umbel; pedicels*

long, 15–60 mm, *outer drooping*; tepals 5–7 mm, pinkish, greenish or brownish; stamens not protruding. **Habitat** Dry, rough calcareous grassland, usually on steep, S-facing slopes. **Dist**. Native. Scattered throughout England; rare elsewhere. (All Europe except extreme S.) **Fls** Jul–Aug.

Wild Onion/Crow Garlic
Allium vineale

Stems To 120 cm, smooth. **Leaves** 2–4, cylindrical, hollow. **Flowers** Umbel 2–5 cm across, with bulbils only (var. *compactum*), with flowers and bulbils (var. *vineale*), or rarely with flowers only (var. *capsuliferum*); 1 bract; tepals 2–4.5 mm, pink or greenish white; stamens protruding or not. **Habitat** Dry calcareous or neutral grasslands, hedgerows, roadsides, weed of cereal crops, coastal cliffs; to 455 m. **Dist**. Native. Widespread in Britain N to central Scotland, becoming coastal further N; S Ireland. (Most of Europe except extreme N.) **Fls** Jun–Jul.

Three-cornered Garlic
Allium triquetrum

Stems To 45 cm, *sharply 3-angled.* **Leaves** 2–5, to 40 cm long, 5–17 mm wide, *flat, keeled beneath.* **Flowers** Drooping, in 3–15-flowered umbel, rather lax and 1-sided, without bulbils; *2 bracts*; tepals 10–18 mm, white with longitudinal green stripe; stamens not protruding. **Habitat** Roadsides, hedge banks, waste ground. **Dist.** Introduced. Naturalised escape from cultivation, widespread and increasing. S and SW Britain, S Ireland; scattered but spreading elsewhere. (W Mediterranean.) **Fls** Apr–Jun.

Daffodils ▶ *Narcissus*

Familiar bulbous perennials. Flowers either solitary or arranged in few-flowered umbels with a single thin, papery bract, the spathe, and with a trumpet-like or ring-like corona inserted between tepals and stamens; 6 tepals, all alike, usually spreading; 6 stamens; ovary inferior. There are numerous varieties, cultivars and hybrids, which are increasingly becoming naturalised on roadsides, banks and waste ground. The only native British daffodil is *N. pseudonarcissus* ssp. *pseudonarcissus.*

Daffodil
Narcissus pseudonarcissus

Habitat Damp, open woods, coppice, heathland, commons, old pastures, on mildly acid soils. **Dist.** Native and widespread to N England, E Wales; scarce in E England. Widely naturalised in East Anglia, Wales, Scotland; absent from Ireland. (W and central Europe.) **Fls** Feb–Mar.

Snowdrop
Galanthus nivalis

Bulbous perennial to 25 cm. **Leaves** 2, glaucous, linear, flat. **Flowers** Solitary, nodding, up to 40 mm across, white; spathe of 2 fused bracts, deeply divided at tip; tepals free, in 2 whorls, inner whorl smaller, emarginate, with green patch near incision. **Habitat** Damp woodlands, hedge banks, churchyards, parks; to 370 m. **Dist.** Probably introduced. Naturalised throughout BI, but rare in N Scotland, Ireland. (Most of Europe except N.) **Fls** Feb–Mar.

NARTHECIACEAE

Bog Asphodel
Narthecium ossifragum

Glabrous, rhizomatous perennial to 40 cm. **Leaves** *Mostly basal*, up to 30 cm long × 5 mm wide, often curved, similar on both surfaces, *erect and* Iris-

like. **Flowers** 6–20 in a raceme; *tepals golden yellow*; 1 style; *filaments densely hairy, anthers orange.* **Fruits** Capsule. **Habitat** Abundant plant of acid bogs, wet heaths, flushes; to 1005 m. **Dist**. Native. Widespread in N and W Britain; local in S England. (N and W Europe.) **Fls** Jul–Sep.

TOFIELDIACEAE

Scottish Asphodel
Tofieldia pusilla

Similar to a small *Narthecium*. **Stems** To 20 cm. **Leaves** Mostly basal, to 4 cm × 2 mm. **Flowers** 5–10 in a short, dense inflorescence; *tepals greenish white*; 3 *styles*; filaments glabrous, anthers greenish yellow. **Habitat** Wet calcareous hillside flushes, springs, mountain stream sides; to 975 m. **Dist**. Native. Widespread in central Scottish Highlands; confined to Upper Teesdale (Yorkshire, Durham) in England. (N Europe.) **Fls** Jun–Aug.

COLCHICACEAE

Meadow Saffron
Colchicum autumnale *(R)

Glabrous perennial with a spherical corm. **Stems** Flowering stem elongating in fruit. **Leaves** Developing in spring, up to 35 × 5 cm, bright glossy green; *plant leafless at flowering.* **Flowers** *1–3, Crocus-like, appearing in late summer–autumn*; perianth tube 5–20 cm, pale purple; ovary subterranean. **Habitat** Damp permanent meadows, clearings in open woodland, on rich, fertile soils. **Dist**. Native. Locally frequent but declining. Central and S Britain, especially around Severn Valley. (S, W and central Europe.) **Fls** Aug–Oct.

MELANTHEACEAE

Herb Paris
Paris quadrifolia

Distinctive rhizomatous perennial with erect stems, to 40 cm. **Leaves** *Broad, in whorls of 4* at top of stem, 6–12 cm. **Flowers** Solitary; tepals green, outer 4 sepal-like, inner 4 linear; 8 stamens. **Fruits** Black, berry-like. **Habitat** Damp calcareous woodland, grikes in limestone pavement; to 360 m. **Dist**. Native. Widely distributed but rather local throughout Britain. (Most of Europe except Mediterranean.) **Fls** May–Aug.

HERB PARIS

IRIDACEAE
Iris family
....

Differ from the lily family chiefly in having 3 stamens rather than 6; styles are usually 3-branched and ovary is inferior.

Spring Crocus
Crocus vernus

The most commonly cultivated garden crocus. **Leaves** 2–4, present at flowering, 90–150 × 2–8 mm, shorter than or as long as flowers. **Flowers** Spathe present; perianth tube purple, or white only if rest of flower is white; tepals purple or lavender, white, or striped purple and white. **Habitat** Roadsides, parks, churchyards. **Dist**. Introduced. Naturalised as escape from cultivation throughout Britain. (Central and S Europe.) **Fls** Feb–Jun.

Autumn Crocus
Crocus nudiflorus

Stoloniferous perennial. **Leaves** 3–4, not present at flowering, up to 17 cm ×

2–4 mm. **Flowers** Solitary, 50–100 mm across; spathe present; perianth tube white, tinged lilac or purple; tepals purple, not prominently veined. **Habitat** Meadows, pastures, parks, roadsides. **Dist**. Introduced. Naturalised as relic of cultivation, scattered throughout Britain. (SW Europe.) **Fls** Sep–Oct.

Irises ▶ *Iris*
Rhizomatous or bulbous perennials, with sword-shaped leaves often arranged in 2 vertical ranks. The characteristic large, showy flower is regular, with tepals in 2 whorls, the outer ('falls') usually deflexed and the smaller inner ones ('standards') often erect, usually consisting of well-marked basal 'claw' and expanded terminal 'limb'. Three style branches ('crest') lie close above falls and are broad, petaloid and notched at tip. Flowers develop within 2 spathes.

Yellow Iris
Iris pseudacorus

Tall, erect, glabrous, rhizomatous perennial to 150 cm. **Stems** Compressed, smooth, often branched. **Leaves** 15–25 mm broad, about as long as flowering stems. **Flowers** 8–10 cm across, *yellow*; pedicels about as long as ovary. **Habitat** Shallow margins of ponds, lakes, rivers and dykes, marshes, fens, wet woods; lowland to 480 m. **Dist**. Native. Widespread and common throughout BI. (Most of Europe.) **Fls** May–Jul.

Stinking Iris
Iris foetidissima

Dark green perennial to 80 cm, with *strong, unpleasant smell* when bruised.

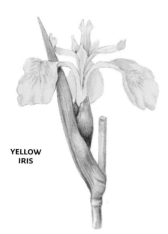

YELLOW IRIS

Montbretia
Crocosmia × crocosmiiflora

Stoloniferous, clump-forming perennial with flattened corms. **Stems** To 90 cm, unbranched or with 1–2 branches. **Leaves** 5–20 mm wide, shorter than stem, sword-like, *prominently veined on both surfaces*. **Flowers** 10–20 in a one-sided spike, *deep orange*, 2.5–5 cm across, irregular; tepals spreading, lobes about as long as tube. **Habitat** Hedge banks, roadsides,

Stems Unbranched, angled on one side. **Leaves** As long as or longer than flowering stem. **Flowers** *c.*8 cm across, *purplish livid*, rarely yellowish; spathes 2–3-flowered; pedicels 4–5× as long as ovary. **Fruits** *Seeds conspicuous, orange-red.* **Habitat** Dry woods, hedge banks, scrubby sea cliffs, usually on calcareous soils. **Dist**. Native. Locally frequent. S Britain to N Wales. (S and W Europe.) **Fls** May–Jul.

woods, waste ground. **Dist**. Introduced as garden plant in 1880 (native of S Africa). Naturalised throughout BI, especially in W. (W Europe.) **Fls** Sep–Nov.

DIOSCOREACEAE
Black Bryony and yams

Black Bryony
Tamus communis

Climbing, dioecious perennial with large, subterranean tuber. The only British member of the tropical yam family. **Stems**

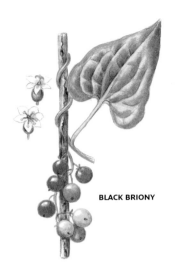

BLACK BRIONY

To 20 m or more. **Leaves** 3–15 × 2–10 cm, *dark glossy green, ovate, base cordate.* **Flowers** 4–5 mm across, in lax, axillary, spike-like raceme, to 15 cm; tepals pale green. **Fruits** *Waxy red berry.* **Habitat** Hedgerows, wood margins, on well-drained neutral or calcareous soils. **Dist**. Native. Widespread and common throughout England, Wales. (S and W Europe.) **Fls** May–Jul.

ORCHIDACEAE
Orchids
••

The distinctive flowers of orchids are strongly irregular and highly modified for insect pollination and are unlikely to be confused with any other group of plants. The perianth consists of 6 free tepals in 2 whorls of 3. The outer 3 (sepals) and 2 of the inner whorl (petals) are all more or less similar whilst the lowest petal or lip (*labellum*) is large, conspicuous and usually much modified and often extended behind into a hollow 'spur'. The stamens and stigmas are borne on a special structure, the *column*, in the middle of the flower. There is 1 stamen with the pollen in 2, often stalked, sticky masses, the *pollinia*.

The 2 fertile stigmas are located at the base of the column, the third stigma often forming a sterile protrusion, the *rostellum*, which may function to prevent self-pollination. The seeds are numerous, minute and dust-like.

White Helleborine
Cephalanthera damasonium VU.

Stems Leafy; flowering stem to 60 cm. **Leaves** Ovate, 5–10 cm. **Flowers** *Erect, sessile, remaining closed*, in 3–12-flowered spike; *bracts longer than ovaries*; outer tepals obtuse; labellum shorter than other tepals; hypochile pouched, with orange patch; epichile heart-shaped, with orange keels on upper surface; ovary glabrous. **Habitat** Shady chalk and limestone woodlands, especially Beech. **Dist**. Native. Local but widespread. S England. (Most of Europe except N.) **Fls** May–Jun.

Marsh Helleborine
Epipactis palustris
*(NI)

Attractive orchid with creeping rhizome. **Stems** To 50 cm. **Leaves** 5–8, spirally arranged. **Flowers** Stalked, in 7–14-flowered inflorescence; outer tepals brownish or purplish green, hairy on outside; inner tepals whitish with purple veins; labellum strongly constricted; hypochile with erect lobe on each side;

epichile white with red veins; rostellum persistent. **Habitat** Marshes, fens, wet pastures, dune slacks, often forming large colonies. **Dist**. Native. Local and declining. Widely distributed in England, Wales, Ireland; very rare in Scotland. (All Europe except extreme N.) **Fls** Jun–Aug.

Violet Helleborine
Epipactis purpurata

Similar to *E. helleborine*, but *flowering stems often clustered*, tinged violet below; leaves narrower, ovate-lanceolate to lanceolate, grey-green or tinged purplish; bracts longer than flowers; flowers pale greenish white; *interior of hypochile mottled violet inside; epichile at least as long as broad, with 2–3 smoothly ridged basal bosses.* **Habitat** Shaded mixed woodlands, coppice, usually on base-rich or calcareous soils. **Dist**. Native. Rather local but widely distributed in central and S England. (NW and central Europe.) **Fls** Aug–Sep.

Broad-leaved Helleborine
Epipactis helleborine

Stems 1–3 flowering stems, to 80 cm. **Leaves** Spirally arranged, broadly ovate, dull green. **Flowers** Drooping, greenish to dull purplish, in 15–50-flowered inflorescence; *interior of hypochile dark reddish brown; epichile wider than long, with 2 wart-like bosses at base,* tip reflexed; rostellum large, persistent. **Habitat** Woods, hedge banks, roadsides, dune slacks, limestone pavement, on mildly acid to calcareous soils. **Dist**. Native. Widely distributed throughout BI, N to central Scotland. (Most of Europe except extreme N.) **Fls** Jul–Oct.

Bird's-nest Orchid
Neottia nidus-avis *(NI)

Rhizomatous, *saprophytic* perennial, *without green leaves*. Roots in a dense mass resembling a bird's nest; *whole plant yellowish brown.* **Stems** Flowering stem to

50 cm, stiffly erect, glandular, densely covered by brownish scales. **Flowers** Yellowish brown, spur absent, honey-scented, in cylindrical, spike-like inflorescence; labellum 2× as long as outer tepals, with 2 broad, widely spreading lobes. **Habitat** Deep humus of shaded calcareous woodlands, especially Beech woodlands on chalk. **Dist.** Native. Declining. Throughout BI, but scarce outside S England. (Most of Europe except extreme N.) **Fls** May–Jul.

Common Twayblade
Neottia ovata (*Listera ovata*)

Stems Flowering stems solitary, to 75 cm, glabrous below, pubescent above, *with pair of broad, sessile, opposite leaves somewhat below middle.* **Leaves** 5– 20 cm. **Flowers** *Yellowish green, inconspicuous,* in a lax, spike-like raceme, 7–25 mm; tepals ovate, all ± same length, outer connivent; labellum deeply divided at tip into 2 linear lobes. **Habitat** Grassland, open woodland, hedgerows, scrub, dune slacks, limestone pavement, disused quarries, on calcareous or mildly acid soils. **Dist**. Native. Frequent and sometimes abundant. Throughout BI. (Most of Europe except extreme N.) **Fls** Jun–Jul.

Lesser Twayblade
Neottia cordata (*Listera cordata*)

Small, inconspicuous orchid. **Stems** Flowering stem solitary, reddish, 6–10 cm, with *pair of spreading, shiny, ovate leaves about halfway up stem.* **Flowers** Tiny, 6–12 forming inflorescence, 1.5–6 cm; outer tepals greenish, inner reddish on inside; labellum 3.5–4 mm, reddish, pendulous, divided about halfway into 2 linear, tapering lobes. **Habitat** Damp, shaded acid habitats; to 1065 m. **Dist**. Native. N England, N Wales, Scotland, Ireland. (All Europe except S.) **Fls** Jun–Sep.

Autumn Lady's-tresses
Spiranthes spiralis

Stems Flowering stem to 20 cm, with appressed bract-like scales. **Leaves** Ovate-elliptic, glossy green; *those of current season forming lateral overwintering rosette* with or after flowers and withering the following summer before flower spike develops. **Flowers** *Very small, in tightly spiralled 5–15-flowered spike*; bracts 6–7 mm, *tepals all ± equal, lip unloded*; spur absent.

Habitat Downs, hill pastures, meadows, cliff tops, dunes, lawns, on calcareous soils. **Dist**. Native. Declining. Widely distributed in S England; scattered in N England, Ireland; coastal in Wales. (All Europe except N.) **Fls** Aug–Sep.

Creeping Lady's-tresses
Goodyera repens

AUTUMN LADY'S-TRESSES

Orchid with creeping rhizomes. **Stems** Flowering stems to 35 cm, glandular-hairy, scaly. **Leaves** *In basal rosette*, ovate-lanceolate, *conspicuously net-veined*, evergreen. **Flowers** Small, sweet-scented, in slender spike, 3–7 cm, with a slight spiral twist; bracts green, 10–15 mm; tepals all ± same length; labellum shorter than tepals, unlobed; spur absent. **Habitat** Mature pine woods; to 335 m. **Dist.** Native in Scotland, especially NE; naturalised on pine plantations in Cumbria, Norfolk. (Central and N Europe.) **Fls** Jul–Aug.

Greater Butterfly-orchid
Platanthera chlorantha

Stems To 40 cm. **Leaves** Usually 2 basal leaves, large, to 15 × 5 cm, elliptic, blunt; upper stem leaves bract-like. **Flowers** 18–23 mm across, greenish white, heavily fragrant at night, in lax spikes to 20 cm; bracts about as long as ovary; outer tepals spreading; labellum long, narrow, to 16 mm; spur long, to 28 mm, curved downwards and forwards; pollinia 3–4 mm, widely diverging below. **Habitat** Woods, scrub, meadows, pastures, downs, usually on well-drained calcareous soils; to 460 m. **Dist.** Native. Throughout BI, but rather local. (Most of Europe, but absent from parts of N, E and SW.) **Fls** May–Jul.

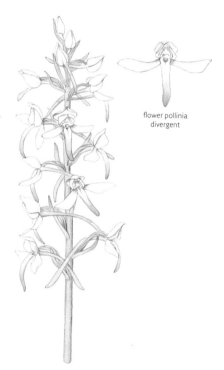

flower pollinia divergent

Lesser Butterfly-orchid
Platanthera bifolia VU.

Similar to *P. chlorantha*, but stem to
30 cm; leaves to 9 × 3 cm; flowers
11–18 mm across; labellum 6– 12 mm;
spur 15–20 mm, almost horizontal; pollinia
*c.*2 mm, vertical, parallel. **Habitat** Heathy
grassland, moorland, wood margins, scrub,
on acidic to calcareous soils; to 365 m. **Dist**.
Native. Local, declining. Throughout BI,
but commoner in N and W. (All Europe,
but rare in Mediterranean.) **Fls** May–Jul.

converging into a hood; labellum 3-lobed,
with 2 vertical ridges or 'guide-plates' on
upper surface; spur to 14 mm, as long as
or longer than ovary. **Habitat** Well-drained
calcareous grassland, scrub, roadsides, dunes,
dune slacks. **Dist**. Native. Locally frequent
throughout BI, but becoming coastal to N.
(Most of Europe except N.) **Fls** Jun–Aug.

Small-white Orchid
Pseudorchis albida VU. *(NI, R)

Stems Flowering stems to 30 cm. **Leaves**
3–5 main leaves, oblong-lanceolate. **Flowers**
2–2.5 mm, greenish white, in dense-
flowered cylindrical spike; bracts about as
long as ovary; tepals converging with
3-lobed labellum, making flowers appear ±
tubular; spur short and blunt, shorter than
ovary. **Habitat** Well-drained hill pastures,
mountain grasslands,
stream sides; to
550 m. **Dist**. Native.
Widespread in
upland Britain but
declining. (NW, W
and central Europe.)
Fls Jun–Jul.

flower pollinia
parallel

**CHALK FRAGRANT
ORCHID**

**PYRAMIDAL
ORCHID**

**SMALL-WHITE
ORCHID**

Pyramidal
Orchid
*Anacamptis
pyramidalis*

Stems Leafy; flowering
stems to 50 cm. **Leaves**
Lower leaves 8–15 cm,
oblong-lanceolate,
keeled. **Flowers** Rosy
purple, in dense-
flowered, ± conical or
rounded spike; outer
tepals spreading, rest

Chalk Fragrant Orchid
Gymnadenia conopsea

Stems Flowering stems to 40 cm. **Leaves** Lower ones 3–5, narrowly oblong-lanceolate, keeled, to 15 × 3 cm. **Flowers** Inflorescence a ± dense-flowered cylindrical spike; bracts about as long as flowers; flowers small, pinkish-red, very fragrant; outer lateral tepals spreading; labellum 3-lobed; spur 11–16 mm, almost 2× as long as ovary. **Habitat** Dry calcareous grassland. **Dist.** Native. Widely distributed throughout BI to 610 m, but commoner in S. (Most of Europe.) **Fls** Jun–Aug.

Frog Orchid
Coeloglossum viride VU.

Stems Flowering stem to 25 cm, reddish, slightly angled above. **Leaves** 2–5. **Flowers** Greenish, tinged brownish purple, in rather lax cylindrical spike, 1.5–6 cm; lowest bracts often longer than flowers; outer tepals converging to form hood; labellum 3.5–6 mm, oblong, parallel-sided, 3-lobed at tip; spur short, *c.*2 mm. **Habitat** Calcareous grasslands, dunes, mires, flushes, limestone pavement, scree, roadsides; to 915 m. **Dist**. Native. Scattered throughout BI, but declining. (Most of Europe, but only in mts in S.) **Fls** Jun–Aug.

Spotted-orchids and marsh-orchids ▶
Dactylorhiza
A particularly complicated group, largely because of the amount of variation within the species and the ease with which they hybridise. It is often not possible to identify individual plants with certainty. Leaves are spotted or unspotted, the lower with sheathing bases, and the upper intermediate with the bracts and not sheathing, although they may clasp the stem. The flowers have a spur, usually <10 mm long; the 3 upper tepals are incurved; the lateral sepals are spreading, erect or downcurved, and the labellum is usually shallowly 3-lobed. The shape and markings of the labellum are important diagnostic characteristics, together with the number of sheathing leaves.

Common Spotted-orchid
Dactylorhiza fuchsii

The commonest British orchid, often occurring in large numbers. Very variable, with a number of named subspecies and varieties. **Stems** Flowering stem to 50 cm. **Leaves** With dark, ± transversely elongated spots, oblong-lanceolate; lowest leaves broad, blunt. **Flowers** Pale to deep pink, occasionally white, in dense, cylindrical, many-flowered spike; bracts about as long as ovaries; labellum deeply divided

into 3 ± equal lobes, middle lobe slightly longer than lateral; spur 5.5–10 mm. **Habitat** Neutral and calcareous grasslands, roadsides, open woodlands, marshes, fens, dune slacks, quarries, embankments; to 530 m. **Dist.** Native. Widespread throughout most of BI. (Most of Europe except parts of S.) **Fls** Jun–Aug.

Heath Spotted-orchid
Dactylorhiza maculata

Similar to *D. fuchsii*, but leaves with ± circular spots; lowest leaves lanceolate, acute; flowers almost white to pale pink and deep pink; middle lobe of labellum much smaller and usually shorter than broadly rounded lateral lobes. **Habitat** Heaths, moors, bogs, mountain grassland, on acid soils; to 915 m. **Dist.** Native. Throughout BI, but commoner in N and W, and scarce and declining in parts of English lowlands. (Most of Europe except SE.) **Fls** Jun–Aug.

Early Marsh-orchid
Dactylorhiza incarnata

Stems Flowering, to 60 cm. **Leaves** ± erect, yellow-green, hooded at tip. **Flowers** Lowest bracts much longer than flowers; outer tepals ± erect; sides of labellum strongly reflexed soon after flower opens so looks narrow from in front; spur 6–8.5 mm. **Habitat** Bogs,

fens, marshes, wet meadows, dune slacks. **Dist.** Throughout BI, declining especially in S. (Most of Europe, rare in Mediterranean.) **Fls** May–Jul. **Ssp.** 5, well-marked, very variable, with different habitats:

Southern Marsh-orchid
Dactylorhiza praetermissa

Tall, robust orchid. **Stems** To 70 cm tall and 5 mm diam. **Leaves** Rather grey-green, unspotted, or rarely ring-spotted (f. *junialis*). **Flowers** Rich pinkish purple, in rather dense inflorescence; labellum usually wider than long, shortly 3-lobed, slightly concave, markings predominantly fine dots; spur 6–9 mm. **Habitat** Damp meadows, marshes, fens, dune slacks. **Dist.** Native. Widespread in England, Wales, N to Humber. (NW Europe.) **Fls** Jun–Jul.

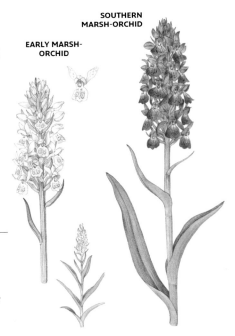

SOUTHERN MARSH-ORCHID

EARLY MARSH-ORCHID

Northern Marsh-orchid
Dactylorhiza purpurella

Stems Flowering stems to 30 cm. **Leaves** Usually 5–8, ± stiffly spreading, dull green or grey-green, unspotted. **Flowers** Rich deep purple, in short, broad, dense, rather flat-topped inflorescence; bracts purplish; labellum 7–9 mm wide, flat, diamond-shaped, sub-entire or obscurely 3-lobed, markings rather indistinct loops, lines; spur to 9 mm. **Habitat** Wet meadows, fens, marshes, road verges, dune slacks. **Dist.** Native. Britain N of Humber, W Wales, N Ireland. (NW Europe.) **Fls** Jun–Jul.

Dist. Native. Local and declining, but can form large colonies. Throughout Britain N to Tees; central and W Ireland. (Most of Europe except N.) **Fls** May–Jun.

Early-purple Orchid
Orchis mascula

Stems Flowering stems to 60 cm. **Leaves** Basal leaves in a rosette, usually with purple-black spots. **Flowers** Purplish crimson, in a rather lax spike, 4–15 cm; bracts about as long as ovary; lateral pair of outer tepals (sepals) spreading then folded back; rest of tepals converging; labellum 8–12 mm, sides reflexed, 3-lobed, central lobe longer than laterals, notched; spur as long as or longer than ovary, curved upwards. **Habitat** Woods, coppice, calcareous grassland, pastures, hedge banks, roadsides, on base-rich soils; to 880 m. **Dist.** Native. Widespread and common throughout BI. (W and W-central Europe.) **Fls** Apr–Jun.

Green-winged Orchid
Anacamptis morio *(NI, R)

Stems Flowering stems to 40 cm. **Leaves** Unspotted. **Flowers** Deep purple, through pale pink to almost white, in rather lax, few-flowered inflorescence, 2.5– 8 cm; tepals converging to form hood, outer tepals with conspicuous greenish or greyish veins; labellum broader than long, 3-lobed, lateral lobes folded back; spur about as long as ovary. **Habitat** Old permanent pastures, hay meadows, churchyards, sand-dunes.

**EARLY-PURPLE
ORCHID**

Bee Orchid
Ophrys apifera *(NI)*

Attractive, distinctive orchid. **Stems**
Flowering stems to 45 cm. **Leaves** 5–6
basal leaves, greyish green. **Flowers** Rather
large, in 2–7-flowered inflorescence; outer
tepals (sepals) deep pink, 10–15 mm,
oblong; inner tepals linear, greenish;
labellum 10–15 mm, resembling abdomen
of bumble-bee, strongly convex, velvety,
*central lobe ending in long, tooth-like
appendage, curved back beneath lobe so as
to be invisible from above.* **Habitat** Short,
dry calcareous grassland, scrub, dunes,
lawns, roadsides, limestone pavement. **Dist**.
Native. Throughout Britain to N England,
widespread but local in S; scattered in
Ireland. (S, W and central Europe.)
Fls Jun–Jul.

GLOSSARY

Achene Small, dry, single-seeded, indehiscent fruit, e.g. that of buttercup. (*See* illustration.)

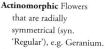

achene

Actinomorphic Flowers that are radially symmetrical (syn. 'Regular'), e.g. Geranium.

actinomorphic

Acuminate Gradually tapering to a point. *See* diagram of cordate leaf.

Alternate (of leaves) Individual leaves are neither opposite nor whorled on stem.

Annual A plant that completes its life cycle from germination to seed in a single season.

Anther The pollen-containing part of the stamen, situated at the tip of the filament.

Apocarpous A plant with individual carpels that are separate and not fused to form a single ovary (*see* p.13).

Apomictic Producing viable seed without fertilisation; in effect, cloning by seed.

Appressed Pressed close to another organ but not fused to it, e.g. hairs on a stem.

Archaeophyte Although not thought to be native, a plant long established in the British Isles and certainly present since before 1600.

Aristate With an awn or stiff bristle.

Ascending Sloping or curving upwards at an oblique angle.

Auricle Small, ear-like projections at the base of a leaf, especially in grasses.

Axillary Arising in the axil of a leaf or bract.

Base-rich Soil or water rich in minerals such as calcium or magnesium that produces a non-acid neutral or basic reaction (cf. 'Fertile').

Berry Fleshy fruit with usually several seeds, without a hard stony layer surrounding seeds.

Biennial A plant that completes its life cycle in two growing seasons and does not flower in the first, e.g. Foxglove.

Bifid Deeply split into two.

Brackish Refers to water or wet soils that are salty but less saline than sea water; especially marshes and dykes close to the sea.

Bract (*see* p.12).

Bulb Underground organ consisting of a short stem bearing a number of fleshy scale leaves, the whole enclosing next year's flower bud, e.g. an onion.

Bulbil A small bulb arising in the axil of a leaf or in an inflorescence.

Calcicole A plant usually found on calcium-rich soils, e.g. over chalk or limestone.

Calcifuge A plant usually found on calcium-poor acid soils, e.g. heath and moorland.

Calyx The sepals of a flower.

sepal (calyx)

Capitulum The head-like inflorescence of a member of the Asteraceae family.

capitulum

Capsule A dry, dehiscent fruit consisting of more than one carpel.

Carpel A unit composed of the female part of the flower (*see* p.13).

Carr Woodland or scrub that develops on permanently wet soils.

capsule

Casual An introduced plant that does not become established.

Cladode A green leaf-like lateral shoot.

Compound (of a leaf) Comprised of several distinct leaflets, e.g. palmate, pinnate.

Cordate Refers to the shape of base of leaf blade.

cordate

Corm Short, bulb-like underground stem that, unlike a bulb, does not consist of fleshy scale leaves (cf. 'Tuber').

Corolla The petals of a flower.

Corymb An inflorescence in which all the flowers are more or less at the same level but whose stalks arise from different points on the stem (adj. corymbose) (*see* p.14).

Crucifer Name commonly given to members of the Brassicaceae (= Cruciferae).

Cuneate Refers to the shape of base of leaf blade.

Cuspidate (of a leaf) Abruptly drawn out to a sharp narrow point.

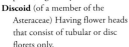

cuneate

Decumbent Refers to stems that lie on the ground or are prostrate and tend to rise up at the tips (cf. 'Ascending').

Decurrent (of leaves) With the base prolonged down the petiole or stem as a wing.

Deflexed Bent sharply downwards.

Dioecious Having male and female flowers on separate plants, e.g. Holly.

Discoid (of a member of the Asteraceae) Having flower heads that consist of tubular or disc florets only.

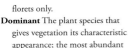

decurrent

Dominant The plant species that gives vegetation its characteristic appearance; the most abundant species.

Drupe A fleshy fruit with one or more seeds, each of which is surrounded by a stony layer, e.g. plum.

discoid

Endemic Native to one country or a small area. If used without qualification, then refers here to the British Isles.

Entire (of a leaf) Neither toothed nor serrated.

Epicalyx A calyx-like whorl outside the true calyx, e.g. as in *Potentilla*.

Eutrophic (of soil or water) Especially rich in nutrients, particularly nitrogen and phosphorus; extremely fertile.

epicalyx

Falcate Sickle-shaped.

Filament The stalk of the stamen.

Filiform Thread-like.

Fimbriate With a fringe-like margin.

Floret A highly modified individual small flower, e.g. of Asteraceae.

Flush Area of wet ground with moving ground water, e.g. margin of upland spring.

Follicle A dry, dehiscent fruit consisting of a single carpel, splitting along one side.

Fruit The ripe seeds together with the structure surrounding them, which may be either dry (e.g. a nut) or fleshy (e.g. a berry).

Glabrous Without hairs.

Gland Small, globular vesicle containing oil or resin, with or without a stalk, on the surface of any part of a plant.

Glaucous With a blue-green or grey-green hue.

Herb Any non-woody plant (not same as culinary definition).

Herbaceous Green, soft and with a leafy texture.

Hispid Coarsely and stiffly hairy, e.g. Viper's-bugloss.

Hyaline Thin and translucent.

Hybrid Offspring that results from a cross between two different species.

Incurved Bent gradually inwards.

Inferior (of a flower) With the perianth inserted above the ovary, and the ovary embedded in, and fused with, the receptacle (*see* p.13).

Inflorescence The flowering part of the stem, including the flowers, branches and bracts (*see* p.14).

Internode The part of the stem between two adjacent nodes (*see* p.12).

Introduced Not native. In this book it refers to plants brought into the British Isles either accidentally or intentionally since about 1600 (sometimes referred to as 'neophytes').

Involucral Forming an involucre.

Involucre Bracts that form a more or less calyx-like whorl around or just below a condensed head-like inflorescence, e.g. Asteraceae.

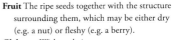

involucre

involucral bract

Irregular (of a flower) Divisible through the centre of the flower in only one longitudinal plane to produce two identical halves that are mirror images of each other (syn. 'Zygomorphic'), e.g. dead-nettles.

irregular

Keel The lower petal or petals when these are shaped like the keel of a boat, e.g. gorse.

Labiate Name commonly given to members of the Lamiaceae (= Labiatae).

Lanceolate (*See* illustration.)

Latex A milky juice, usually poisonous or a skin irritant.

Leaching The process of removing the nutrients from the upper layers of the soil by the downward movement of rain water.

Legume 1. Name commonly given to members of the Fabaceae (= Leguminosae) family.
2. Fruit (pod) of a member of the Fabaceae.

Ligulate (of the inflorescence of a Composite). Consisting of ray florets only, e.g. Dandelion; strap-shaped.

Limb The flattened, expanded terminal part of a corolla, the base of which is tubular.

Lip A group of petals or tepals united together and sharply differentiated from the rest.

Lobed (of leaves) Divided, but not into separate leaflets.

Mesotrophic Soil or water that is neither extremely fertile (eutrophic) nor extremely infertile (oligotrophic).

Monocarpic (of a perennial) Flowering only once.

Monoecious Having unisexual flowers, but with the male and female flowers on the same plant.

Mucronate (of a leaf) With a short bristle-like tip.

Native Thought to have arrived in an area by means of natural dispersal (i.e. not introduced).

Neophyte *See* 'Introduced'.

Node The point on a stem where leaves are attached (*see* p.12).

Nut Dry, one-seeded, woody, indehiscent fruit, e.g. sorrels.

Ob- (as prefix) Inverted, e.g. obovate, a leaf that is broadest above the middle, as opposed to ovate, a leaf that is broadest below the middle.

Oblong (*See* illustration.)

Obovate (*See* illustration.)

Obtuse Blunt.

Opposite Of two organs that arise at the same level on opposite sides of a stem.

Orbicular Rounded. (*See* illustration.)

Ovary The part of the carpel containing the ovules (*see* p.13).

Ovate (*See* illustration.)

Ovoid (of a solid object) Egg-shaped.

lanceolate

lobed

Ovule The organ inside the ovary containing the egg and seed after fertilisation.

Palmate Divided into separate leaflets, with all the leaflets arising from the tip of the petiole.

Panicle A much-branched inflorescence (*see* p.14).

Pedicel The stalk of a single flower.

Peduncle The stalk of an inflorescence.

Peltate (of a leaf) Having its lower surface attached to the stalk. (*See* illustration.)

Perennial A plant that lives for more than two years, flowering in the second year and regularly or irregularly thereafter.

Perianth A collective term for the sepals and petals, or the tepals if these are not differentiated into calyx and corolla.

Petiole The stalk of a leaf.

Pinnate (of a leaf) Having separate leaflets along each side of the leaf stalk. (*See* illustration.)

Pollinia The pollen masses of the stamens of orchids.

Procumbent Lying along the ground.

Proliferous An inflorescence that produces small plantlets instead of flowers.

Pubescent Hairy.

Raceme (*see* p.14).

Radiate (of a Composite inflorescence) Having disc florets in the centre and ray florets around the periphery (daisy-like).

Ray (of an inflorescence) The primary branch of an umbel.

Receptacle The enlarged tip of the stem that bears the flower parts (*see* p.13).

Recurved Curved backwards.

Regular (of a flower) Radially symmetrical (syn. actinomorphic).

oblong

obovate

orbicular

obovate

ovate

peltate

pinnate

ray

Revolute Rolled back from the tip or margin.

Rhizome A horizontal underground root-like stem.

Rotate (of a corolla) With a short tube and spreading lobes.

Runner A creeping stem, rooting and producing plantlets at its nodes.

Salt-marsh Vegetation that develops on soft inter-tidal mud.

Saprophyte A plant lacking chlorophyll and deriving its nourishment from decaying organic matter, usually in association with a fungus.

Scape A leafless flower stalk.

Scarious Thin, dry, pale and membranous.

Scrub Vegetation dominated by shrubs and young trees.

Seed Technically the fertilised ovule. The sexual reproductive structure of the plant, which germinates to produce the plant of the next generation.

Sepal An individual segment of the calyx.

Sessile Without a stalk.

Sheathing (*See* illustration.)

Shrub A woody plant like a small tree but with several stems that arise from the base rather than a single trunk.

Simple (of a leaf) Not compound, i.e. not composed of several distinct leaflets.

sheathing

Spathe A large bract enclosing or subtending a flower or inflorescence.

Spike (*see* p.14).

Spur A slender, tubular, often nectar-secreting projection that usually extends from the rear of a flower.

spur

Stamen The male reproductive structure of a flowering plant (*see* p.13).

Stigma The receptive tip of the style (*see* p.13).

Stipule A leafy outgrowth from base of the petiole.

Stolon A creeping stem, rooting at the nodes and producing young plants along its length.

stipule

Style The elongated terminal portion of the carpel, bearing stigma at its tip (*see* p.13).

Subulate Flat and awl-shaped, tapering from base to apex.

Sucker A shoot originating below ground.

Superior (of a flower) With the ovary inserted above the origin of the perianth (cf. 'Inferior' (*see* p.13)).

subulate

Tendril A climbing, thread-like, twining tip to a branch, leaf or petiole. (*See* illustration.)

Tepal The individual segment of a perianth when the sepals and petals are not differentiated.

tendril

Terete (usually of a stem) Smooth, cylindrical and more or less circular in section.

Tomentose Densely covered in soft hairs.

Trifoliate (of a leaf) Consisting of three leaflets.

Trigonous (of a stem) Bluntly three-angled.

Triquetrous (of a stem) Sharply three-angled.

trifoliate

Tube (of a flower) The fused basal part of a calyx or corolla.

Tuber A swollen underground stem or root, surviving for one year (cf. 'Corm').

Umbel An inflorescence in which the pedicels all arise from the same point on the peduncle (*see* p.14).

Umbellifer Name commonly given to members of the Apiaceae (= Umbelliferae).

Vein A strand of strengthening and conducting tissue running through a leaf (syn. nerve).

whorled

Whorl Three or more organs arranged in a circle around an axis, e.g. a whorl of leaves on a stem, or the corolla as a whorl of petals (adj. whorled).

Zygomorphic *See* 'Irregular'.

zygomorphic

INDEX